C.
CONTEMPORARY   urban   NTICE-HALL
              erformance   TICS SERIES
                              ARA, *Editor*

published

ROBERT C. FRIED
University of California at Los Angeles

FRANCINE F. RABINOVITZ
University of Southern California

Prentice-Hall, Inc.
Englewood Cliffs, N.J. 07632

COMPARATIVE URBAN POLITICS
A PERFORMANCE APPROACH

Library of Congress Cataloging in Publication Data

Fried, Robert C
  Comparative urban politics, a performance
approach.

  (Prentice-Hall contemporary comparative politics
series)
  Includes bibliographical references and index.
  1. Municipal government.   2. Comparative
government.   I. Rabinovitz, Francine F., joint
author.   II. Title.
JS67.F74   320.8   80-10810
ISBN 0-13-154351-2

COMPARATIVE URBAN POLITICS:
A PERFORMANCE APPROACH
Robert C. Fried and Francine F. Rabinovitz

Printed in the United States of America

10   9   8   7   6   5   4   3   2   1

PRENTICE-HALL INTERNATIONAL, INC., London
PRENTICE-HALL OF AUSTRALIA PTY. LIMITED, Sydney
PRENTICE-HALL OF CANADA, LTD., Toronto
PRENTICE-HALL OF INDIA PRIVATE LIMITED, New Delhi
PRENTICE-HALL OF JAPAN, INC., Tokyo
PRENTICE-HALL OF SOUTHEAST ASIA PTE. LTD., Singapore
WHITEHALL BOOKS LIMITED, Wellington, New Zealand

CONTENTS

FOREWORD

The organization of the Contemporary Comparative Politics Series is based on a number of assumptions and guidelines that are worth calling to the reader's attention. Foremost among these is that the undergraduate student of comparative politics is less interested in political science than we might hope, but more capable of synthetic analysis than we may imagine. If this is so, then it would be an enormous mistake to pretend to organize an introductory series around one or more half-baked "theories" of politics or political systems—theories that are difficult for even the more hardened members of the profession to digest. It would seem equally debatable whether the undergraduate student has a strong desire to learn in depth the institutional arrangements and workings of any single political system, whether that system be as established as that of Great Britain or as new and exotic as that of Tanzania.

What, then, can we expect of those undergraduates who study comparative politics? First, I think that they are quickly turned off by simplistic or spurious efforts to lend the discipline a theoretical elegance it manifestly does not possess; second, that saturation treatments of single political systems are as unpalatable today when the countries are individually packaged as they were when several countries appeared between the same hard covers; third, that the undergraduates sittting in our classrooms might very well be turned on if they learned what sorts of things political scientists do and what kinds of knowledge of the political process they can glean from the things we do. These things, incidentally, would involve not merely data gathering on some aspect of the political system, but also speculative and normative considerations about the relationship between politics and the good life. We can expect that if the things to be written and lectured about are carefully chosen and intelligently organized, the undergraduate will display a striking capacity to synthesize information and to develop skills in analyzing political phenomena at least as impressive as, say, those of a New York taxi driver, a voluble parent, or a political orator.

Another major assumption underlying the organization of the series is that the topics included should not reflect a commitment to an institutional or behavioral, normative, or empirical approach. If members of the profession are still battling about such things, let them spare undergraduates the arid, scholastic, and essentially unproductive nature of such encounters. The authors of this series are neither bare-facts empiricists nor "cloud-ninety" political moralists; they neither sanctify nor abominate institutional or behavioral anaylsis, but would rather use whatever methods are available to enlighten the reader about important aspects of political life. To emphasize the important is also to be relevant, and our correlative assumption here is that the student who wants political science to be "relevant" does not mean by this that it should be banal, simple-minded, or unsystematic.

Since no series can tell us everything about politics, we have had to choose what we consider to be the important, relevant, and reasonably integrated topics. Such choices are always arbitrary to some extent. However, we have sought to accord attention to certain standards and ubiquitous institutions as well as to newer conceptual and analytical foci that have provoked a good deal of recent research and discussion. Thus, the series currently has volumes within it that deal with comparative legal cultures, comparative political elites, and comparative legislatures; but it also includes works on comparative political violence, comparative revolutionary movements, and solidiers in politics.

Future volumes will represent what we believe is an interesting and useful mosaic that should be appealing to those who teach, those who learn about, and all of those who try to understand politics.

Joseph LaPalombara

New Haven

PREFACE

High-school history books sometimes place the Age of Exploration in the fifteenth and sixteenth centuries, but wrongly so, for it is still with us. In the last decades of the twentieth century, not only do we explore the mysteries of the moon, but we also seek to discover, describe, and understand the experiences of people living in what for all practical purposes could be the moon—the world of other countries and other continents. In this book, we explore places that can be even farther and more exotic than the moon: our own cities.

Exploration means more than arriving and staying somewhere; it means observing from a sophisticated viewpoint. In this book, we try to determine how and in what ways the quality of life in cities reflects the quality of politics and government. Rather than describe how political and governmental institutions vary from city to city, we look for the *consequences* of those variations for the quality of life lived by "ordinary" people. We study and describe differences among cities in such areas as health, education, housing, poverty, and transportation. Then we ask, "To what extent are these variations the product of politics and government? How do the political and governmental processes enhance or detract from the quality of cities as places in which to live?"

Our answers to such fundamental questions are still only exploratory. Our knowledge about cities still comes more from impressions and stereotypes than from solid evidence, because the world's 2000 cities display a dazzling diversity. No two cities are identical. Every city is a unique combination of characteristics, defying generalizations about the urban experience.

Most people who will read this book are urbanized, because the late twentieth-century world is led by cities. All cities are comparable human products: they are the products of past human efforts (history), of current human relationships, and of international change. In this book we look at what cities have in common and at what makes them better or worse places in which to live.

The accent in this book is on performance—on the outcome of institutional arrangements and institutional achievements. Our knowledge of arrangements is good; our knowledge of achievements is less so. Too many countries are unwilling or unable—mostly unable—to make available data about the quality of life in their cities. Thus we have to build theory about comparative urban performance on the basis of incomplete data. At least half of the world's cities remain either off limits on political grounds or unmapped—beyond the reach of the modern census. Thus the generalizations we offer remain tentative and exploratory.

We thank the Ford Foundation for its generous grant. The UCLA Academic Senate has also provided invaluable support. The many research assistants who have contributed to this enterprise will recognize their contribution and here receive acknowledgment of our gratitude. William Hanna must be specially thanked for his critical reading—as detailed as it was perceptive—of an earlier version of this book. Many other comparative urbanists have contributed to our understanding of cities around the world: our footnotes and references acknowledge only a small portion of our indebtedness.

Robert Fried
Francine Rabinovitz

THE POLITICS OF URBAN PERFORMANCE

1

For most of history, political life has centered on the control of rural, agrarian societies. With few people living in cities, local government has mostly been rural government. National government attention has been turned towards external affairs. Government and politics have played little role in people's lives. During the past hundred years the situation has been changing everywhere, transforming rural into urban societies, making government and politics more important to more people than ever before, shifting urban problems and politics to the center of national and even international concern. In 1960, about 40% of the world's population lived in cities; by the year 2000, about 50% will be living in cities. As Table 1-1 shows, the proportion of urban population in big cities has already risen nearly as high in the Third World as in the more developed areas.

How the needs and demands of 3 billion urban residents will be met is of prime concern to all countries, large and small, rich and poor, democratic and dictatorial, communist and noncommunist. The urbanization of societies is urbanizing national politics and government; it is also urbanizing local government. Local government has increasingly become urban, suburban, and metropolitan government. National and state governments now dedicate much of their anxieties, energies, and resources to urban affairs. In studying comparative urban government, we are, thus, studying an increasingly important segment of political life.

1-1 APPROACHES TO THE STUDY OF COMPARATIVE
URBAN POLITICS

THE PERFORMANCE APPROACH

In this volume, we shall study the urban segment of political life by concentrating on the problem of urban performance. By urban performance, we mean the comparative ability of governments to meet the needs, demands, and expectations of

Table 1-1   World Population: Trends in Urban-Rural Distribution, 1920-2000

Population Category	1920	1940	1960	1980	2000
WORLD					
Total	1860	2295	2990	4325	6110
Rural	1500	1725	2000	2545	3020
Urban	360	570	990	1780	3090
Agglomerated[a]	267	432	760	1354	2337
Big cities[b]	107	181	352	—	—
Percent urban	19	25	33	41	51
MORE DEVELOPED REGIONS					
Total	576	820	975	1195	1440
Rural	415	435	395	345	280
Urban	260	385	580	850	1160
Agglomerated[a]	198	304	450	661	901
Big cities[b]	93	146	221	—	—
Percent urban	39	47	59	71	80
LESS DEVELOPED REGIONS					
Total	1185	1475	2015	3130	4670
Rural	1085	1290	1605	2200	2740
Urban	100	185	410	930	1930
Agglomerated[a]	69	128	310	693	1436
Big cities[b]	14	35	131	—	—
Percent urban	8	13	20	30	41

Source: UN Center for Economic and Social Information, Publication no. 139, December 19, 1969.

[a]Population of localities with at least 20,000 inhabitants.
[b]Population of agglomerations with at least 500,000 inhabitants.

the various groups concerned with the quality of urban life. The problems of cities can be found in varying forms and degrees throughout the world, problems such as traffic congestion, slums, chaotic growth, and urban violence. Urban problems beset a wide variety of social and political systems; and, thus, no country can escape the emergence of some form of urban crisis. How that crisis is perceived, defined, and measured, however, varies a good deal. In some countries, particularly those with a low degree of urbanization, the urban crisis would seem, at least to outside observers, to be mild. In those countries, there are relatively few people living in cities and they may make few demands on government; the real crisis in those nations would seem to lie in the rural crisis of the countryside. But even in relatively unurbanized countries, local observers often consider the problems and tensions of the cities to be critically important—even more important than the problems and tensions of the rural areas—perhaps because of the greater political clout of urban interests in national politics.

Whether looking at the cities of highly advanced nations or those of the Third World, students of urban performance are interested in such questions as:

- Why do some cities have higher crime rates than others?
- Why are people better housed in some cities than in others?
- Why do people pay more taxes in some cities than in others?
- Why is building regulated much more strictly in some cities than in others?
- Why do some cities provide more ample and sanitary drinking water for their inhabitants than others?
- Why do some cities have higher employment rates than others?
- Why do some cities provide many more cultural activities for their inhabitants than others?
- Why do some cities provide cheaper, swifter transportation than others?
- Why are services administered more evenly or equitably among districts in some cities than others?
- Why are some cities more innovative in their policies and programs than others?
- Why is there greater social and economic equality in some cities than in others?
- Why is there greater social and economic opportunity in some cities than in others?
- Why do some cities provide greater welfare for their disadvantaged citizens than others?
- Why is there more violence and disorder in some cities than in others?
- Why are citizens treated more considerately and with more equal consideration by government officials and civil servants in some cities than in others?
- Is high performance in one sector associated with high performance in other sectors? Do cities with low crime rates tend also to have low-cost, abundant, and good-quality drinking water, police protection, planning, and housing?
- Why are citizens in some cities much more satisfied with city government performance than in other cities? Are citizens more satisfied with government and urban life where conditions are best by objective measurement?

Students of comparative urban performance are also interested in some broader methodological and theoretical questions, such as:

- What are the ways in which performance can be measured? How do different social groups perceive and evaluate city government performance? What do they expect from government? What standards do they apply? What is the impact of their standards on government performance? How do the standards of ordinary people differ in nature and impact from those of professional groups?
- What is the impact of political variables on comparative government performance as contrasted with economic or cultural variables? Are performance differences among cities determined by the nature of the socioeconomic environment and the level of achieved socioeconomic development, or are political factors also important in shaping differences in the quality of life from city to city?
- How can performance be changed or improved? Are the factors identified as crucial in determining the level of performance subject to deliberate manipulation and change by public decision makers and citizens?

The more we know about the causes of differential performance, the more may be able to shape performance itself. The study of comparative urban polit offers the prospect of developing action-related, socially relevant knowledge. satisfactory theory of comparative urban performance should indicate what th critical performance variables are and highlight the most effective strategies for manipulating those variables. Are performance differences among cities highly related to the rapidity of population growth? Then perhaps this is the crucial point with which to give public policy leverage: programs designed to adjust growth rates may permit us to raise performance levels in a variety of functional areas. Are performance differences mostly related to the political orientations of leadership groups? Then attempts to change the ideology of community leaders may be the best strategy for improving performance. Unfortunately, our ignorance about the relative importance of various factors in shaping performance levels is great. The opportunity for useful study is correspondingly vast.[1]

ALTERNATIVE PERSPECTIVES

There are, of course, other approaches than that of performance analysis to the study of urban affairs, generally, and urban politics and government, in particular. We characterize these approaches as:

1.   the urban-*politics* approach,
2.   the urban-*administration* approach,
3.   the urban-*problems* approach,
4.   the urban-*development* approach.

The Urban-Politics Approach[2]   The urban-politics approach focuses on the struggle for power in the city; it stresses political activity, rather than government outputs or the consequences of outputs for the quality of life. The urban-politics approach looks at who is active (and inactive) in city politics, what they seek to gain by being active, and what they get out of participation. Urban politics is seen as a game in itself, with no necessary connection to what urban government does or fails to do. The distribution of influence is taken as the key dependent variable to be explained, rather than, as in our book, one of the independent variables to explain comparative urban performance. This alternative approach derives from the fact that some of urban politics is not performance-oriented and that some performance is not related to politics. Urban political systems, according to the urban-politics approach, are (or can be) compared in terms of their patterns of participation and decision making—their degree of oligarchy or pluralism; the number and kinds of interest groups; the nature and functioning of political machines; the political cultures and subcultures of various groups involved in community affairs; the degree to which group interest or influence is specific to particular issues.

The Urban-Administration Approach[3]   The urban-administration approach goes to the other extreme by stressing outputs as much as the urban-politics approach stresses inputs. The urban-administration approach emphasizes the operations of the institutions of urban government (local, metropolitan, state, or national). It looks not so much at individuals and groups trying to win influence, as at legislative and administrative types trying to get a job done. The approach asks how policies are adopted and implemented within and for urban areas. Much of the emphasis is on organizational behavior, which may be explained in terms of legal and financial rights and obligations or organizational decision rules and role structures. There is often a reformist element in this approach, which sees in organization and, especially, in reorganization, a means of changing conditions within the city or city government.

The Urban-Problems Approach[4]   The urban-problems approach views urban affairs in terms of a particular social problem—housing, employment, racism, poverty, education, health, crime, transportation, pollution—and what concretely may be done about this problem through public policy and programmatic action. Urban affairs are seen through the lens of the technical specialist in a particular professional field. Politics and the government structure become relatively unimportant compared to the way an urban problem is perceived and the legislation and administration that are designed to cope with that problem. The concern is with identifying, defining, and solving the kinds of social problems found exclusively, predominantly, or, perhaps, more acutely in urban areas. Urban affairs are studied in terms of mobilizing professional skill and public support to work on such problems as welfare dependency, slums, dwindling tax revenues, unemployment, violent disorders, crime, discrimination, segregation, and environmental degradation. The "problems" approach focuses on how and by whom problems are perceived; how and by whom they are defined; and how and by whom they are being solved or, at least, attacked. Those adopting this approach often ask such questions as: Are urban problems unique to urban areas? Are solutions to urban problems likely to be found locally, regionally, or nationally? Does everyone agree on what major problems and solutions are? To what extent are problems likely to persist, go away by themselves through benign neglect, or yield to public action?

The Urban-Development Approach[5]   The urban-development approach is focused not so much on the quality of urban life as on the impact of urbanism on national development. Urbanization is seen not as a local, but as a national problem. The primary question is: How does the growth of cities affect the goals of national economic and political development? Urban affairs, seen collectively, become independent rather than dependent variables—the causes rather than the effects. From this perspective urban affairs are no more important than rural affairs. Rural-urban interaction with national variables is the object of concern and study. The functioning of cities and their governments is looked at as part of an integrated national system of urban and rural communities—a system that has

profound consequences for the rate and pattern of demographic, economic, and institutional change. From the urban-development perspective, the key questions are: What is the best pattern of urban-rural spatial development for the purposes of promoting rapid economic growth, minimizing social and individual disruption, and maximizing the achievement of national identity and national goals? Is the growth of cities or of particular urban areas good or bad from the standpoint of economic or political development and stability? Can and should something be done to regulate (through planning) the pace and pattern of urban growth? Does urbanization—(whether it is the growth of city populations, the growth in the urban share in the national population, or the diffusion of urban ways of life to rural areas) represent "progress"? From the urban-development perspective, it may seem rational and enlightened to reduce the level of urban performance—to build fewer roads, *not* to increase the water supply—so as to reduce the external attractiveness of cities for migrants and to achieve a preferred pattern of national territorial development. From that perspective, it may seem rational to reduce the capabilities of urban units in the interests of balanced national development.

We have preferred in this book to adopt the performance approach because we feel that it is likely to provide understanding of important aspects of comparative urban politics and, eventually, to help in the formulation of effective urban policy. The performance approach starts with *outcomes* of urban processes—the differences among cities in the way people live and the quality of urban life—and attempts to identify the impact on these intercity variations of differences in politics: how people are governed, by what kinds of political forces, by what policies, under what organizational arrangements, with what distribution of rights and authority. We are broadly interested in the question: To what extent does politics seem to matter in determining the distribution of services and satisfactions among the people living in cities around the world?

The performance approach has, to be sure, a number of difficulties. A crucial one is the problem of isolating the role of politics and government in urban life so that the impact of politics can be weighed and compared to that of other kinds of variables—economic, demographic, cultural, or historical. The quality of life in cities is the product of many things besides politics: the nature of the international economy, historical traditions, the pattern of race relations, class structure, the operations of the market, regional migration trends, and the like. It is often difficult to identify in an objective manner the extent to which politics—the distribution of power and the distribution of values among the powerful—is responsible for the health, safety, and welfare of an urban community. In some cases, where the scope of government is extremely broad, as in communist systems, the impact of politics, being so nearly total, is quite identifiable. Where the scope of government is less than total, it is often very hard to tell how much of urban quality to attribute to government, private action, the environment, or chance.

The second difficulty has to do with the nesting of urban performance in various nonlocal patterns of influence. Urban governmental autonomy in many countries is quite limited; this means that local environmental conditions and local

governmental structures may have less impact on what happens in the local community than events occurring at the regional, national, or the international level.
One has only to remember the impact of the world energy shortage on life-styles in
cities (and to imagine what the consequences of thermonuclear warfare might be) to
see how important international factors can be in the life of cities today. Urban performance is affected by variables that are not urban or neatly localized for us to
study. The nesting phenomenon—the intermeshing of influences from local, regional, national, and international levels—is a complicating assumption, but one that
we must make.

1-2 ISSUES IN THEORY BUILDING

UNITS OF COMPARISON: CITIES VERSUS URBAN AREAS

Comparing cities is more difficult than comparing nations because the units of
analysis at the national level are more clearly identifiable. The boundaries of the
demographic entities we think of as cities are seldom clearly defined. What makes a
settlement a "city" or "urban" is not self-evident, nor are the kinds of settlements
one should include in the comparative study of urban areas. Should urban areas be
defined by size, density, occupational structure, or style of life? Is the urban community basically a labor market, a communications grid, a commutation area, or a
community based on common norms, loyalties, and identifications? In many parts
of the world, there are local government units with densely settled and sizeable
populations (as many as 30 to 50 thousand people), yet the major economic activity
is farming. Are these giant peasant villages to be considered cities simply because, as
settlements, they have a certain size and density? Italian rural sociologists deny that
settlements in which more than two-thirds of the labor force is engaged in agriculture should be classified as urban. In the case of Philippine, Spanish, and Latin
American *municipios,* the total municipal population may be large, but relatively
few people may be living in conditions of urban density or life-style.[6]

Most often, the definition of "city" that we are forced to use is the city as
defined by law. Any local government jurisdiction of a certain minimum size is
considered—for the purposes of legalistic definition—to constitute a city. But the
legal city does not necessarily correspond to the economic, demographic, or political
city. The jurisdiction of a local government may include only a small portion of the
geographic city. Many people who work in the city, who are influential in city
politics, who drive in or through the city, who study in the city, or who buy in the
city's commercial establishments may live outside the central city's boundaries. The
total urbanized area, the total human settlement, may be governed by a number—
sometimes large—of separate, mutually independent local governments. Conversely,
the territory of a city as defined by law may include a number of people living in
rural styles and engaged in rural occupations. The Hispanic *municipio,* as we have
said, typically contains not only an urban core, but a sizeable rural component.
Thus, if one compares only legal cities and conditions within them, one may be

comparing rather different types of human settlements by leaving out the urban components outside the legal city and, at the same time, bringing into the comparison rural components that happen to reside within the legal city.

The unit-of-analysis problem makes comparison difficult because it means that the data base for theory building may contain different kinds of objects. Countries vary in the kind and amount of urban statistics they collect, save, or allow to be published. They also vary in the statistical concepts they use to define urban areas. Statistics are usually provided on the basis of legal jurisdiction, which may or may not coincide with the urbanized area. There may be "contaminating" rural elements in the urban data for some countries, but not for others. Even if one is concerned primarily with the process of urbanization, i.e., the spatial agglomeration of population in cities rather than with local performance, the conceptual differences among countries may be important because one may be unable to isolate the urban component of performance within the statistical aggregate.

Definitional differences can produce quite different conclusions on comparative urban performance. Urban conditions may seem better in one country than in another simply because the former country defines any jurisdiction with more than 10,000 people as urban, whereas the latter reduces the threshold to 2500 people. Using the lower threshold will probably reduce the level of performance achieved since it is more likely than not to bring in rural settlements with traditionally lower levels of performance. Analyzing census materials for the period 1955 to 1963 in 123 countries, a United Nations team found that sometimes striking differences could be produced by using national definitions of "urban," on the one hand, and a standard international definition, on the other. As Table 1-2 shows, the correlation between the two measures of urbanization is virtually nil.

It is our view that the study of comparative urban politics is concerned with the way urban settlements and metropolitan areas (that is, "geographic" cities) are governed. Thus we may have to study the behavior and performance of many non-urban or not specifically urban governments, such as rural and suburban governments, state or provincial governments, and national governments, as well as the behavior of city governments as such. Most of our urban data is collected by and for units of government with jurisdictions that may or may not include the urban entities in which we are interested and that may or may not provide the bulk of available public services. The problem is compounded by the fact that in many cities, "private" governments (political parties, churches, voluntary organizations, etc.) may provide important services, thereby making government activity unnecessary. Unfortunately, we do not have the kind of information about "private" government that we have about official governments.

THE STRATEGIES OF COMPARISON

One of the crucial issues in building comparative urban theory is a strategic one, involving the question: Which cities, however defined, should we compare? Does it make sense to compare all the great cities of the world?[7] Given the enormous variety

Table 1-2 The Importance of Definition: National vs. Uniform International Definitions of "Urban"

	Percentage of Total Population Classified in National Census as Urban	Percentage of Total Population Living in Localities of 10,000 or More Inhabitants
Ghana	23.1	17.0
South Africa	46.7	38.2
South West Africa	23.5	9.2
Togo	9.6	7.7
Barbados	4.9	89.1
British Honduras	53.9	36.3
Canada (1956)	66.6	41.9
Dominican Republic	30.5	95.0
Mexico	50.7	35.4
Puerto Rico	44.1	32.0
United States	69.9	54.3
Brazil	45.1	32.2
Venezuela	62.5	53.0
Japan	56.3	83.1
Korea	24.5	72.2
Philippines	29.9	90.7
Austria	50.0	42.8
Belgium	66.4	48.0
Denmark	69.0	53.4
Finland	55.9	32.2
France	63.0	46.0
Italy	47.7	60.0
Netherlands	80.0	59.6
Poland	47.7	37.8
Sweden	72.8	48.1

Source: United Nations Economic and Social Council, "Statistical Concepts and Definitions of Urban and Rural Population: National, Regional and World-Wide," July 11, 1967.

of urban contexts from country to country and region to region, should we instead attempt to make comparisons *within* multinational regions, (for example, comparing Latin American, Asian, European, or African cities)?[8] Given the great variety within these multinational regions, should we restrict our comparisons to the cities of the same nation-state?[9] Should we compare only cities belonging to regions that have reached similar levels of technology and development; only cities with the same general type of political economy (communist or noncommunist); or only cities with the same general type of political structure (autonomous democratic versus centralized autocratic)?[10]

Ideally, a comparative theory of urban performance should deal with performance in all countries, at all levels of development, within all kinds of institutional matrices. However, the most comprehensive kind of comparison—admittedly an ideal to be realized—is also the most difficult kind to make. When one compares urban government performance in a variety of countries or even on a single continent and finds inequalities of performance, how is one to know whether these are due to national policy, traditions, ideology, social structure, economic development level, government structure, legislative and fiscal patterns, or distribution of power? All of these factors are apt to differ from country to country.

Comparing urban performance within a single country allows us to hold some national factors constant in order to identify the impact of particular regional or local forces shaping performance. Comparisons within countries (or even within states) are also more feasible than world-wide or regional comparisons because we are more apt to have the necessary information in comparable form. Comparable information about cities in various countries of the world is scarce.[11] As Table 1-3 shows, a large proportion of the metropolitan areas of the world are to be found in countries such as the Soviet Union and China, which have, hitherto at least, been difficult to study.

Even within most countries, however, there is wide variation in the economic, culultural, and legal contexts in which cities are governed. Institutional diversity within countries is particularly great in the federal systems which allow each subnational government (state, province) to make its own allocation of rights and obligations to local governments. In the United States, India, or West Germany, each state makes its own rules on how cities are to be governed. Differential performance among United States, Indian, or German cities may thus be due to different institutional arrangements from state to state.

Table 1-3   Location and Emergence of Metropolitan Areas
in the World, 1950-1970

(Number of Areas of 100,000 or More in 1950, 1960,
and (estimated) 1970 by Country)

By Continent:

AFRICA	*1950*	*1960*	*1970*
Algeria	4	5	5
Libya	1	2	2
Morocco	6	8	10
Sudan	1	1	1
Tunisia	1	1	1
United Arab Republic	7	12	15
Dahomey	0	0	1
Ghana	1	3	5
Guinea	0	1	1
Ivory Coast	0	1	2
Mali	0	1	1
Nigeria	7	12	19
Senegal	1	1	1
Sierra Leone	0	1	1
Togo	0	0	1
Ethiopia	1	2	2
Kenya	1	2	2

Table 1-3   Location and Emergence of Metropolitan Areas
in the World, 1950-1970 (continued)

(Number of Areas of 100,000 or More in 1950, 1960,
and (estimated) 1970 by Country)

By Continent:

AFRICA

	1950	1960	1970
Madagascar	1	1	1
Malawi	0	0	1
Mauritius	0	0	1
Mozambique	0	1	1
Somalia	0	0	1
Southern Rhodesia	1	2	2
Tanganyika	0	1	1
Uganda	0	1	1
Zambia	0	0	3
Angola	1	1	1
Cameroon	0	1	2
Central African Republic	0	0	1
Congo, Brazzaville	0	1	1
Congo, Democratic Republic of the	2	4	5
South Africa	10	12	17
Total, Africa	46	78	109

NORTH AMERICA

	1950	1960	1970
Canada	14	17	20
United States of America	119	154	178
Total, North America	133	171	198

LATIN AMERICA

	1950	1960	1970
Costa Rica	1	1	1
El Salvador	1	1	2
Guatemala	1	1	1
Honduras	0	1	1
Mexico	10	17	23
Nicaragua	1	1	1
Panama	1	1	1
Cuba	3	3	6
Dominican Republic	1	1	2
Haiti	1	1	1
Jamaica	1	1	1
Puerto Rico	1	2	2
Bolivia	1	1	2
Brazil	16	33	36
Guyana	0	1	1
Colombia	8	11	15
Ecuador	2	2	2
Peru	1	2	4
Surinam	0	0	1
Venezuela	3	5	0

(Number of Areas of 100,000 or More in 1950, 1960,
and (estimated) 1970 by Country)

By Continent:

LATIN AMERICA	*1950*	*1960*	*1970*
Argentina	11	15	16
Chile	3	4	6
Paraguay	1	1	1
Uruguay	1	1	1
Total, Latin America	69	107	127

ASIA	*1950*	*1960*	*1970*
Taiwan	7	9	12
China	99	124	139
Hong Kong	1	1	1
North Korea	4	7	9
South Korea	8	9	17
Macao	1	1	1
Mongolia	0	1	1
Ryuku Islands	0	1	1
Japan	64	113	133
Burma	3	3	5
Cambodia	1	1	1
Indonesia	11	21	25
Laos	1	1	1
Malaysia	2	3	6
Philippines	7	8	10
Singapore	1	1	1
Thailand	2	2	3
North Vietnam	2	2	5
South Vietnam	1	3	4
Afghanistan	1	2	3
Ceylon	1	1	2
India	178	198	226
Kashmir	1	2	2
Nepal	1	1	1
Pakistan	11	16	20
Total, Asia	408	531	629

EUROPE			
Denmark	3	3	4
Finland	3	3	3
Ireland	2	2	2
Norway	2	2	4
Sweden	3	3	5
United Kingdom	57	57	57
Austria	5	5	5
Belgium	5	5	5

**Table 1-3   Location and Emergence of Metropolitan Areas
in the World, 1950-1970 (continued)**

(Number of Areas of 100,000 or More in 1950, 1960,
and (estimated) 1970 by Country)

By Continent:

EUROPE	1950	1960	1970
France	23	37	42
West Germany	40	40	41
Netherlands	12	16	17
Switzerland	5	6	7
Bulgaria	2	4	6
Czechoslovakia	5	5	6
East Germany	10	11	11
Hungary	3	4	5
Poland	12	15	16
Romania	5	12	14
Albania	0	1	1
Greece	2	3	3
Italy	26	31	41
Portugal	2	2	2
Spain	24	25	30
Yugoslavia	8	13	19
USSR	114	160	202
Total, Europe (and Soviet Asia)	373	465	548
OCEANIA			
Australia	6	8	10
New Zealand	3	3	5
Total, Oceania	9	11	15
WORLD TOTAL	1038	1363	1626

Source: Calculated from Kingsley Davis, *World Urbanization 1950-1970 Volume I:
Basic Data for Cities, Countries, and Regions* (Berkeley: Institute of International
Studies, University of California, 1969), pp. 163-233.

The more dimensions along which cities vary, the harder it is to isolate the
causes of differential behavior among them. But the search for relatively homogeneous contexts within which to make comparisons is limited by the fact that the
more homogeneous the environment, the fewer the city governments one is apt to
be dealing with and the riskier becomes any generalization based on a smaller and
smaller number of units. This is, of course, a major difficulty with case studies of
individual cities.

URBAN DATA FOR COMPARISON

A third issue in comparative urban studies involves the information base on which
to build empirical theory. Materials on urban government exist for relatively few
countries. Statistical materials are available more for the cities in developed indus-

trial societies than for the cities in developing and communist societies. Where urban data exist, they are sometimes not satisfactory for investigations of performance. They indicate how much municipal governments spend or plan to spend, for example, without indicating the impact of spending–the actual services delivered, public satisfaction with service levels, or policy goals achieved. For some crucial dimensions of government performance, particularly those involving integrity (that is, honesty and due process), there are few reliable indicators, certainly few comparative statistics. Some urban governments are more corrupt than others; some are much less affected than others by what we Americans call the principles of due process and equal protection. Yet in this vital area of performance, information is seldom available; when available, it is seldom useful for making meaningful comparisons.

There is a systematic bias in the kinds of performance data which are made available and those which are not. We tend to learn a lot about the physical and monetary outputs of government, but little about the regularity and responsiveness of the governmental process. We tend to learn a good deal about how much is spent, but little about what spending achieves. Urban governments tend to tell us a lot about their efforts and activities, but little about the distribution of their efforts and activities among the various groups in the urban area.

We often have to compare performance in terms of per-capita spending, yet per-capita figures can be highly misleading. The same per-capita figure–say $500 per pupil in the city schools–can be an average of $300 in some schools and $700 in others; or it can be an average of $500 in all the schools of the city. The same level of per-capita expenditures on education might hide the existence of radically different distribution policies. In cities where severe social cleavages are tied to a pattern of spatial segregation, the distributional aspect of government outputs is obviously important. But statistics on distribution are seldom collected and, if collected, seldom published because of their politically explosive nature.

Statistical materials vary also in reliability. Per-capita figures, for example, have to be treated with discretion because the number of "heads" in a city is so often uncertain. When performance measures for a city are worked out, based on services of facilities per person, we tend to assume that the number of persons benefiting from or using the service is known. In fact, even in the most advanced societies, there is seldom a precise knowledge of how many people there are in a city at any given time. The population of cities varies according to the time of day (nighttime residents and visitors vs. daytime residents and commuters) and the time of year. Tourist cities have extremely variable populations. Not only that, but even the steady residential population is difficult to know precisely. Many, probably most, cities have a segment of the population that does not want to be counted: people in trouble with the law, people living in a city without official permission from the police, or people living in the city who have entered the country illegally. The number of illegal residents of Los Angeles, for example, is estimated at between 500,000 and 1,000,000 people! There is also the problem of census taking in lower class or dangerous neighborhoods: in many cities, census takers hesitate or refuse to enter certain neighborhoods or houses, or they simply don't want to bother. Even in

Moscow—located in a country with supposedly totalitarian control over individual behavior—the authorities found from the 1970 census that they had been under-estimating the city's population by several hundred thousand.[12]

Ideally, we would like to be able to produce a theory of urban government based on statistically validated, empirical generalizations. We would like to be able to say, for example, that the greater the degree of urban "home rule," or the more democratic a city government, the higher the government's performance in terms of integrity, responsiveness, and effectiveness. Unfortunately, many basic factors in performance are not reducible to statistical analysis. The more qualitative and sub-jective aspects of government performance are difficult to measure and quantify, as are some of the factors that shape performance.

Performance is most easily measured and explained when the performance criteria can be made measurable and accessible: when people can translate their notions of performance into quantitative indicators. Sometimes performance levels can be expressed in terms of what are called *interval scales,* where the precise nu-merical differences in performance can be plotted. Sometimes performance can be measured less precisely by means of *ordinal scales,* which indicate the rank-order of performance without indicating the amounts of difference between the perfor-mance levels. In many instances, however, we have no scale to measure performance, and only impressionistic judgments can be made.

The second step in developing a theory of performance involves the search for the possible correlates or causes of variations in performance. Assuming that we can find measurable indices of performance, the next step is to determine what variables seem to be associated with those variations. Suppose we decided to measure the performance of cities by using a measure of housing quality, such as the average number of persons per room in a city. We will find a wide range of performance on this scale, such as shown in Chapter Two. The next step is to examine the literature on cities and housing to identify the possible correlates or causes of differences in housing crowdedness. At this point we often come up against a major problem: some of the possible causes of performance (such as different national housing poli-cies) are just as difficult to operationalize as the types of performance themselves. Often, considerable ingenuity must be exercised in order to devise ways of testing the importance of particular variables in shaping urban performance.

Some possible causes are easily tested, others are not. If our data are biased in favor of certain factors over others because measures of those factors are more easily accessible, our conclusions and our recommendations may be biased as well. For example, one of the questions facing the student of comparative urban govern-ment is precisely the question of the importance of local politics and political ac-tion in shaping urban performance. Some studies of state and local performance in the United States have suggested that political factors—compared to social and economic factors, such as the level of economic development—are relatively unim-portant in determining the quantity and quality of what government produces. If this is so, the possibilities of improving urban performance directly (that is, locally) would be slim compared to the possibilities of improving performance by acting on forces that shape the level of economic development.

If economic forces are decisive and difficult to act upon—at least at the local level—responsibility for urban performance will rise to governmental levels with greater leverage over economic growth. If the facts of regional, national, or international economics set basic constraints on what services and amenities can be provided in a city, local action will be futile: local performance will be judged in terms of local ability to get higher level authorities to act. This logic seems to lie behind proposals to alleviate the urban crisis in country after country. Most reform schemes look to action at higher governmental levels or by new, higher governmental levels, such as metropolitan or regional governments, as the only way of raising local performance. Local political action, then, becomes important only insofar as it creates capabilities for securing aid from higher levels. The possibilities for local self-determination conversely depend on success in securing resources while retaining freedom of action from higher levels. But this whole issue may, in fact, be a product of distortions based on biases in the data upon which comparative studies have been mounted. Local political factors may be crucial in shaping performance, but simply not reducible to easily measurable form.

CONCEPTS FOR COMPARISON

Even when we have reliable and comparable data on urban performance, we often lack adequate concepts with which to organize them into intelligible form, that is, theory. Despite all the attention that has hitherto been paid to urban institutions and processes and to such matters as urban governmental forms and community power structures, we have few generally accepted typologies to describe the environments of performance or the type of performance itself.

So, for example, though we are very much interested in whether or not the degree of democracy in a city has consequences for city policy, there is no standard concept of democracy that would allow us to relate degrees of democracy to city performance. We face the same problem with another key institutional variable—autonomy—the degree to which a city government is free to make its own policies for the community. Does greater local autonomy make for higher performance? This is an assumption made by many people, but without a standardized definition of autonomy, we are hard pressed to know whether the assumption is empirically valid. In dealing with comparative urban performance, we can only stipulate definitions of key terms, knowing that some readers may disagree with our definitions and, therefore, our findings.

Just as there are no agreed-upon concepts of democracy or autonomy to help us in understanding the input side of performance, there are no generally accepted ways of describing or evaluating performance outcomes. Therefore, theory building in comparative urban performance must start by identifying the performance criteria used by various social, professional, and political groups and by attempting to see how well various cities measure up to these standards. In our view, there are no absolute standards of urban performance, absolute in the sense that they universally hold or are "scientific." People apply different standards and make varying assessments of urban performance. Some citizens prefer minimal government and low taxation; others desire a high level of services and are willing to pay for them; still others prefer a system which allows them to provide services for themselves, but not much for others. Some find a certain amount of disease or environmental degradation "normal" and acceptable; to others within that city or in different cultures, the same condition might seem intolerable. Practices that seem proper in law enforcement in one community might outrage people in another community or another group within the same community.

Just as ordinary people apply varying subjective standards to urban performance, so do those whose education or training make them sophisticated in their assessments. Thus, city planners do not agree among themselves on what constitutes a well-planned or an ideal community. Some planners admire well-ordered, designed environments; others prefer spontaneity, disorder, or "ordered anarchy." No greater consensus is to be found among other professional groups concerned with performance in such fields as education, welfare, public health, transportation, or housing.

Some performance standards are nonetheless rather widely shared: those involving public health, sanitation, housing conditions, education and literacy, water supply, street paving and lighting, parks and gardens, food inspection, building regulation, and business and occupational licensing. There would be no great disagreement in any international body that epidemics should be prevented; streets be paved and lighted; houses be safely constructed and not crowded with more than one family per room; parks be provided; children be educated; some transportation and means of communication be made available, and so on. There might be sharp disagreement, however, on how important these objectives or needs are compared to other societal or personal goals.

Thus, for example, tens or hundreds of thousands of migrants in Calcutta "by skimping on housing, civic amenities, privacy and sanitation . . . manage to save a maximum of their earnings to send home to their families in rural villages."[13] Poor environmental conditions may be a price some are willing to pay to achieve more important personal goals, such as supporting families back in rural areas. Similarly, communist governments, although accepting many of the same performance criteria as Western governments, consider civic amenity less important than rapid industrialization and consider investment in urban infrastructure a relatively unprofitable form of investment compared to other means of stimulating economic development. Thus, even when the same criteria are held, they may be given different priority by different groups, organizations, and cultures.

Just as there are few universal standards for urban performance, there are few universally defined urban problems. A problem exists because there is a perceived gap between actual performance and someone's performance standards or expectations. Problems are culturally, socially, and individually defined: there is seldom consensus concerning the nature and intensity of urban problems. One man's problem (for example, noise pollution) may provide another man's enjoyment (for example, music). One individual may see the absence of an expressway as a gap to be filled, whereas someone living in the part of the city concerned may see that absence as a means of protecting his or her neighborhood against outside traffic or overdevelopment. Many people in the community may not see police brutality as a problem, but other community segments may consider this to be the major problem in their city.

Not only do individuals and social groups differ in the way they perceive and define urban problems—members of the learned professions also develop "tunnel vision." Professions tend to concentrate on a few issues in the community and disregard other aspects of the community or even the side effects of their own activities. The highway engineer is apt to reduce "the urban problem" to a matter of traffic congestion and measure the adequacy of his solutions in terms of dollars and cents. The sociologist looks at urban transportation in different terms and sees the highway department *creating* problems by disrupting neighborhoods. The comparative urbanist cannot assume that what is seen as an urban problem from one perspective is similarly viewed from another.

The reader will not find an attempt here to press universally valid criteria for urban performance. We evaluate and attempt to explain performance by stipulating a set of performance criteria—integrity, responsiveness, and effectiveness—that we find personally persuasive and that also seems to have some measure of general acceptance. In the absence of a party line or other infallible pronouncement on what constitutes good performance, there is likely to be a number of different and, perhaps, equally valid perspectives. Our underlying assumption is pluralistic: good performance, we believe, lies in the eyes of the observer. We tend to answer the question, "Whose city?" by saying: "Everyone's."

Comparative urban studies are significant because they deal with the problems of an increasingly large segment of the world's population. We can learn much about urban problems by studying them comparatively. While doing so, we shall be learning a good deal about society and government generally: we shall be studying how different governments and societies define and cope with their own form of urban crisis. The systematic study of comparative performance in dealing with urban problems will, we hope, help to produce a better understanding of the nature and causes of these problems and consequently a greater capability to solve them.

The difficulties in formulating a comparative theory of urban government performance are several: they involve

1. ambiguities in definition of units of analysis;
2. lack of information about performance;
3. lack of agreed on concepts and categories for such key variables as "democracy," "autonomy," "output," "values," and "power";
4. enormous variation in the legal, political, social, cultural, and economic context of urban government from country to country and within countries;
5. the difficulty in isolating the *causes* of performance differentials;
6. the lack of universal standards for performance or universally defined urban "problems"; and
7. the ethnocentric or culture-bound nature of many of our urban concepts, research techniques, and working assumptions.

Students of comparative urban government, can, however, take heart from the fact that much of the world's city building lies in the fiture. Between now and the year 2000, as much housing will have to be built as now exists. We hope we may be able, through comparative study, to learn just enough about urban performance by that time to be able to shape cities to fit the needs and expectations of a wide variety of people.

THE PERFORMANCE OF CITY GOVERNMENTS 2

2-1 INTEGRITY IN URBAN GOVERNMENT

Since there are as many valid performance standards as there are people, a theory of urban performance must start with the criteria that we think constitute good performance. We think there are three fundamental standards: integrity, responsiveness, and effectiveness. We assume that the performance of urban governments can validly be assessed in terms of three sets of values:[1]

- *Integrity and human rights.* To what extent are public decisions made and administered honestly, impartially, legally, openly, and considerately? To what extent do city officials (or officials governing the city) act with restraint and fairness when affecting citizen's lives and property? To what extent are mechanisms available by which citizens, at little cost to themselves, can challenge the legality of official action? How effective are the mechanisms for scrutinizing the legality of official actions and for redressing grievances?
- *Responsiveness.* How well does the government perform in the eyes of the community? How receptive is government to movements for change? How extensive is citizen participation in government? How intensive is the search by government to discover community preferences? How intensive are government efforts to provide the community with information about past decisions and future alternatives? How representative of the community is the staffing of city institutions? How effective are the mechanisms, such as the mass media, for expressing criticism of governmental performance?
- *Effectiveness.* How well does the government achieve its goals, solve or alleviate problems, search for new solutions, minimize costs, and provide for minimal standards of health, safety, and welfare?

It is, of course, easier to enunciate criteria for performance than it is to turn such criteria into operational instruments of measurement. This is particularly the case with the first set of criteria—those relating to what we have called governmental integrity. Some urban governments are clearly more corrupt, discriminatory, exploitative, secretive, and immune from challenge than others, but we have little precise knowledge about the distribution of these traits of integrity today or in the past. Our notions of the extent and distribution of corruption derive from periodic and spectacular incidents and from our informal civic training in cynicism, rather than from accurate surveys of municipal pathology.

CROSS-SECTIONAL COMPARISONS

There are, of course, few surveys of corruption; studies of corruption either generalize that corruption is well-nigh universal or that it is to be found only in particular types of countries ("modernizing" or "non-Western" countries) or cities with particular types of party systems ("machines"). Some cities are, however, clearly more corrupt than others; that is, in those cities it is necessary (or possible) to bribe officials in order to secure the performance (or nonperformance) of official duty; it is common for officials to extort bribes, embezzle funds, and award jobs and contracts to friends, supporters, and relatives. In the less corrupt cities of the world, officials obey the law; comply with their duty to enforce the law; make decisions on the basis of standards of impartiality, fairness, and merit; and, in general, use their authority in ways that could be defended as legitimate in the courts and in the press. In the less corrupt cities of the world, a motorist is less likely to be shaken down by a policeman demanding a bribe and is less likely to be able to fix a ticket. In such cities, one is less apt to be able (or forced) to buy a favorable zoning decision or to be required to pay off certain officials in order to obtain a business license, an apartment in public housing, or even a bed in a public hospital.

Table 2-1 illustrates how one might rank the parts of the world in terms of the incidence of municipal corruption. This ranking is based not only on reports from the various parts of the world, but also on the authors' personal experiences and impressions derived from having lived and worked for periods of time in North America, Latin America, and Europe. The ranking is very tentative.[2]

It is much easier to make comparisons with regard to those aspects of integrity that involve, not so much the shadow world of corruption as, the more overt and institutionalized world of human rights. Corruption is not unrelated to human rights, to be sure; for the use of office for personal gain may involve the violation of

Table 2-1 Comparative Municipal Corruption in the World

Least Corruption			*Greatest Corruption*
Northwest Europe	United States	Southern Europe	Latin America
China?	Commonwealth	Eastern Europe	Asia
East Germany?	Tunisia	USSR	Africa
North Vietnam?	Singapore		Middle East

individual rights. But, on the other hand, a strict and Puritanical law-oriented administration may also be one that heavily emphasizes the rights of the government over the rights of the individual. Communist city governments sometimes have little corruption, but they have been reluctant to develop mechanisms and principles that would allow private individuals to challenge the propriety or legality of public actions. Communist justice is heavily weighted in favor of collective, over individual, interests. Western notions of legality and the rule of law—concepts involving due process—are considered out of place in proletarian dictatorships. Government officials in communist cities are much less concerned with legality and individual legal rights than their Western counterparts.

Table 2-2 gives an estimate of the distribution of civil liberties in cities around the world, based on a survey of Freedom House, for the year 1978.

We can also compare the cities of the world in terms of equal protection. Here we ask not whether government officials use office to pursue private interests, or whether they ignore individual rights in the pursuit of private or indeed collective interests; but rather we ask whether they act impartially in deciding among legitimately competing interests. Is government authority used to work against or to reinforce social differences and inequalities based on class, occupation, race, ethnicity, sex, political affiliation, or religion? Are people from all kinds of groups given substantially equal consideration by those governing the city? Or are members of some groups treated as political enemies, pariahs, or second-class citizens? Are government officials engaged in active efforts to promote minority rights and more favorable treatment for minorities?

Just as all cities have some degree of petty corruption, all have some degree of class discrimination by government. No city has a completely homogeneous population so that everyone is treated with equal respect and consideration. In the communist cities, where class differences are said not to exist, the party, government, military, production, and cultural elites typically receive disproportionate shares of scarce consumer goods, including housing space. Even in the most egalitarian of cities—those of China—there are sizeable class differences in the housing space allocated to individuals with different roles in the governing and productive process.

Class differences challenge the impartiality of government in all cities. In some cities—those with racial, religious, ethnic, or political minorities—class cleavages constitute only one source of potential discrimination among many. There are minorities vulnerable to discrimination in many cities around the world. In Table 2-3 we give a crude comparative estimate of the distribution of minority rights among some cities of the world. The problems of racial minorities in American cities have received enormous (and deserved) attention in recent times, though, quite likely, the situation has been much worse for minorities of various kinds in other countries of the world—countries which are more discreet about reporting unfavorable conditions or more accustomed and indifferent to traditional forms of inequality.[3] Tolerance for political opponents varies enormously. It is virtually nonexistent in many cities of the world, including cities that have good records with regard to social equality. Even the religiously, ethnically, and racially homogeneous

Table 2-2 Comparative Civil Liberties in World Cities, 1978

Greatest Protection						Least Protection
1	2	3	4	5	6	7
Brussels	Santo Domingo	Bogotá	La Paz	Rio de Janeiro	Kabul	Tirana
Sydney	Helsinki	Georgetown	Dacca	Santiago, Chile	Algiers	Bangui
Vienna	Paris	Casablanca	Taipei	Abidjan	Buenos Aires	Addis Ababa
San Jose (Costa Rica)	Athens	Kingston	Karachi	Managua	Rangoon	Hanoi
Montreal	Cologne	Tegucigalpa	Mexico City	Accra	Tripoli, Libya	Kampala
Dublin	Calcutta	Madrid	Cairo	Budapest	Shanghai	Mogadiscio
Tokyo	Tel Aviv	Dakar	Quito	Nairobi	Havana	Bamako
Amsterdam	Rome	Istanbul	Lagos	Tananarive	Prague	Ulan Bator
Oslo	Lisbon	Colombo	Kuala Lumpur	Teheran	East Berlin	Conakry
Auckland	Caracas		Monrovia	Jakarta	Moscow	Baghdad
Stockholm			Kuwait City	Manila	Amman	Sofia
Geneva			Guatemala City	Bangkok	Montevideo	Pyongyang
London				Belgrade	Damascus	
NEW YORK				Lusaka	Dar es Salaam	
Copenhagen				Tunis	Johannesburg	
				Khartoum	Kinshasa	
				Seoul	Bucharest	
				Warsaw	Asunción	

Source: Adapted from the table, "Comparative Survey of Freedom," *Information Please Almanac* 1979, pp. 130-131. This table is based on a survey by Freedom House, "Freedom in the World: Political Rights and Civil Liberties, 1978," available from Freedom House, New York. The estimates in the *Almanac* are for nations; these have been adapted to cities.

Table 2-3 Comparative "Equal Protection" among Urban Governments

Greatest Discrimination			Least Discrimination
South African cities (race) Tropical African cities (Asians) Vietnamese cities (Chinese)	United States Southern cities (race)	Soviet cities (politics, religion)	Chinese cities Northern and Western European cities (foreign workers?)

Scandinavian countries practiced discrimination against the working classes and poor, granting them the right to vote in Sweden, for example, only after World War I. Women were given the right to vote in Switzerland only in the 1960s.

COMPARISONS OVER TIME

Cities can be ranked not only at one point in time, but also across time. Although our across-the-board comparative assessment of liberalism at any given time is and, in the nature of things, must be extremely impressionistic, the same is not true for judgments regarding changes in liberalism over time—at least with regard to particular cities and countries. We can say with a good deal of certainty that the degree of corruption declined drastically, for example, in Chinese cities between 1950 and 1960; American cities between the 1880s and the 1950s; English cities between the 1770s and the 1850s; and Cuban cities between the 1940s and the 1960s. Urban political history is replete with examples of reform movements that attempt, sometimes with enduring success, to "clean up" municipal government; to stop the buying and selling of permits, jobs, contracts, and immunities; and to bring an end to chronic misfeasance (performance of a lawful act in an unlawful manner), malfeasance (performance of unlawful acts), and nonfeasance (failure to perform duties required by law). Urban elections—in those cities in the world where they exist—are much less corrupt than in the eighteenth or nineteenth centuries, when bribery, intimidation, and voting by show-of-hands were regular features of local elections.

A similar liberalization process can be observed with regard to civil liberties and equality before the law. There are few cities in the world in which individuals do not have greater legal protection and greater legal equality today than members of their families had a few generations back. Arbitrary and discriminatory government was normal rather than exceptional before the American and French Revolutions. While the full liberalizing impact of those revolutions has still to be felt in many places, almost everywhere urban government has become liberal in principle, if not in practice. Racial, religious, or class discrimination may be practiced, but it is no longer embodied in the law as it was, for example, in France before 1789; in

Russia before 1917; in Germany before 1918; or in the American South before the 1950s and 1960s.

COMPARATIVE RESPONSIVENESS

As with other forms of performance, responsiveness in urban government can be measured in three ways: (a) the extent, variety, and utilization of formal procedures that attempt to make urban government responsive; (b) informal but suggestive indicators of responsiveness, such as bureaucratic recruitment patterns, patterns of service distribution (who gets what share of city services, jobs, and contracts; who gets what share of the better jobs, services, or contracts); and (c) subjective perceptions of performance: who feels most satisfied with performance, most fairly treated, most efficacious in approaching government with a problem and obtaining satisfaction.

Responsiveness relates not so much to how (that is, with what due process) public functions are performed (integrity), or how well they are performed (effectiveness), but to the nature of the functions themselves: who wants them performed and at what cost? Responsiveness means congruence between community preferences and urban public policies. Responsiveness exists when people living in a city feel that government is doing enough and performing well enough to justify the costs it incurs. It exists also when people feel that government is not being too responsive to improper or illegitimate demands. Responsiveness has to be measured both objectively and subjectively since people in the community may not correctly perceive the level of performance or the extent to which government is trying to be responsive.

How do the city governments of the world rate in terms of responsiveness? In terms of the formal structures of government, those city governments which enjoy considerable decentralized autonomy; which are run democratically; which are characterized by competition among political parties and interest groups; which are subject to the scrutiny of competing and independent media of communication are probably much more responsive—at least to local preferences—than cities run by centrally appointed officials; those run by oligarchies; those governed without openly and legitimately competing parties, groups, and media. Even greater responsiveness can be produced where local electorates are empowered to decide issues directly—through the local referendum. If these institutions mean (as they likely mean) greater responsiveness, then the rank-order of Table 2-4, Comparative Urban Government Responsiveness, makes some sense. The assumption is: Urban governments formally designed to be locally responsive are more likely to be responsive in fact than urban governments not designed to be locally responsive.

In terms of formal procedures designed to enhance responsiveness, American cities are difficult to beat. Consider only:

- the number of directly elected officials
- the degree of local municipal autonomy

Table 2-4 Comparative Political Rights (Responsiveness) in World Cities, 1978

Most Responsive — *Least Responsive*

1	2	3	4	5	6	7
Sydney	Tokyo	Nicosia	Dacca	Cairo	Algiers	Kabul
Brussels	Helsinki	San Salvador	Beirut	Seoul	Buenos Aires	Tirana
Vienna	Athens	Santo Domingo	Casablanca	Jakarta	Bogotá	Sofia
San Jose (C.R.)	Calcutta	Kuala Lumpur	Dakar	Tananarive	Santiago	Rangoon
Montreal	Tel Aviv	Georgetown	Rio de Janeiro	Managua	Havana	Kinshasa
Dublin	Rome	Guatemala City		Taipei	Quito	Addis Ababa
Amsterdam	Kingston			Lagos	Karachi	East Berlin
Oslo	Lisbon			Panama City	Dar es Salaam	Conakry
Auckland				Lima	Belgrade	Port-au-Prince
Stockholm				Asunción	Warsaw	Baghdad
Geneva				Damascus	Tegucigalpa	Ventiane
London				Lusaka	Budapest	Pyongyang
NEW YORK				Manila	Amman	Ulan Bator
Copenhagen				Salisbury	Kuwait City	Maputo
Caracas				Singapore	Monrovia	Bamako
Cologne				Freeport	Katmandu	Tripoli
Paris				Khartoum	Accra	Moscow
					Abidjan	Kampala
					Montevideo	
					Tunis	
					Bangkok	

Source: See source for Table 2-2.

- the ability of voters to recall elected officials
- the ability of voters to make or veto laws and policies through the initiative and referendum
- the dependence of administrators on politicians, and the latter's dependency on freely given voter support
- the freedom of individuals and groups to organize, publicize their criticisms and demands, and petition for redress of grievances
- the freedom of the press and other media
- the proliferation of interest groups
- the numerous devices for consulting public opinion, such as hearings, advisory committees, public opinion surveys
- the ease with which communities can become independent municipal corporations

It may also be that American cities, given the free enterprise system and freedom of movement, may have more responsive urban government since people are free (if not always financially able) to move to localities that suit them best.

One can, of course, challenge this ranking (and we expect our readers will). Two challenges are of particular interest. The first argues that formal structures of government do not necessarily create or guarantee breadth of responsiveness. What really counts is the attitude of decision makers: do they deliberately seek out the preferences of the broadest number of groups when making decisions? Do they attempt to consult as many groups as possible before making decisions? Do they seek out the opinions and preferences of the less organized, the less articulate groups in the community? One can argue that even the officials of a central government appointed to rule a city may be more disposed to cater to local preferences than some officials elected by, accountable to, but not always responsive to the local community. Officials responsible to higher levels of government may be more responsive or attempt to be more locally responsive than local officials. It is quite possible, in fact, for higher-level officials to be more responsive than locally responsible officials to certain parts of the local community—particularly to local minorities. This was certainly the case with federal judges and administrators, compared to local officials, via-à-vis racial minorities in the cities of the American South.

This brings us to the second challenge. Some Marxists would argue that true responsiveness to the interests of the entire community, in general, and to the interests of the working class and of the poor, in particular, is possible only under conditions of proletarian dictatorship—the dictatorship of Communist parties. Given capitalistic economic and social relationships and the power of capitalistic propaganda, it is impossible, say the Marxists, for the lower classes to perceive their true interests and to press them effectively in the political arena. Only when guided by a Communist party—conscious of the true, long-term interests of humanity—can such groups achieve responsive government. Under communist control, they say, decentralization and political competition are unnecessary, even harmful; under capitalist conditions, decentralization and political competition are useless.

Even noncommunist leftists have traditionally been hostile or indifferent to local autonomy and democracy because of the feeling that the necessary radical changes in society could be made only through action at the national or international levels. Democratic socialists have generally looked to centralization rather than decentralization as the means for transforming society or at least equalizing conditions among the social groups in various parts of their countries. In recent times, however, even socialists have had greater sympathy for decentralization, local participation, and community self-government as intrinsic values.

Democratic socialists do not subscribe to the theories of "virtual" representation advocated by the communists; they do not, that is, believe that control by the communists necessarily means a higher form of responsiveness—responsiveness to the long-term interests of all communities. But they are likely to think that only where the working and lower classes are organized into Labor, Socialist, or Communist parties will they receive a proper share of attention and consideration from public authorities. Thus it can be argued that American cities, though possessing in unusual degree the traits of decentralized autonomy and referendum-type democracy, are not and cannot be as responsive to the poor as cities in other decentralized, democratic systems where the poor have separate and specific political representation. The fact that most American cities have nonpartisan electoral systems is said to militate against responsiveness to lower-class interests.[4]

We might also note that, again in terms of formal structure, American city councils tend to be much smaller—and *perhaps* less representative as a consequence—than city councils in the other advanced democracies, as shown in Table 2-5. Also, as we shall document in Chapter 4, American voter registration laws create the smallest pools of eligible voters of any of the advanced democracies.[5] Nonetheless, the preponderance of evidence based on formal structures of government suggests that responsiveness to the general public is as high in American cities as it is anywhere.

Evidence based on recruitment of officials (the distribution of office) and on the allocation of government services and sanctions is simply not available, except for American cities. In no other country do we have data on who gets what (positive goods or negative sanctions) from urban government. Evidence from the few American studies on the subject seem to indicate that the prime beneficiaries of urban government in the United States are the poor and the rich; those in between seem less favored.[6] Whether this is a pattern common to other advanced countries is not known. The pattern of allocations in communist or Third World cities is also not known, although evidence points in the direction of relative equality in the communist cities and sharp inequality in Third World cities.

Evidence about comparative responsiveness based on actual surveys of how people in various cities of the world evaluate performance is fragmentary. Only one cross-national study has been made in this area—the famous *Civic Culture* survey of the early 1960s. This classic study of government in five nations by Gabriel Almond and Sydney Verba found striking differences in the way people expect (or in 1960 expected) to be treated by local officials and the police in the United States, Britain,

West Germany, Italy, and Mexico.[7] Table 2-5 gives some support to the idea that decentralized, democratic urban governments are more responsive or give the impression of being more responsive than governments which are more controlled from above or controlled by an authoritarian political party. Most observers would rank the urban governments of the five nations in the same order in terms of decentralized competitiveness as they are ranked in the Almond-Verba survey data.

Responsiveness is difficult to measure comparatively in that, subjectively at least, it depends so much on expectations. A government may be judged responsive even when it does nothing, if people expect it to do nothing. A government may be judged unresponsive even when it tries hard and does much, simply because people's expectations are high. Protest demonstrations in a city may be a sign of unresponsiveness—failure of government to do what people expect it to do. They may also be a sign of responsiveness—the result of previous governmental responsiveness to protest. Still, there are differences among the city governments in the world in the degree to which they tolerate protest and the degree to which they can and will act against widespread and intense community preferences. There is greater toleration of protest and avoidance of unpopularity in the advanced democracies than in the authoritarian Third World or the totalitarian communist world. But despite their tolerance and their sensitivity to public opinion, even in the advanced democracies, there is a widely held, strong, and growing feeling that government is simply not responsive enough to the interests of the ordinary person.[8]

Table 2-5   The Comparative Representativeness of City Councils:
Persons per Council Representative (1970s). U.S. cities
in capital letters

PERSONS PER CITY COUNCIL REPRESENTATIVE

less than 10,000	10-25,000	25-50,000	50,000 +
PROVIDENCE	Stuttgart	Kyoto	SAN FRANCISCO (65,000)
Malmö	Copenhagen	Munich	CHICAGO (67,000)
Bristol	The Hague	Marseilles	BOSTON (71,000)
Manchester	Sapporo	ST. LOUIS	WASHINGTON (84,000)
Antwerp	Glasgow	CLEVELAND	NEW ORLEANS (85,000)
Oslo	Cologne	ATLANTA	SAN DIEGO (87,000)
Liverpool	Rotterdam	HONOLULU	Paris (91,000)
Le Havre	Vienna	DENVER	PHILADELPHIA (115,000)
Stockholm	Lyon	NEWARK	HOUSTON (154,000)
Düsseldorf	Amsterdam	BALTIMORE	DETROIT (168,000)
Birmingham		Edmonton	LOS ANGELES (188,000)
Strasbourg			NEW YORK (213,000)
Hannover			
Frankfurt			
Bern			
Bonn			
Sheffield			
Bradford			

Source: R. Fried, *World Handbook of Cities,* Ch. 9.

As we suggested in Chapter One, there are no universal, scientific standards by which to judge the effectiveness of city governments or the government of cities—how well urban problems are solved (or at least managed). How one judges urban government performance depends on how one defines urban problems (or the urban crisis) and how one defines the proper role of government in dealing with those problems. Urban politics everywhere turns precisely on the question of what the important problems are (*whose* problem is most important) and what the government (at various levels) ought to do about them. Some people consider many aspects of city life as problematical and requiring government action, whereas others may take a more fatalistic approach. People everywhere are aware of problems in their own lives, but not as aware of problems in other neighborhoods or in the spheres of community life in which they do not participate. People thus define and rank a city's problems differently. They define government's responsibility to act differently. They also have different perspectives on who should pay the costs of acting on city problems (either in taxes, displacement, program priorities, or ideological distaste). Performance standards vary within the cities of every country; not surprisingly, they vary also from city to city within countries and among countries.

Nevertheless, in spite of intracity, intercity, and international differences in standards, some agreement does exist on what governments ought to try to achieve in the provision of urban security and amenity. There is probably a consensus that cuts across national, ideological, sexual, generational, and class boundaries to the effect that cities should

- be reasonably safe for lives and property;
- be reasonably free from preventable types of health hazards;
- have safely constructed, uncrowded, and decently equipped housing;
- have neighborhoods with paved, lit, drained, and cleansed streets;
- have ample and convenient shopping facilities;
- have adequate supplies of potable water, electricity, and fuel;
- ensure minimal provision of food, shelter, and clothing to all;
- be adequately provided with means of transportation and traffic control;
- provide widespread access to communications through mass media and telephone and postal service;
- provide adequate numbers of recreational, cultural, religious, and educational facilities;
- have enough jobs for all desiring employment;
- have minimal social breakdown and degradation (begging, drug addition, suicide, prostitution, family desertion, illegitimacy);
- be adequately provided with services for the elderly, youth, low-income groups, and the handicapped;
- provide some measure of general private comfort;
- finance the provision of public services through fairly assessed and equitable means of raising revenues and through sound financial management.

For a variety of reasons, it is not possible to make comprehensive and precise comparisons in all of these areas of performance for cities in all areas of the world. Even if we had the measures and the data, we would not have the space. What we can do, in the remaining part of this chapter, is to make some illustrative comparisons in a variety of performance areas—comparisons that may help to indicate the range and distribution of performance among the cities in the world.

Safety   Which are the safest cities in the world for lives and property? One way of measuring this is to look at the incidence of violent crime. Unfortunately, many countries like the USSR and the People's Republic of China publish no crime statistics. There are, moreover, problems in making comparisons for those cities for which we have statistics. Crimes are defined differently from country to country, and even from state to state within countries. Then, too, there are differences from country to country and city to city in the extent to which crimes are reported by people to the authorities and are in turn, reported by the local authorities to central statistical offices. In the case of American cities, we know there is a large gap between crime rates as reported to the FBI by local police departments and crime rates as revealed by direct surveys of criminal victimization.*

Be that as it may, if we look at available comparative statistics and surveys, we find that American cities are less safe in terms of violent crime than any other city in the advanced world and less safe than many cities in the Third World! Table

*There seems to be an even greater discrepancy between officially reported crime and victim reported crime in Australian cities. Victimization surveys, such as that conducted by Gallup International, show a pattern of criminality in Australian cities much like that in United States cities. Statistics based on police reports, however, show a much lower incidence of street crime, as in the tables on murder, robbery, rape, and assault shown in Table 2-6.

Question: "During the last five years have any of these happened to you: Has your home been broken into or an attempt made to? Has money or property been stolen from you or other household members? Been personally assaulted physically?" (PERCENT YES)

	United States	Canada	United Kingdom	France	Italy	West Germany	Benelux	Scandinavia	Brazil	Mexico	India	Japan	Australia	Africa
House Broken Into?	17	12	7	8	4	5	7	8	11	23	8	3	14	21
Property Stolen?	26	21	16	11	11	8	2	18	20	28	9	7	25	21
Assaulted Physically?	4	5	5	3	1	2	0	4	7	20	6	2	5	11

Source: The Gallup Organization, *Human Needs and Satisfactions: A Global Survey, SUMMARY VOLUME* (June 1977), pp. 217-18.

2-6 shows that American cities lead much of the world in homicide, robbery, assault, and rape.

Tokyo, with about the same number of people as New York, had 196 murders in 1973 compared to 1680 in New York; 361 robberies compared to 72,750; 426 reported instances of rape compared to 3735. The New York Police shot 314 suspects in 1971; in the three-year period 1968-1971, the British police (protecting 50 million people) wounded or killed six people.[9]

The record of American cities with regard to property safety is only slightly better, as shown in Table 2-7. The lack of safety in American cities is reflected in opinion surveys taken in American and non-American cities about the community problems. When one asks about city problems in European, Japanese, or Indian cities, crime is seldom, if ever, mentioned, even as a minor problem. When one asks the same question about community problems in the United States, street safety emerges as a salient concern.[10] Clearly the absence of public safety is one of the major failures in American urban performance. As Table 2-8 shows, American cities seem to have an abnormally high rate of injury and death from fire—a rate double or even triple the rate in other advanced nations, the communist countries, and Third World countries.[11]

Table 2-6   Comparative Personal Safety in Cities (1970s)*

Relatively Safe Cities			*Relatively Unsafe Cities*
Homicides per 100,000 People			
0-2.4	*2.5-4.9*	*5-9.9*	*More than 10*
Bern	Sydney	BOSTON	WASHINGTON
Toronto	Montreal	Rotterdam	BALTIMORE
Amsterdam	PITTSBURGH	MILWAUKEE	CLEVELAND
Madrid	Nagoya	PORTLAND	ST. LOUIS
London	PROVIDENCE	HONOLULU	Pretoria
West Berlin	MINNEAPOLIS	BUFFALO	ATLANTA
Oslo	Osaka	SAN DIEGO	NEWARK
Calcutta	Palermo	Amsterdam	SAN FRANCISCO
Bombay	SEATTLE	Copenhagen	PHILADELPHIA
Mexico City	Warsaw	Munich	ALBUQUERQUE
Antwerp	Bonn		CHICAGO
Rome	Vienna		CLEVELAND
Tokyo	Edmonton		BALTIMORE
Essen			DALLAS
Yokohama			MIAMI
Sheffield			HOUSTON
Hong Kong			Taipei
Bradford			NEW YORK
			MEMPHIS
			DETROIT
			NEW ORLEANS
			ATLANTA
			Rio de Janeiro
			Athens

Table 2-6   Comparative Personal Safety in Cities (1970s) (continued)

Relatively Safe Cities			*Relatively Unsafe Cities*

Assaults per 100,000 People

0-99	*100-199*	*200+*	
Sydney	BOSTON	SAN FRANCISCO	
Dortmund	CLEVELAND	WASHINGTON	
Bologna	HOUSTON	BALTIMORE	
Rio de Janeiro	Tokyo-to	ST. LOUIS	
Warsaw	Essen	Sheffield, England	
Yokohama	Hong Kong	Bonn	
	Vienna	Edmonton	
	Bradford (199)		

Rape Rate per 100,000 People

0-10	*11-25*	*26-50*	*50+*
Montreal	Oslo	SAN FRANCISCO	ATLANTA
Toronto	Zürich	NEW YORK	DETROIT
Copenhagen	Stockholm	CHICAGO	DALLAS
Vienna	Warsaw	BOSTON	LOS ANGELES
Sydney	Munich		ST. LOUIS
MILWAUKEE	West Berlin		NEWARK
Tokyo	PHILADELPHIA		WASHINGTON, D.C.
Hong Kong	Göteborg		Bradford, England (65)
Yokohama	Hamburg		
	PROVIDENCE		
	Bonn		
	Bern		
	Edmonton		

Robberies per 100,000 People

1-99	*100-199*	*200-299*	*Over 300*
Taipei	Montreal	ST. LOUIS	SAN FRANCISCO
Toronto	BOSTON	Hong Kong	WASHINGTON
Sydney	PITTSBURGH	Edmonton	BALTIMORE
Mexico City			HOUSTON
Tokyo-to			NEW YORK
Sheffield			NEWARK
Bonn			DETROIT
Vienna			PHILADELPHIA
Singapore			Warsaw
Bradford			
Yokohama			

*For the specific dates involved for each city, see R. Fried, *Word Handbook of Cities,* Ch. 1.

Table 2-7   Comparative Property Safety in Cities in the 1970s

Relatively Safe Cities		Relatively Unsafe Cities	

Burglaries per 100,000 People

0-999	1000-1999	2000-2999	Over 3000
CLEVELAND	BOSTON	SAN FRANCISCO	Stockholm
PITTSBURGH	WASHINGTON		
Montreal	BALTIMORE		
Toronto	HOUSTON		
Glasgow	ST. LOUIS		
Hong Kong	Sydney		
Singapore	Philadelphia		
Warsaw	Bonn		
Athens	Vienna		
	Bradford, England		
	Edmonton		

Car Thefts per 100,000 people

0-500	500-999	1000+
Toronto	Sidney	BOSTON
Montreal	SAN FRANCISCO	CLEVELAND
PITTSBURGH	WASHINGTON	PROVIDENCE
Oslo	BALTIMORE	NEWARK
West Berlin	HOUSTON	
Zürich	ST. LOUIS	
Helsinki	NEW YORK	
Hamburg	CHICAGO	
Sheffield	Copenhagen	
Bonn	Göteborg	
Bern	SEATTLE	
Vienna	Stockholm	
Singapore	DALLAS	
	PHILADELPHIA	
	LOS ANGELES	
	Edmonton	

Source: R. Fried, *World Handbook of Cities,* Ch. 1.

In absolute terms, American cities also perform poorly with regard to traffic safety, although as with every safety measure, there is considerable variance among American cities. The traffic fatality rate per 100,000 people in some American cities seems to be five or six times higher than in cities such as Tokyo, Paris, Barcelona, Ahmedabad (India), or Denver, Colorado. (See Table 2.9 or 2.1.) The American record improves greatly only when one takes into account the number of automobiles circulating in American cities—more per person than in any other cities in the world. In terms of auto fatalities per 10,000 autos, the performance of American cities is excellent. In those same terms, the performance of Soviet cities—

Table 2-8   Comparative Safety from Fires (1970s)

Relatively Safe Cities			Relatively Unsafe Cities

Death Rate from Fire per 100,000 People

0-0.9	1.0-1.9	2.0-2.9	3.0+
Rio de Janeiro	London	LOS ANGELES	PHILADELPHIA
Munich	Vienna	Edmonton	CHICAGO
Delhi	Tokyo-to		Naples
Singapore	Taipei		
Budapest	Nagoya		
Madras	Manila		
Cairo	Seoul		
Alexandria	Jakarta		
Pusan	Osaka		
Kyoto	Bonn		
Baghdad	Bradford		
Sapporo	Yokohama		
Mexico City			
Hong Kong			
Singapore			

Injury Rate from Fire per 100,000 People

0-4.9	5-9.9	10-14.9	15+
Ahmedabad	Alexandria	Tokyo-to	Naples
Belo Horizonte	Budapest	London	PHILADELPHIA
Cairo	Kanpur	Madras	
Delhi	Kobe	Osaka	
Jakarta	Munich	Bradford	
Pusan	Nagoya		
Rio de Janeiro	Sapporo		
São Paulo	Seoul		
Singapore	Yokohama		
Taipei	Hong Kong		
Teheran	Edmonton		
Bonn			
Singapore			

Source: R. Fried, *World Handbook of Cities,* Ch. 1.

which have extremely few automobiles—is quite bad; Hedrick Smith reports in *The Russians* that the Soviet traffic fatality rate is ten times the American rate (in proportion to the number of cars), at least partly because Russians drive at night, even on open highways, using only their parking lights.[12]

If it is the responsibility of government to assist in protecting citizens against many forms of accidental death (automobile, fire, explosion, drowning, food poisoning, floods, building collapse, falling objects, etc.), the general death rate from accidents may reflect the comparative effectiveness of regulatory capabilities

Table 2-9 Comparative Safety from Automobiles in Cities (1970s)

Relatively Safe Cities   *Relatively Unsafe Cities*

Auto Fatalities per 100,000 People

0-4	4-9	10-19	20+
DENVER	CHICAGO	BUFFALO	ATLANTA
Barcelona	NEW YORK	SAN FRANCISCO	BALTIMORE
Ahmedabad	London	PITTSBURGH	LOUISVILLE
Tokyo	Mexico City	LOS ANGELES	PHOENIX
Paris	East Berlin	BOSTON	SAN DIEGO
Sheffield	Osaka	PHILADELPHIA	SEATTLE
	Rio de Janeiro	NEW ORLEANS	CLEVELAND
	Milan	NEWARK	MIAMI
	Madras	Montreal	Belo Horizonte
	Manila	Prague	Bogotá
	Taipei	São Paulo	Copengagen
	Jakarta	Bangalore	Bonn
	Naples	DETROIT	Vienna
	Teheran	Munich	
	Stockholm	Hamburg	
	Hong Kong	Singapore	
	Yokohama	Glasgow	
	Athens	Bangkok	
		West Berlin	
		WASHINGTON	
		Calcutta	
		Istanbul	
		Budapest	
		Warsaw	
		Zürich	
		Geneva	
		Bradford, England	
		Edmonton	

Auto Fatalities per 10,000 Autos

0-4	5-9	10-19	20+
LOS ANGELES	Prague	Jakarta	Bangkok
Milan	Kyoto	Rio de Janeiro	Delhi
Barcelona	Munich	Singapore	Kanpur
CHICAGO	Hamburg	Manila	Teheran
PHILADELPHIA	West Berlin	Mexico City	Istanbul
Tokyo	Paris	Glasgow	Recife
London	Copenhagen	São Paulo	Calcutta
Osaka	Bonn	Warsaw	Belo Horizonte
Naples	Vienna	Madras	Seoul
NEW YORK	Bradford, England	Hong Kong	Pusan
Stockholm	Athens		
Sheffield			
Yokohama			
Edmonton			

Source: R. Fried, *World Handbook of Cities,* Ch. 1.

of various urban governments (It may also reflect the effectiveness of the medical care system, since death rather than injury rates are concerned.) If this is so, the record of American cities as shown in Table 2-10, would seem to be rather good.

Health   One of the better indicators of comparative community health is the infant death rate: the frequency of death during an infant's first year. Table 2-11 gives statistics that show the huge gap between the richer and poorer countries and the moderately good performance of United States cities. The infant death rate can also be measured as a proportion of all deaths in a city. Table 2-12 shows the enormous health gap among the cities of the world: in some cities, infants constitute less than 2% of deaths, in others, more than 30%.[13]

One can also measure comparative community medical care—which is not always the same as community health. Here, too, the contrasts are striking, though not always the contrasts one expects (for example, Rotterdam and Sheffield and persons per doctor). Medical personnel—physicians, dentists, and pharmacists—abound in some cities and are rather scarce in others, as Table 2-13 shows.

These tables, of course, understate the health gap among the world's cities. Figures on infant deaths err on the optimistic side since a large proportion of deaths in Third World cities go unregistered and three-quarters of the registered deaths occur without medical certification. One of the health problems in Third World cities is the lack of information on the extent and nature of health problems. But even if precise information is not available, we do know that many cities in the world are still plagued with infectious and parasitic diseases such as cholera, dysentery, gastroenteritis, diphtheria, polio, and measles, whereas in other cities of the world, few people suffer or die from these preventable illnesses.

Comparative suicide rates may measure the extent of community mental health. Table 2-14 gives the suicide rates for all people, and for young people, in particular.

Table 2-10   Comparative Safety from Accidents in Cities (1970s)

Relatively Safe		Relatively Unsafe
Accidental Death Rate per 100,000 Residents		
10-39	40-59	60+
Tokyo	Stockholm	Rio de Janeiro
Taipei	Zürich	East Berlin
Kyoto	Copenhagen	Bologna
NEW YORK	Geneva	Recife
LOS ANGELES	Bonn	
Montreal	Seoul	
Hong Kong	Prague	
Vienna	Bern	
Singapore		
Yokohama		
Edmonton		

Source: R. Fried, *World Handbook of Cities,* Ch. 1.

Table 2-11   Comparative Infant Death in Cities (1970s)—Infant Death Rate per 100,000 Live Births

0-9	10-19	20-29	30-39	40-49	50-59	60-69	70-79	80-89	90+
Taipei	Tokyo	ATLANTA	Panama	Buenos Aires	Havana	New Delhi	Accra	Quito	Freetown (127)
Bern	East Berlin	DENVER	Bangkok	Bucharest		Manila	Mexico City	Colombo	Tunis (99)
	Hamburg	DETROIT	Milan	Tashkent		Lisbon	Rio de Janeiro	Bombay	Cairo (141)
	Kiev	NEW ORLEANS	Turin	Athens			São Paulo	Madras	Alexandria (106)
	Kyoto	Baghdad	Sofia	Budapest			Ahmedabad	Naples	Belo Horizonte (105)
	Leningrad	Barcelona	Bologna				Bogotá		Istanbul (114)
	London	West Berlin	Palermo				Brasília		Recife (229)
	LOS ANGELES	Birmingham, England	Belgrade						
	Madrid	CHICAGO							
	Osaka	Moscow							
	Paris	Munich							
	Yokohama	NEW YORK							
	Amsterdam	PHILADELPHIA							
	Copenhagen	Prague							
	Oslo	Rome							
	Göteborg	Saigon							
	Stockholm	Warsaw							
	Geneva	Vienna							
	Zürich	Brussels							
	Sydney	Leipzig							
	Melbourne	Dublin							
	Bonn	Manchester							
	Hong Kong	Glasgow							
	Singapore	Vienna							
	Bradford								
	Edmonton								

Source: R. Fried, *World Handbook of Cities*, Ch. 2.

Table 2-12 Comparative Infant Deaths in Cities in the 1970s—Infant Deaths as a Percentage of All Deaths

Very Low Infant Death Rate (Less than 2%)	Low Rate (2-5%)	Moderately High (5-10%)	High (10-20%)	Very High (20-30%)	Extremely High (30%+)
Stockholm	Leningrad	Hong Kong	Naples	Accra	Freetown
Göteborg	Moscow	Sofia	Palermo	Kinshasa	Mexico City
Zürich	Wellington	Valencia (Spain)	Kingston	Belo Horizonte	Fortaleza
Geneva	Sydney	Belgrad	Panama City	São Paulo	Quito
Bern	Birmingham, England	Bucharest	Kuala Lumpur	Colombo	Brasília
Oslo	Warsaw	Reggio Calabria	Porto Allegre	Bombay	Manila
Amsterdam	Łódź	Rome	Rio de Janeiro	New Delhi	Bangkok
Hamburg	Glasgow	Turin	Taipei	Madras	Cairo
West Berlin	Budapest	Milan	Baghdad	Amman	Recife
Leipzig	Cologne	Bologna	Havana	Calcutta	
Paris	Frankfurt	Athens	Tashkent	Hyderabad	
Vienna	Marseilles	Dublin		Istanbul	
Antwerp	Lille	Barcelona			
Prague	ATLANTA	Singapore			
Copenhagen	DENVER				
Brussels	DETROIT				
East Berlin	NEW ORLEANS				
Bonn	NEW YORK				
	Tel Aviv				
	Kyoto				
	Tokyo				
	Kobe				
	Salzburg				
	Helsinki				

Table 2-12 Comparative Infant Deaths in Cities in the 1970s—Infant Deaths as a Percentage of All Deaths (continued)

Very Low Infant Death Rate (Less than 2%)	Low Rate (2-5%)	Moderately High (5-10%)	High (10-20%)	Very High (20-30%)	Extremely High (30%+)
	CHICAGO				
	LOS ANGELES				
	Taipei				
	London				
	Hong Kong				
	Singapore				
	Bradford, England				
	Yokohama				
	Edmonton				

Source: R. Fried, *World Handbook of Cities*, Ch. 2.

Table 2-13   Comparative Availability of Medical Care (c. 1970)

Persons per Doctor

1000+	500-1000	335-500	200-333	Less than 200
Jakarta	Milan	Calcutta	Warsaw	Kiev
Manila	Sapporo	Bucharest	LOS ANGELES	Moscow
Ahmedabad	Belo Horizonte	Prague	Budapest	Leningrad
Alexandria	Yokohama	Barcelona	Paris	Tashkent
Tunis	Rome	Rio de Janeiro	Munich	Tel Aviv
Mexico City	São Paulo	NEW YORK	Kyoto	Bonn
Baghdad	New Delhi	Recife	PHILADELPHIA	
Istanbul	Teheran	Göteborg	CHICAGO	
Port-au-Prince	Cairo	Amsterdam	Tokyo	
Addis Ababa	The Hague	Utrecht	East Berlin	
Rotterdam	Zürich	Turin	Naples	
Sein-et-Marne	Geneva	Oslo	Osaka	
Dakar	Göteborg	LOS ANGELES	Tokyo-to	
Kinshasa	CHICAGO	Stockholm	Manila	
Hong Kong	Bologna	Bern	Athens	
Singapore	Bradford,	Vienna	Belgrade	
Sheffield	England	Edmonton	West Berlin	
Yokohama			Hamburg	
Athens			Helsinki	
			Copenhagen	

Persons per Dentist

3000+	1999-2999	1000-1999	Less than 1000
Port-au-Prince	The Hague	Tokyo	LOS ANGELES
Accra	London	Tokyo-to	Warsaw
Addis Ababa	Milan	Belo Horizonte	Paris
Baghdad	Leningrad	Hamburg	CHICAGO
Jakarta	Moscow	NEW YORK	Oslo
São Paulo	Tashkent	Vienna	Göteborg
Istanbul	Yokohama	Zürich	Helsinki
Madras		Geneva	Stockholm
Manila		LOS ANGELES	Bern
Dakar		West Berlin	Athens
Kinshasa		PHILADELPHIA	
Kharkov		East Berlin	
Recife		Paris	
Rio de Janeiro		Prague	
Naples		Lódź	
Teheran		Bucharest	
Singapore		Bonn	
Amsterdam		Edmonton	
Rotterdam			
Cairo			
Taipei			
Seoul			
Mexico City			
Kiev			
Hong Kong			
Bradford,			
England			

Table 2-13   Comparative Availability of Medical Care (c. 1970) (continued)

Persons per Pharmacist

15,000+	1999-2999	1000-1999	Less than 1000
Port-au-Prince	Prague	PHILADELPHIA	Warsaw
Kinshasa	East Berlin	LOS ANGELES	Edmonton
Recife	Belgrade	CHICAGO	
Hong Kong	Budapest	Bucharest	
	Zürich	Turin	
	Bern	Paris	
	Singapore	Hamburg	
	Bradford,	Munich	
	England	West Berlin	
		Vienna	
		Bonn	
		Yokohama	

Source: R. Fried, *World Handbook of Cities,* Ch. 2.

Housing   The performance gap among the world's cities in housing is extreme. In some cities of the world, like Calcutta, hundreds of thousands of people have no housing at all; they sleep on sidewalks, railway platforms, under bridges, in boats, or in caves. Table 2-15 gives some idea of the differences among cities (only for those living in dwellings), showing the percentage of dwellings with running cold water inside the dwelling. Piped water inside the dwellings is well-nigh universal in North America, Western Europe, and Australia; if less common in Japan and Eastern Europe (80-90% on the average), in some countries, it is rather rare. Private flush toilets (Table 2-16) are nearly universal in American, British, Swiss, Canadian, and Italian cities; somewhat less common (80% to 90%) in parts of Western Europe (Scandinavia, Netherlands, West Germany); uncommon in some French cities; and scarce in Japan. Private baths or showers (Table 2-17) are standard in North American and Australian cities, and much less common in European cities and the cities of the Third World. Less than half the dwellings in Paris, Copenhagen, Essen, Tokyo, or Vienna have private baths or showers. Table 2-18 shows that a number of major cities in the advanced world with cold climates (for example, Vienna, East Berlin, Prague, Amsterdam, London, and Essen) have little central heating. Central heating is standard in North American cities and in the wealthiest cities of Europe, such as Stockholm and Zürich.

Most people in the world apparently would prefer to live in single-family dwellings in a suburban residential density.[14] Table 2-19 shows the distribution of one- and two-family dwellings in the cities of the advanced world. They appear to be common in North America, West Germany, and Australia, but rare in Europe. Home ownership is sometimes regarded as a positive goal of housing policy. Table 2-20 shows the extent to which home ownership is spread throughout the world's cities.

Table 2-14 Comparative Suicide Rates per 100,000 People

0-9.9	10-19.9	20-29.9	30+
Barcelona	PHILADELPHIA	Göteborg	Warsaw
PROVIDENCE	WASHINGTON	Dortmund	West Berlin
NEW YORK	DETROIT	MIAMI	Copenhagen (43)
MEMPHIS	CLEVELAND	LOS ANGELES	Stockholm (58)
Taipei	Yokohama	Vienna	
BIRMINGHAM	NEW ORLEANS	SAN FRANCISCO	
NEWARK	MILWAUKEE	Toronto	
Tokyo	SEATTLE	Zürich	
HONOLULU	PORTLAND	Basel	
CHICAGO	Geneva	Munich	
DALLAS	Cologne	Bern	
Mexico City	DENVER		
Bradford,	Bonn		
England	Singapore		
Athens	Edmonton		
Recife			
Rio de Janeiro			

Suicide Rates for Youths (to age 20) per 100,000 People

Less than 1	1-1.9	2+
Barcelona	Basel	Copenhagen[b]
WASHINGTON	Bonn[d]	Toronto[a]
West Berlin		Göteborg[a]
Munich		Zürich[c]
Cologne		Warsaw (6.6)
Hamburg		Vienna[e] (2.0)
Tokyo		Singapore (2.2)
Nagoya		Yokohama (2.3 to age 19) (5.57 to
Bradford,		age 24)
England[d]		Edmonton[e] (2.4)
Recife[a]		

[a] to age 24
[b] to age 25
[c] to age 30
[d] to age 18
[e] to age 21

Source: R. Fried, *World Handbook of Cities,* Ch. 2.

Table 2-15 Comparative Housing Quality in Cities (c. 1970): Running Water—Percentage of Dwellings with Running Water

0-10%	20-30%	30-40%	50-60%	60-70%	70-80%	80-90%	90-100%
Kinshasa	Port-au-Prince	Cairo	Addis Ababa	Belgrade	Łódź	Tokyo	WASHINGTON
	Saigon	Tunis	Accra	Moscow	Ravenna	Kyoto	SAN FRANCISCO
	Santo Domingo		São Paulo		Lima	Nagoya	ST. LOUIS
	Managua		Mexico City		Prague	Cracow	PHILADELPHIA
			Algiers		Warsaw	Warsaw	NEW YORK
			Havana		Budapest	Montevideo	Lille
						Paris	Nantes
						Barcelona	Dresden
						Madrid	Bordeaux
						Athens	Toronto
						Vienna	Paris
							Florence
							Rome
							Leipzig
							East Berlin
							Stockholm
							Zürich
							Geneva
							London
							Amsterdam
							Buenos Aires
							Lisbon
							Helsinki
							Bonn
							Hong Kong
							Singapore
							Bradford
							Yokohama
							Athens

Source: R. Fried, *World Handbook of Cities*, Ch. 2.

Table 2-16 Comparative Housing Quality in Cities (c. 1970): Private Toilets

Percentage of Dwellings with Private Flush Toilet (c. 1970)

0-10%	10-20%	20-30%	30-40%	40-50%	50-60%	60-70%	70-80%	80-90%	90-100%
Hong Kong	Osaka	Tokyo		Lille	Singapore	Paris	Marseilles	Birmingham, England	Düsseldorf (90)
Pyongyang		Kyoto		Bordeaux		Lyon	Stuttgart	East Berlin	Bonn (19)
		Nagoya		Lima		(Hong Kong)a	London	Rotterdam	Utrecht (92)
		Athens					Vienna	Hamburg	Malmö (93)
								Warsaw	Amsterdam (94)
								West Berlin	Stockholm (97)
								Munich	Florence (98)
								Cologne	Genoa (98)
								Göteborg	Bologna (98)
								Nice	Rome (99)
								Trieste	Bern (99)
								London	All United States
								Bonn	cities (99)
								Bradford, England	Melbourne (98)
									Montreal (99)
									Toronto (98)
									Edmonton (98)
									Yokohama (94)

aFigures from Hong Kong may not reflect only private facilities, but may also include shared facilities. The figures, kindly supplied by the Office of Census and Statistics, Hong Kong, vary sharply from the figures in other sources.

Source: R. Fried, *World Handbook of Cities*, Ch. 3.

Table 2-17 Comparative Housing Quality in Cities: Private Bath

Percentage of Dwellings with Private Bath or Shower (c. 1970)

0-10%	30-40%	40-50%	50-60%	60-70%	70-80%	80-90%	90-100%
Hong Kong	Osaka	Essen	Łódź	Frankfurt	Bari	Stockholm	Geneva
	Paris	Lille	Augsburg	Kyoto	Nice	Basel	Lausanne
	Moscow	Copenhagen	Dortmund	Düsseldorf	Taranto	Florence	ST. LOUIS
		Hannover	Cologne	Marseilles	Utrecht	Zürich	BOSTON
		Tokyo	Stuttgart	Amsterdam	Grenoble	Birmingham,	NEWARK
		Nuremberg	Lyon	Munich	Venice	England	NEW YORK
			Bordeaux	West Berlin	Göteborg	Bern	Toronto
			East Berlin	Rotterdam	Genova	Bologna	Montreal
				The Hague	Oslo	London	Bradford
				Hamburg	Bonn		Edmonton
				Vienna	Yokohama		
				Athens			

Source: R. Fried, *World Handbook of Cities*, Ch. 3.

Table 2-18   Comparative Housing Quality in Cities: Central Heating

Percentage of Dwellings with Central Heating (c. 1970)

0-10%	10-20%	20-30%	30-40%	40-50%
HONOLULU	Vienna	Amsterdam	Leeds	Bordeaux
	MIAMI	Essen	LOS ANGELES	Frankfurt
	Leipzig	NEW ORLEANS	SAN DIEGO	Marseilles
	East Berlin	Stuttgart	Cologne	Düsseldorf
	Prague	Venice	Florence	Paris
		Glasgow	West Berlin	Bonn
		Birmingham, England	Bologna	
		Lille	Trieste	
		Bradford, England	Oslo	

50-60%	60-70%	70-80%	80-90%	90-100%
Hamburg	Nice	PORTLAND	CHICAGO	MINNEAPOLIS
DALLAS	SEATTLE	BUFFALO	Baltimore	OMAHA
Genoa	SAN FRANCISCO	Basel	BOSTON	Malmö
Copenhagen		ST. LOUIS	PITTSBURGH	Lausanne
Grenoble		Rome	Bern	Stockholm
Montreal		Warsaw	Geneva	NEW YORK
Moscow			Zürich	Helsinki
			NEWARK	Toronto
			WASHINGTON	Edmonton
			DETROIT	
			Philadelphia	

Source: R. Fried, *World Handbook of Cities,* Ch. 3.

Most of these data concern regularly built housing in regularly constructed districts. Much of the world's population, however, does not live in such housing, but rather in structures built neither to code standards nor on legally occupied land. Table 2-21 gives an idea of the extent to which people in some cities live in squatter settlements, often without running water, electricity, sewerage, paved streets, or the other facilities considered a normal part of the "urban way of life." Cities with large squatter settlements also tend to have extremely overcrowded housing, as measured by persons per room (Table 2-22).

Communications Development   Another measure of the quality of urban life is access to communications, one way of measuring which is to look at the distribution of telephones among the households of a city. Table 2-23 shows that telephones are standard in American urban households (80%-90%) while practically absent in some major cities in Europe.

Table 2-19 Comparative Housing Quality: One-and Two-Family Dwellings (Detached and Semi-Detached) as a Percentage of all Dwellings (c. 1970)

0-10%	10-20%	20-30%	30-40%	40-50%	50-60%	60-70%	70-80%	80-90%
The Hague	NEW YORK	PROVIDENCE	Montreal (c)	Montreal (m)	LOS ANGELES	KANSAS CITY	Bremen	Perth
Paris (c)	Göteborg	CHICAGO	SAN FRANCISCO	West Berlin	PITTSBURGH	BALTIMORE	PHOENIX	
Amsterdam	BOSTON	BUFFALO	CINCINNATI	Düsseldorf	Munich	DALLAS	ALBUQUERQUE	
Rotterdam	Copenhagen	Oslo	ST. LOUIS	Frankfurt	DETROIT	SAN DIEGO	OKLAHOMA CITY	
Geneva	Bonn	London	WASHINGTON	MIAMI	DENVER	PHILADELPHIA	COLUMBUS, OHIO	
Lausanne		Paris (m)	CLEVELAND	NEW ORLEANS	SEATTLE	Hamburg		
Basel		Athens	MILWAUKEE	HONOLULU	Yokohama+	PORTLAND		
NEWARK			Quebec	MINNEAPOLIS		HOUSTON		
Stockholm			Bern	Stuttgart		MEMPHIS		
Helsinki				Essen		OMAHA		
Rome				Cologne		VANCOUVER		
Vienna				ATLANTA		Edmonton		
Bradford				Dortmund				
				Toronto				

U.S. cities = % 1 unit; West Germany = % 1 and 2 family units; Swiss cities = % 1 and 2 family units; Scandinavian cities = % "småhus"; United Kingdom = detached & semi-detached + "detached houses and tenement houses"; (c) = central city; (m) = entire metropolitan area.

Source: R. Fried, *World Handbook of Cities*, Ch. 3.

Table 2-20 Comparative Housing Quality in Cities: Private Ownership

Privately Owned Dwellings as a Percentage of All Dwellings (c. 1970)

0-10%	10-20%	20-30%	30-40%	40-50%	50-60%	60-70%	70-80%
Vienna	Frankfurt	NEW YORK	Bologna	ST. LOUIS	HOUSTON	DETROIT	Melbourne
Geneva	Düsseldorf	WASHINGTON	SAN FRANCISCO	LOS ANGELES	PHILADELPHIA	OMAHA	São Paulo
Lausanne	Essen	NEWARK	CHICAGO	BALTIMORE	PITTSBURGH	INDIANAPOLIS	
Amsterdam	Hannover	Utrecht	Montreal	CLEVELAND	DENVER	PHOENIX	
Zürich	Cologne	Strasbourg	Bremen	London	SAN DIEGO	ALBUQUERQUE	
West Berlin	Munich	Montreal	Toulouse	HONOLULU	DALLAS	Perth	
Helsinki	The Hague	Paris	Nancy	Bari	Swansea	Bradford,	
Bern	Hamburg	Nottingham	Manchester	Leeds	Bristol	England	
	Stuttgart	BOSTON	PROVIDENCE	ATLANTA	BIRMINGHAM		
	Stockholm	Lyon	MIAMI	Lille	PORTLAND		
		Bonn	Nice	Birmingham,	MEMPHIS		
		Singapore	Sheffield	England	KANSAS CITY		
			Genoa	OAKLAND	Toronto		
			Grenoble	East Berlin	Yokohama		
			NEW ORLEANS	Florence	Athens		
			CINCINNATI	BUFFALO	Edmonton		
			Rome	MILWAUKEE			
			Venice	Nantes			
			Montevideo	MINNEAPOLIS			
			Mexico City	Toronto			
				Tokyo-to			

Source: R. Fried, *World Handbook of Cities*, Ch. 3.

Table 2-21   Comparative Housing Quality in Cities:
Legality of Tenure

Percentage of Population in Squatter Settlements (1960s)

Calcutta	75	Dakar	30
Ankara	60	Santiago (Chile)	25
Mexico City	46	Jakarta	25
Caracas	40	Istanbul	21
Dar-es-Salaam	36	Lima	20
Rio de Janeiro	33	Manila	20
Kuala Lumpur	33	Singapore	15
Karachi	33	Bogotá	15
		Rome	3

Sources: Charles Abrams, *Man's Struggle for Shelter in an Urbanizing World* (Cambridge, Massachusetts: MIT Press); Morris Juppenlatz, *Cities in Transformation* (Santa Lucia, Queensland: University of Queensland Press, 1970), p. 15; Robert C. Fried, *Planning the Eternal City: Roman Politics and Planning Since World War II* (New Haven: Yale University Press), p. 116.

Table 2-22   Comparative Urban Housing: Crowding

Persons per Room (c. 1970)

High Comfort (.5-.6)	Moderate Comfort (.7-.9)	Moderate Overcrowding (1.0-1.9)	Extreme Overcrowding (2.0+)
Göteborg	Rome	Tokyo	Algiers
Stockholm	Venice	Osaka	Bombay
ATLANTA	Geneva	Cracow	
Hamburg	Bologna	Warsaw	
CHICAGO	Lausanne	Bari	
LOS ANGELES	Bern	Birmingham,	
DETROIT	HONOLULU	England	
London	MIAMI	East Berlin	
Manchester	Zürich	São Paulo	
PHILADELPHIA	Cologne	Lisbon	
Montreal	NEWARK	Prague	
Toronto	WASHINGTON	Belgrade	
Brussels	NEW YORK	Vienna	
Copenhagen	Frankfurt	Moscow	
Oslo	Helsinki	Yokohama	
Bonn	Paris		
Bradford	Athens		
Edmonton			

Source: R. Fried, *World Handbook of Cities,* Ch. 3.

Table 2-23   Comparative Access to Communications in Cities: The Telephone

Percentage of Households with Telephones (c. 1970)				
0-10%	10-20%	20-30%	30-40%	40-50%
Amman	Lille	Tel Aviv	Paris	Oslo
Seoul	Marseilles	Leicester	Rome	West Berlin
Casablanca	Bordeaux	Utrecht	Hamburg	Helsinki
Karachi	Leipzig	Nice	The Hague	Ottawa
Lima	Budapest	East Berlin	Venice	Montreal
Damascus	Palermo	Madrid[a]	Florence	Milan
Bangkok	Kyoto	Buenos Aires	Cologne	Munich
São Paulo	Naples	Barcelona	Leeds	Frankfurt
Addis Ababa	Glasgow	Rotterdam	Kyoto[a]	Düsseldorf
Jakarta	Nottingham	Edinburgh	Glasgow[a]	Stuttgart
	Dortmund	Salzburg	Antwerp[a]	Lisbon[a]
	Birmingham, England	Vienna	Athens[a]	Melbourne[a]
	Leningrad[a]	Oxford	Bradford	Sydney[a]
	Kiev[a]	Amsterdam		Brussels[a]
	Mexico City[a]	Bologna		Prague[a]
	Manila[a]	Warsaw[a]		
	Istanbul[a]	Johannesburg[a]		
	Caracas[a]	Belgrade[a]		
	Rio de Janeiro[a]	Budapest[a]		
	Bogotá			
	Moscow[a]			

50-60%	60-70%	70-80%	80-90%	90-100%
Hamburg	London	Lausanne	NEW YORK	SEATTLE
Vancouver	Montreal[a]	Bern	ATLANTA	PORTLAND
Göteborg	Copenhagen[a]	Basel	CHICAGO	MILWAUKEE
Toronto	Bonn	MIAMI	BOSTON	HONOLULU
Geneva	Vienna	Tokyo[a]	PHILADELPHIA	PITTSBURGH
Oslo		Helsinki[a]	DETROIT	MINNEAPOLIS
Rome[a]		Yokohama	SAN FRANCISCO	OMAHA
Turin[a]			Geneva[a]	Edmonton
Osaka[a]			Stockholm	
Amsterdam[a]			Zürich	

[a] Estimates

Source: R. Fried. *World Handbook of Cities,* Ch. 5.

Transportation Facilities   A popular measure of the quality of urban transportation is the diffusion of the automobile. Transportation planners and energy conservationists may frown upon the car as a means of transportation, but ordinary people around the world seem determined to defy their judgment. Table 2-24 shows the diffusion of automobiles among households in various cities, ranging from the cities in communist countries with few cars to American and Swiss cities in which auto ownership is standard. Cities like Los Angeles, with a car for every two persons, contrast sharply with cities like Baghdad or Bucharest, with one auto for every three or four hundred persons.

Enemies of the motor car measure the quality of urban transportation by the quality of public rather than private means of transportation. Table 2-25 compares cities in terms of relative reliance on public transportation for commutation. Table 2-26 shows the comparative availability of nonpersonal transportation in the form of taxis.

Public Facilities   One measure of the quality of public services available to people in different cities is indicated by the public library system. (Table 2-27)

Affluence   In much of the world, including many places with collectivist governments, the performance of regimes is evaluated in terms of the material standards of living in private households. When the city of East Berlin, for example, wants (in its statistical yearbook) to demonstrate "progress" since 1949, it shows improvements, to be sure, in the numbers of physicians and dentists per 10,000 people; in the numbers of nursery and kindergarten places per child; and in the teacher/pupil ratio in the public schools. But it also prominently features improvements in such things as central heating, bathroom equipment, washing machines, refrigerators, automobiles, and food consumption.[15] Although the quality of publicly provided goods and services is often an important measure of urban government performance, the basic performance test applied by ordinary people seems to be the distribution and quality of private goods. To many, probably most, people the quality of urban life is judged by the ability to make a living and to acquire an increasing number of private consumer goods.

By this test, the best performing cities are those with the highest standards of living measured in terms of private consumption, taking into account the comparative cost of living in various places. We have already made some comparisons in living standards when we provided tables on housing, telephones, and automobiles. Table 2-28 shows how various cities in the world rank in terms of widely desired or standard items of household comfort and mobility. Data on household equipment are available for rather few cities in the world. These data suggest that urban affluence is concentrated in relatively few parts of the world. North America, with 6% of the world's population, has 48% of the world's telephones. Europe (without the USSR), with 12% of the world's population, has 29% of the world's telephones. Latin America, Africa, and Asia, with 75% of the world's population, have 17% of the world's telephones (without Japan, only 8%). North America likewise has 46% of the world's passenger cars, Europe another 35%. North America and Europe, with 18% of the world's population, have 77% of the world's telephones and 81% of the world's passenger cars. The USSR with 6.5% of the world's population, has 0.4% of the world's telephones.[16]

Table 2-24 Comparative Urban Mobility: Automobiles

	Percentage of Households with One or More Autos (c. 1970)							
0-10%	20-30%	30-40%	40-50%	50-60%	60-70%	70-80%	80-90%
Warsaw	East Berlin	Copenhagen	Leeds	London	Stockholm	Melbourne	DETROIT
Shanghai	São Paulo	Vienna	Birmingham	WASHINGTON	Zürich	PHILADELPHIA	DENVER
Moscow			Göteborg	Paris	CHICAGO	Toronto	LOS ANGELES
Leningrad			Bradford	Montreal		Vancouver	Geneva
						Bonn	Edmonton

Source: R. Fried, *World Handbook of Cities*, Ch. 6.

Table 2-25 Comparative Urban Transportation: Reliance on Public Transportation (c. 1970)

	Percentage of Communication by Public Transportation						
0-10%	10-20%	20-30%	30-40%	50-60%	60-70%	80-90%	90-100%
PHOENIX	DALLAS	ATLANTA	Catania	Rome	NEW YORK	London	Moscow
SAN DIEGO	PORTLAND	ST. LOUIS	NEW ORLEANS	Bern	Milan		
HOUSTON	BIRMINGHAM	The Hague	Innsbruck	Bradford			
DENVER	HONOLULU	CLEVELAND	SAN FRANCISCO				
LOS ANGELES	MEMPHIS	BALTIMORE	CHICAGO				
	SEATTLE	Salzburg	PHILADELPHIA				
	DETROIT	Rotterdam	WASHINGTON				
		PITTSBURGH	NEWARK				
			BOSTON				
			Cologne				
			Essen				
			Düsseldorf				
			Dortmund				
			Bonn				

Source: R. Fried, *World Handbook of Cities*, Ch. 6.

Table 2-26   Comparative Urban Transportation: The Availability of Taxis

Persons per Taxi (c. 1970)			
2000+	1000-1999	500-999	1-499
Dortmund	San Francisco	Rome	WASHINGTON, D.C.
LOS ANGELES	Stuttgart	Vienna	Oslo
Bradford	Pittsburgh	Helsinki	Paris
Peking	MILWAUKEE	NEW YORK	Lagos
	Budapest	Frankfurt	Athens
	East Berlin	Cairo	Montreal
	Bonn	London	Copenhagen
	CLEVELAND	BALTIMORE	Tokyo
	Seattle	Düsseldorf	Stockholm
	The Hague	Bern	Mexico City
		Hong Kong	NEW ORLEANS
		PHILADELPHIA	Vienna
		CHICAGO	Warsaw
		ST. LOUIS	BOSTON
			Yokohama

Source: R. Fried, *World Handbook of Cities,* Ch. 6.

But if the cities of North America and Europe are affluent compared to cities in the rest of the world, this does not mean that poverty has been eliminated in those cities. Although the poor in the affluent cities (as we shall see) enjoy what people in the Third World or much of the communist world might consider affluence, they suffer from relative and, sometimes even absolute, deprivation. American cities, although they probably provide the highest standard of living for a larger proportion of their residents than any other cities in the world, are notorious for their squalid slums, high unemployment, and sizeable numbers of people living below officially defined minimal standards for income.[17]

Finance   High performance in cities is expensive, and it is getting more expensive. Large amounts of capital have to be raised to create and maintain schools, hospitals, highways, sewerage systems, transit systems, water supply systems, airports, libraries, police and fire stations. Large amounts of money are needed to pay for the salaries and pensions of municipal service workers and to cover the growing deficits of public transportation systems. One of the major challenges to urban government is to raise the revenues needed to cope with the demand for services and, at the same time, not strain the capacities or tolerance of the taxpayers.

Direct comparisons among city governments in terms of finance are difficult since urban services are provided by such a different mix of institutions from city to city, even within the same country. In some cities, services may be privately provided and paid for; in others they may be provided or at least paid for by metropolitan governments, state governments, national governments, or international

Table 2-27   Comparative Access to Information: Public Library Systems

Books per Resident (c. 1970)

(0.01-0.49)	(0.50-0.99)	(1-1.99)	(2-5)	(5+)
Osaka	Tokyo	Copenhagen	Munich	Liverpool
Vienna	Hamburg	Stockholm	Warsaw	Birmingham,
Turin	Madras	Oslo	CINCINNATI	England
Istanbul	Montreal	Hannover	MINNEAPOLIS	London
Singapore (0.43)	Frankfurt	Rio de Janeiro	Budapest	East Berlin
Hyderabad	Taipei	CHICAGO	Bucharest	Manchester
New Delhi	Recife	Prague	SEATTLE	Leningrad
Sapporo	Mexico City	SAN DIEGO	Edinburgh	Prague
Seoul	São Paulo	PHILADELPHIA	Göteborg	BOSTON
Hong Kong (0.2)	Cairo	LOS ANGELES	Tashkent	
Manila	Rome	Paris	Glasgow	
Saigon	ALBUQUERQUE	Zagreb	Birmingham	
Teheran	MIAMI	Toronto	Bradford	
Amman		Berlin	BALTIMORE	
Ahmedabad		NEW ORLEANS	BUFFALO	
Jakarta		NEW YORK	CLEVELAND	
Dacca (0.05)		Milan	DENVER	
Lahore (0.6)		Bonn	GRAND RAPIDS	
Kabul (0.005)		Vienna	KANSAS CITY	
Yokohama (0.31)		ATLANTA	MILWAUKEE	
		BIRMINGHAM	MINNEAPOLIS	
		CHARLESTON, S.C.	NEWARK	
		DALLAS	OAKLAND	
		DETROIT	PROVIDENCE	
		HONOLULU	ST. LOUIS	
		HOUSTON	SALT LAKE CITY	
		INDIANAPOLIS	SAN FRANCISCO	
		LOUISVILLE	SEATTLE	
		MEMPHIS	WASHINGTON, D.C.	
		OKLAHOMA CITY		
		OMAHA		
		PHOENIX		
		PITTSBURGH		
		PORTLAND		
		SAN DIEGO		
		Edmonton		

Source: R. Fried, *World Handbook of Cities,* Ch. 7.

agencies. Thus, one cannot necessarily tell the quantity or quality of local services
from the amount of money spent by the local general government of the city; other
agencies (such as an independent water, sanitation, or school district) may be responsible for services that in some cities are provided by the local general government.

Table 2-28   Comparative Urban Affluence:
              The Equipment of Households (c. 1970)

| | Percentage of Households with | | | | |
	Washing Machine	TV	Auto	Refrigerator	Telephone
London	46	91	52	88	62
Paris	50	75	55	85	34
East Berlin	60	91	21	93	35 (estimate)
LOS ANGELES	53	94	83	100	88
Zürich	78			74	90 (estimate)
Munich	51				
Bonn	70	90	70	95	69
Vienna	40	73	38	91	69
Tokyo	98	87	24	98	75
Geneva	70			82	
Leeds	80	96	46	68	32
Montevideo	26	30		66	
Bern	77			77	77

Source: R. Fried, *World Handbook of Cities,* Ch. 8.

Some useful comparisons can nonetheless be made. We can compare the incidence of taxation by all levels of government in particular cities. Table 2-29 shows the remarkable differences in tax pressure from high points in Scandinavia and the Netherlands to low points in such cities as Beirut, Hong Kong, and Madrid. Government takes 41% of the gross income of mechanics in Amsterdam and 51% of the gross income of personnel managers in Stockholm; this amounts to about double the amount of taxes (including social security taxes) paid by workers and managers in American cities!

City governments typically borrow large amounts of money in order to finance capital improvements like schools, bridges, or waste treatment plants. Sometimes, less justifiably, they borrow money to cover their current running expenses. There are major differences among the cities of the world in the degree to which they have incurred a sizeable municipal debt, as shown in Table 2-30. At a certain point, however, interest charges begin to eat up sizeable chunks of the operating budget. Table 2-31 perhaps gives an indication of the comparative solvency (fiscal prudence) of various cities in the world by showing how much of their operating budget must be used to pay off interest charges on borrowed money. (It will be noted that New York City—despite its financial notoriety—is not the most indebted major city in the world or the most deeply mired in interest charges.)

Performance in the fiscal arena can also be compared in terms of efficiency, which can (albeit crudely) be measured in the ratio of personnel costs to total operating expenditures. Table 2-32 shows the rather astonishing proportion going for personnel expenditures in American cities as compared to the other cities in the world.

Table 2-29   Comparative Finance: The Weight of Taxation (1973)

Comparative Taxation: Auto Mechanics

Light Taxation	*Moderate Taxation*	*Heaviest Taxation*
(Less than 15% of Gross Income)	(15-24% of Gross Income)	(25% or more of Gross Income)
Hong Kong	Singapore	Geneva
Beirut	Paris	London
Madrid	Johannesburg	Vienna
Buenos Aires	Sydney	Tel Aviv
Bogotá	Tokyo	Istanbul
Caracas	CHICAGO	Düsseldorf
Rio de Janeiro	Zürich	Oslo
Rome	NEW YORK	Helsinki
Bombay	SAN FRANCISCO	Copenhagen
Athens		Stockholm
Mexico City		Amsterdam
Milan		

Comparative Taxation: Personnel Managers

Light Taxation	*Moderate Taxation*	*Heaviest Taxation*
Hong Kong	Paris	Geneva
Beirut	Bombay	London
Caracas	Milan	NEW YORK
Buenos Aires	Rome	CHICAGO
Johannesburg	Tokyo	SAN FRANCISCO
	Madrid	Zürich
	Athens	Sydney
	Mexico City	Vienna
	Rio de Janeiro	Tel Aviv
	Singapore	Oslo
		Amsterdam
		Düsseldorf
		Bogota
		Helsinki
		Istanbul
		Copenhagen
		Stockholm

Source: Union Bank of Switzerland, *Prices and Earnings Around the World* (Zürich: Union Bank, 1974).

Table 2-30   Comparative Fiscal Health: Per-Capita Municipal Debt

$0-499	$500-999	$1000-1499	$1500+
Lille	CLEVELAND	London	Rotterdam
Barcelona	Montreal	Frankfurt	Manchester
Lyon	Toronto	Palermo	Stockholm
Bordeaux	DETROIT	Birmingham,	Rome
Portland	Oslo	Nottingham	Bern
Vienna	Munich	Zürich	NEW YORK
SAN DIEGO	Dortmund	Glasgow	Amsterdam
Nice	Genoa	Göteborg	
PITTSBURGH	Cologne	Sheffield	
MIAMI	DALLAS	Naples	
MINNEAPOLIS	Copenhagen	ATLANTA	
HONOLULU	BALTIMORE	Bristol	
Stuttgart	DENVER	Bradford, England	
Osaka	SAN FRANCISCO	Edmonton	
Vancouver	PHILADELPHIA		
Kyoto	Milan		
CHICAGO	Bonn		
NEWARK	The Hague		
NEW ORLEANS	BOSTON		
HOUSTON	LOS ANGELES		
Tokyo	Frankfurt		
Turin	Yokohama		

Source: R. Fried, *World Handbook of Cities,* Ch. 10.

In this chapter, we have stressed quantitative measures of performance, but these measures can, of course, mask considerable qualitative performance differences. Persons per doctor assumes that doctors are equal in skill, dedication, equipment, and medicines. A single-family house or owner-occupied dwelling can be a luxurious villa or an adobe hut. The telephones per household may give access to a telephone communication system that works reasonably well or one that malfunctions as a matter of course. Water available for consumption can vary widely in potability. Electrification of households may give access to generating systems of high and steady capacity or to systems with chronic variations and deficiencies in current. Persons per room as a measure does not take into account room size or comfort. Autos per resident does not take into account size, comfort, reliability, or convenience of repair. Plumbing and heating equipment may exist to be counted by census takers, but not function regularly or at all. Public transportation may be cheap, but crowded, infrequent, and unsafe. Households with TVs may have many or few

Table 2-31 Comparative Fiscal Health:
Interest Payments as a Percentage of Operating Budget

Low			High
(less than 5%	5-9%	10-19%	20%+
Helsinki	CLEVELAND	Dortmund	Florence
SAN FRANCISCO	BOSTON	OMAHA	BIRMINGHAM
PORTLAND	SAN DIEGO	KANSAS CITY	Genoa
Vienna	PITTSBURGH	Düsseldorf	Naples
BALTIMORE	LOS ANGELES	Cologne	OKLAHOMA CITY
NEWARK	DETROIT	Palermo	Bologna
ST. LOUIS	CHICAGO	Venice	Rome
DENVER	Munich	LOUISVILLE	
Oslo	Stockholm	DALLAS	
Stuttgart	SEATTLE	NEW YORK	
	Basel	ATLANTA	
	Essen	Geneva	
	NEW ORLEANS	Lausanne	
	PARIS	Milan	
	Bonn	Turin	
	Frankfurt	Edmonton	
	PHILADELPHIA		
	OAKLAND		
	Bern		
	Zürich		
	HOUSTON		

Source: R. Fried, *World Handbook of Cities,* Ch. 10.

hours of broadcasting available, a few or many channels to look at, great or little choice in what they can watch.

There may be telephones, but no telephone book. Hedrick Smith writes:[18]

Another common reference tool that Westerners take absolutely for granted— the telephone book—is an item of almost priceless rarity. One of the momen- tous events during our three years in Moscow [1971-1974] was the publication of a new phone book. Until that moment—and even afterward—Moscow must have ranked as the largest metropolis in the world without a readily available phone directory. Unlike Western telephone companies, the Soviet Ministry of Communications does not automatically provide phone books to subscribers. Nor are they available at pay phones or other public places. . . . The phone book that went on sale in 1973 was the first directory of personal telephone listings to be published in Moscow in 15 years. . . . For a city of eight million people, the printers published 50,000 phone books. They sold out within a few days at city newsstands even though the full four-volume set cost a hefty 12 rubles ($16).

Table 2-32   Comparative Efficiency: Percentage of Operating Expenditures for Personnel

10-20%	20-30%	30-40%	40-50%	50-60%	60-70%	70-80%
Fukuoka	Toronto	Bordeaux	BIRMINGHAM	OMAHA	CHICAGO	DALLAS
Sapporo	Vienna	Copenhagen	Bologna	OKLAHOMA CITY	CLEVELAND	MEMPHIS
Kobe	Yokohama	Düsseldorf	Cologne	HONOLULU	OAKLAND	
Kitakyushu	Osaka	Essen	Dortmund	PHILADELPHIA	PHOENIX	
	Nagoya	Frankfurt	DETROIT	WASHINGTON	PORTLAND	
	Kyoto	Geneva	Göteborg	CINCINNATI	SEATTLE	
	Kawasaki	Hannover	Nuremberg	SAN FRANCISCO		
		INDIANAPOLIS	Vancouver	BALTIMORE		
		Rome	WASHINGTON, D.C.	NEWARK		
		Stockholm	Calgary	BOSTON		
		Stuttgart	Edmonton			
		Tokyo	Milan			
		Zürich	Naples			
		Montreal	Munich			
			KANSAS CITY			
			MIAMI			

Source: R. Fried, *World Handbook of Cities*, Ch. 10.

As for public libraries, the quantitative measures used in Table 2-27 need, of course, to be supplemented with more qualitative indicators: the quality of books available; whether the library service is free; hours of service and physical comfort; distribution among city districts; public access to the stacks; and quality of the professional reference staff. One might also want to compare service in proportion to potential consumers, that is, take into account the proportion of the population that is literate. Kabul, Afghanistan, for example, has one library book for every 200 residents (the "norm" in the West is a book per person), but 90% of the city is illiterate. Providing numbers of books up to Western standards would be an obvious misuse of scarce funds.

Many of the performance measures we have been using in this chapter are averages for the whole city, but we all know that performance, however measured, varies a good deal within every city—among districts, social classes, age groups, racial and ethnic groups, income groups, occupational groups, groups with differing types and amounts of education, groups with differing life-styles and tastes, groups with differing amounts of bargaining power within the political system. Urban politics arises because people contend for larger shares of commonly sought values or for the ability to pursue distinctive values. Some of the tables in this chapter— those dealing with the percentage of households with washing machines, cars, owned dwellings, single-family dwellings, telephones, refrigerators, baths, private toilets, and central heating—do give an idea of distribution within the city. But other figures—such as those dealing with crime rates, health, taxation, or public libraries—are city averages—averages that need to be examined closely in terms of rates for particular kinds of districts or groups. Unfortunately, distribution comparisons (apart from the percentage measures we have just mentioned) are just beginning to be made.

We have tended to stress absolute levels of performance among cities. This does not take into account how far some cities have come—how much progress they have made. Table 2-33 shows how comparative performance can be evaluated over time; it shows how some cities have made outstanding progress since the 1920s in reducing infant mortality, while others have not. More subtle kinds of comparison need to be made than we have been able to make here: comparisons that take into account not only achievement, but difficulties overcome. Absolute comparisons may be much less helpful to policymakers and citizens than comparisons made at given levels of resources, difficulty, and constraint.

In any event, our purpose in this chapter has been illustrative, not exhaustive, comprehensive, or definitive. We have illustrated some of the range of performance that exists among the world's cities. We have shown some of the measures currently available to measure performance. We have shown the kinds of cities for which performance data exist. We are only at the beginning in the process of making refined international comparisons of cities. But some obvious and not so obvious differences have been laid out. In the rest of this book we will try to explain why these differences in performance occur among the cities of the world.

Table 2-33   Comparative Urban Performance: Improvement over Time

Infants Deaths as a Percentage of Live Births

	Rate in 1920s	Rate in 1960s	Percentage Drop
Large improvement			
Moscow	26.2	2.6	−23.6
Leningrad	26.5	2.8	−23.7
Osaka	27.3	3.4	−23.9
Kobe	22.9	2.8	−20.1
Sofia	26.8	6.3	−20.5
Warsaw	20.0	2.9	−17.1
Athens	20.9	8.0	−12.9
Bucharest	23.2	8.9	−14.3
Medium improvement			
ATLANTA	12.3	4.9	− 7.4
London	9.1	2.0	− 7.1
Hamburg	8.3	1.6	− 6.7
Vienna	6.9	1.7	− 5.2
DETROIT	15.7	4.6	−11.1
NEW YORK	10.6	4.0	− 6.6
Wellington	9.6	4.7	− 4.9
Sydney	11.1	3.7	− 7.4
Melbourne	8.9	3.3	− 5.6
Rio de Janeiro	22.6	14.9	− 7.7
No improvement			
Cairo	34.7	34.9	+ 0.2
Naples	17.2	16.5	− 0.7
Bombay	24.8	24.6	− 0.2
Mexico City	35.0	35.2	− 0.2

Source: Calculated from Office Permanent, Institut International de Statistique, *Statistique Internationale des Grandes Villes* (The Hague: Van Stockum, 1931) and International Statistical Institute, *International Statistical Yearbook of Large Towns* (The Hague: ISI, 1970).

MODERNIZATION AND URBAN PERFORMANCE

3

3-1 MODERNIZATION: KEY TO URBAN PERFORMANCE

Of all the theories to explain the performance differences outlined in Chapter 2, the most powerful one is modernization. Cities are most likely to have integrity, responsiveness, and effectiveness in their government when they are located in modernized countries.[1] Modernization is a cluster of processes that causes different kinds of traditional societies to converge towards a common type of society—a society characterized by such things as schools, government bureaucracies, department stores, railways and airlines, hospitals, churches, prisons, and mass media of communications. Note that these institutions are all specialized; in the traditional society, the dominant institutions—the family and the village—were multifunctional, rather than specialized. Thus the modern society is one in which there is a highly developed division of labor and degree of specialization. Where formerly, the family and the village performed all functions necessary for social existence, there are now a growing number of specialized institutions for education (schools), law enforcement (bureaucracies), production (factories, business corporations), exchange (commercial establishments and transportation networks), religion (churches), medical care (hospitals), control of social deviants (prisons), law making (legislatures), communications (the mass media), and territorial control (urban and regional governments).

One is recruited into traditional institutions on the basis of one's birth: one is born into one's family, one's village, one's role, and one's chances in life. Traditional institutions operate on the basis of custom and tradition. They have low productivity. Modern institutions, on the other hand, recruit people on the basis of competence and merit. They are run on the basis of rules deliberately shaped to accomplish specific purposes. Modern institutions are highly productive: only they are capable of producing affluence, literacy, and long life for the mass of the people.

To produce mass well-being—well-being for the ordinary family—requires a variety of interlocking processes: industrialization, the commercialization of agriculture, the diffusion of literacy and training, and the development of the mass media. It requires major shifts in the local structure of power: the replacement of aristocracies whose status is based on birth with middle classes whose status is based on wealth, income, and managerial skill; and the replacement of peasantries with workers, both manual and white collar. These socioeconomic processes are produced, regulated, and guided by a new set of political institutions, including and clustering around, the modern nation-state. Through the legal institutions of the nation-state, behavior is no longer regulated by tradition and custom, but by socially useful laws and regulations administered by impartial bureaucracies. Superstition and lore devoted to the understanding of the supernatural world are displaced by science and technology devoted to the exploitation of the possibilities of this world. The end result is the generation of vast wealth, material comfort, and a growing measure of social equality.

Modernization requires and produces urbanization—the concentration of people into dense settlements. Drawn from villages and farms to the factories and shops of urban centers, men and women become parts of vast national and international markets for labor, goods, and services, as well as members of vast national communities and vast national or international audiences. Their dependency on nature is turned into dependency on the impersonal forces of the market and of government that is offset by a growing collective ability to shape and control the natural environment. In the modernized society, few people produce what they consume or consume what they produce. No longer dependent on family and locality for production, consumption, education, entertainment, medical care, transportation, communication, religion, and moral training, they become dependent on specialized, impersonal, and remote institutions. People accept this new form of dependence for the greater returns that specialization and the division of labor can bring.

Modernization makes possible mass security, affluence, and dignity. Once isolated and self-sufficient (or at least subsistent), individuals, families, and localities are integrated into regional, national, and international networks. Producing for distant markets; consuming imported or distantly produced products; affected by faraway political events, natural disasters, and performance breakdowns, the modern individual and family need government in a way their rural predecessors did not. For modernization produces not only resources, but also tensions, strains, and conflicts—a full agenda of problems for governmental regulation and adjudication. The individual needs government and is encouraged to believe himself or herself as a part-owner of the government, shaping collective decisions with other members of the community.

Table 3-1 summarizes the major processes involved in modernization and shows the impact that these changes have on urban politics and government.[2]

Table 3-1   Modernization and Urban Performance

	Form of Change	*Implications for Urban Performance*
TRADITIONAL SOCIETY	MODERN SOCIETY	
ECONOMY		
Subsistence agriculture	Commercial agriculture	Exodus from rural areas to cities
Barter economy	Money economy	Creation of urban employment in factories, offices
Production for consuption	Production for sale	Economic surplus to support city population and services
Farming as predominant economic activity	Industrialization	Creation of taxable resources
Few taxable resources (little money or spare manpower)	Service economy	Need for urban infrastructure: housing, production, services
Elite production and consumption	Mass production and consumption	Need for government to adjust conflicts of economic interest
Economic self-sufficiency	Economic interdependency	Need for government to ensure vital supplies: such as fuel, food, and medicine
		Dependency on remote (absentee) economic institutions
SOCIAL CHANGES		
Small elite aristocracy	Modern working class	Need for government to adjust relations among individuals from diverse backgrounds
Huge peasant mass	Huge middle class	
Flat pyramid-shaped social structure	Diamond-shaped social structure	
Predominance of face-to-face groups: family and village	Predominance of impersonal organizations	Development of bureaucracies to produce goods and services
Rewards and status based on birth (sex, race, and lineage)	Rewards based on achievement	Linkage of urban groups to regions, national institutions, international processes, ideas, forces
Little social or geographic mobility	High social and geographic mobility	
Localized relationships	Strong regional, national, international relationships and solidarities	Possibility of professional urban bureaucracies
	Competitive status	
	Importance of professional groups	

Table 3-1   Modernization and Urban Performance (continued)

	Form of Change	Implications for Urban Performance
TRADITIONAL SOCIETY	MODERN SOCIETY	

VALUE CHANGES

Localism, xenophobia	Cosmopolitanism: awareness and toleration of many values	Possibility of peaceful coexistence in diverse groups in cities
Inequality as "natural"	Equality as "natural"	Allocation of government services and rights equally to all
Fatalism, concern for world after life spiritualism	Optimism about control over nature Materialism (concern for earthly rewards)	
Resistance to change	Innovation as desirable ("progress")	Constant efforts to improve performance
Time as natural units (movement of sun, moon, stars; life stages); little concept of punctuality	Predominance of artificial time units; time is a value to be budgeted; punctuality a virtue and necessity	Future orientation: planning; regular predictable performance based on clocks, schedules
Magical view of numbers; everyone knows where everything and everyone is	Rational use of numbers: (streets, houses, telephones, taxpayers, residents, routes, buildings, floors, postal zones, policemen, police cars, automobiles, weights, measures, prices, and fees); need for numbers because people and locations are unfamiliar	Possibility of administering large-scale complex urban community
Little specialized or new information	Explosion of technical, specialist forms of knowledge	Possibility of technical, professional urban bureaucracies
Justification through tradition; authority based on precedent	Justification through social utility; authority based on consent	Rationalized government (decisions defensible in terms of the public interest)
Importance of traditional controls of family, church, and village: customary norms	Importance of deliberately created laws and regulations: norms based on law	Need for government to regulate behavior in the absence of shared custom and moral codes
Little formal education	Mass education to provide common background of information and values Scientific, experimental attitude	Need for government to provide mass education

Table 3-1   Modernization and Urban Performance (continued)

	Form of Change	Implications for Urban Performance
TRADITIONAL SOCIETY	MODERN SOCIETY	

COMMUNICATIONS

Little interlocal communication: predominance of dialects	Huge amount of interlocal communication: shared language	Heavy flow of communications between government and community
Small, local audiences	Regional, national, and international audiences	Greater visibility of government and government performance
Predominantly word-of-mouth communication	Impersonal, mass media Importance of written communications	
Mass illiteracy	Mass literacy	Possibility of regulating behavior through written announcements, signs, notices, and information forms
Weak diffusion of new ideas and fashions	Strong diffusion network for new ideas and fashions	Rapid diffusion of new techniques and standards; powerful mass media
Interlocal rivalries	Interregional and international rivalry and competition (need to "keep up with" regional, national, and international standards)	Diffusion of new and higher performance standards and practices
Mass unawareness of events outside the village	Mass awareness of events in the world and in outer space	Pressure on urban government to conform to mass expectations

POLITICS

Localized political systems	National political systems	Domination of urban government by regional and state government Provision of basic civil defense through nation-state National and state regulation of urban affairs: nationalization of urban government
Customary norms	Modern law and legal institutions	Regulation of urban affairs through complex legislation in all spheres of social life; importance of courts of law

Table 3-1   Modernization and Urban Performance (continued)

	Form of Change	Implications for Urban Performance
TRADITIONAL SOCIETY	MODERN SOCIETY	
Government is private property: sale or inheritance of offices	Government belongs to the people	Public accountability of officials Election of officials Subordination of bureaucrats to elected officials
Authority based on birth and custom	Authority based on law, popular choice, consent, and expertise	Modern urban bureaucracies recruited on the basis of achievement norms
Group and individual privileges, no rights	Civic equality; equal rights for all (democratization of privilege)	Government based on "equal protection of the laws"
Government as primarily extractive (taxes, troops); little dependence on performance	Government as provider of services and regulations (exchanged for taxes)	Dependence on government for performance; expectation that government will ensure minimum health, safety, and welfare
Elite participation in government	Mass participation in government: voting, taxpaying, obeying laws, and utilizing services	Expectation of broad responsiveness to the community rather than to elite groups
Little distinction between public and private interest	Public office is a public trust: distinction between private property and income and public property and funds	Conflict-of-interest laws; proliferation of internal and external checks and audits
Little organization	Proliferation of organized interest groups and political associations	Expectation that government responsiveness will be to legitimate organized interests and mass political organizations
Small public sector	Broad public sector: high percentage of GNP in public sector	Resources for broad variety of services; support professional urban bureaucracies
Segregation: little intergroup contact	Desegregated communities: high potential for intergroup conflict	Need for government to adjust conflicts in values and interests
Little care for mass opinion Rarely articulate opinion	Government manipulates, pays attention to public opinion	

Urban government based on law, respect for individual rights, and due process is, thus, a product of modernization. The principles that all individuals in the city have the right to fair treatment and equal consideration; that government officials have only the authority specifically granted to them in law; and that government office is a public trust, not a species of private property—these are modern principles. The spirit of modernization is universalistic (the same rules for all) and rationalistic (rules should have some useful purpose). Institutions are no longer judged by their divine origins or ancient custom, but by their capacity to serve the general public. In premodern society, government is usually considered a species of private property owned by some family. Local authority is transmitted like royal crowns—as private inheritances. Government posts are a form of investment property, which can be bought, sold, and inherited. They are also a privilege to which some family or social group has a prescriptive right. Decisions are made, taxes are raised and spent, and laws are enforced in premodern society not according to publicly known general rules, but at the discretion of the rulers or the few experts in the traditional mysteries. Different laws apply to different places and social groups in each locality. Decisions are made in secrecy. Contracts, jobs, and franchises are awarded to favor friends, relatives, supporters, and members of friendly or high-status groups.

Political modernization, which began mostly in the seventeenth and eighteenth centuries, created a state, a system of government that belongs to no one and to everyone. Government—national and local—was converted from private property into a public trust. Particularistic privileges were converted into universally valid general rules, binding not only on all private subjects or citizens, but on government officials as well. Official authority came to be based not on membership in a privileged social group or the ruler's favor, but on the law and popular sanction. Through law, the community endowed officials with specific and limited authority to carry out the community's will. Law became not a statement of traditional group privileges, but an instrument of community purpose. Explicit rules came to define how contracts, jobs, and franchises were to be awarded, taxes collected, revenues spent, officials compensated, punishments inflicted, and rights protected. Group privileges were converted into the rights of individuals, and modern bureaucracies were created to enforce those rights.

Modernization thus laid the foundations for integrity in government: government under the rule of law with equal protection and due process for all citizens. Thus, the countries with the highest levels of socioeconomic development tend also to have cities with the most integrity in government. Powerful urban middle classes have created systems of government with relatively little corruption and high accountability through such mechanisms as public budgeting and accounting, representative assemblies, detailed statutes and regulations, popular elections, and freedom of the press.

Moreover, as societies modernize, old forms of social prejudice based on race, ethnicity, religion, age, sex, and class tend to diminish, thus providing the underpinning for urban government based on equal protection of the law. In traditional society, social prejudice is not only a matter of custom and informal practice, but it is often based on law: members of different groups have different rights and privileges, such as the right not to pay taxes (for aristocrats in prerevolutionary France), the right to a different court system (for aristocrats in England), the right to live wherever one wishes (denied to Jews in many European cities, whence the original "ghetto"), the right to practice an occupation (restricted to those in craft-guild families), and the right to vote and hold office (restricted to property owners or to members of certain families). Modern societies affirm the principles of civic equality and make efforts, both private and governmental, to equalize life chances.

That there is thus a fairly strong correlation between modernization level and integrity is suggested (though far from proved) by the comparative survey carried out by Gabriel Almond and Sydney Verba in the early 1960s. The higher the GNP, the more likely were people in a country to feel that if they had a problem with the police or bureaucracy, they would be treated much the same as everyone else; the higher the GNP, the more people felt they could do something about an unjust local regulation.[3] See Figure 3-1.

In the cities of the less modernized countries, urban government (whether national or local) is more likely to be corrupt, favoritistic, and arbitrary. Officials like policemen are poorly paid and use their office to extort extra income from the public. Officials are expected to favor their friends, their relatives, people from the same village, or people from the same tribe. Voters expect to be bribed. The group

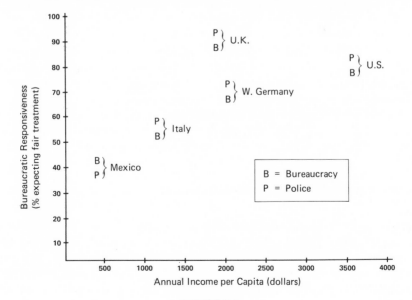

FIGURE 3-1

of professional administrators with modern standards of honesty, efficiency, and technical competence is small and outweighed by corrupt and lawless politicians, soldiers, businessmen, or other private individuals. Controls exercised over local government operations by central administrative agencies and by the courts is ineffective. There are few or no private organizations acting as watchdogs over local performance and pressuring for good government. The press is not likely to be either independent or to pay much attention to local government affairs. Critics of government performance are subject to various forms of intimidation. Auditing of local operations is difficult, given the inadequacy of financial records and irregularity of financial practices. Moreover, hostility among tribal, racial, or ethnic groups is often greater than in advanced societies and, consequently, various forms of public and private discrimination are more likely to exist.

Modernization can produce regularity and due process through such institutions as an independent legislature and judiciary, a free press, active watchdog associations, educated citizens with "good government" standards, professionalized (rational-legal) bureaucracies, tightly defined procedures, and laws against discrimination. But modernization also contains a powerful antiliberal potential. It creates the technology by which to establish totally corrupt and arbitrary government: modern means of suppression, surveillance, and secrecy. It creates an increasing number of impersonal, large-scale bureaucratic organizations with the ability to ignore individual rights. It creates a frenzied search for material welfare that leads to new forms of "honest graft" and new (legal) ways of using government for private profit. Its pressures for social equality may be only partially realized, leaving many forms of inequality and discrimination intact.

Modernization generates potentials. Which potential is realized depends upon the nature of the political system. In the advanced democracies, the integrity potential in modernization is most completely realized, but only at the cost of eternal vigilance. In the communist countries, the integrity potential in modernization is only embryonic, given regime emphasis on effectiveness at any cost. Even the egalitarian component in integrity that communism stresses so heavily is sacrificed in favor of effectiveness. Thus we find in communist cities unequal rewards based on differential work capacities; unequal power based on membership or lack of membership in the ruling party and government elite; and unlimited governmental capacity to discriminate on any basis currently justified by the party line.

3-3 MODERNIZATION AND RESPONSIVENESS

The spirit of modernity is equality—a stress on the common person's welfare, rights, and opportunities. Traditional societies have been elite-oriented, stressing the right of the upper classes to rule and the duty of the lower classes to obey. The great modernization revolutions in the United States (1776) and in France (1789) have proclaimed the right of all people to have a say in running government. Government henceforth is to belong to all, to benefit all, and to justify its demands and authority by showing that it has the support of all. Rather than the people being responsive to the demands of the government elite, now the government elite is to be responsive to the demands of the people. The basic method for securing responsiveness is the popularly elected representative assembly—an assembly that is given the right to shape government policies through laws and appropriations.

Modernization favors the development of governmental responsiveness not only by subjecting government to the control of elected assemblies, but also by reshaping society in the direction of greater social and economic equality. Modernization reduces the traditionally enormous gap in social status, education, and wealth between ruling elites and ordinary people by spreading wealth, income, education, and social standing among the masses of the people. Modernization tends to break down traditional social hierarchies based on race, caste, ethnicity, or religion in favor of a broad middle-class urban social structure. By spreading literacy and education through public school systems, ordinary people are made aware of their political rights and are encouraged to use them. Modernization produces the mass media of communication that allow ordinary people to follow public events and observe how other urbanities are living. As local communities acquire large numbers of educated citizens, central governments become more disposed to allow representatives of local citizens to exercise wide governmental authority through decentralization.

In the less modernized countries, urban government tends to be less responsive. There is less mass awareness of individual rights, of governmental programs, of proposed and past governmental decisions. There is a great status gap between educated governmental officials and the mass of uneducated or poorly educated people. The mass of the people accept government decisions passively; they are less disposed to complain about poor performance or nonperformance, particularly if their legal status as residents or squatters is uncertain. There are few pressure groups to give government officials some idea of what various parts of the community are thinking. Newspapers are read by only a tiny minority and are seldom free from government control. Instead of government by democratic politicians, anxiously competing for public support, there is apt to be government by elites—traditional, military, or single-party—with little concern for public opinion. Instead of decentralized urban government—government by officials who are responsible to local voters—there is apt to be centralized urban government, government by bureaucrats responsible to the top national political elite.

But though urban government is likely to be more responsive in the more modernized countries, there are strong forces even in those countries that work to diminish responsiveness. First of all, though modernization provides the potential for mass control, it also provides the potential for total elite control with a facade of mass participation. Politics again determines which of the potentials in modernization are realized: the democratic or the dictatorial. Some of the most socially and economically advanced countries in the world have dictatorial forms of government. East German or Czech cities, for example, though highly industrialized, educated, and oriented toward social equality, are governed by dictatorial Communist parties. Modernization generates the resources not only for mass influence, but for the suppression of mass influence over government. Modernization allows a single dictatorial party to monopolize control of the bureaucracies of the modern state, the modern mass media, the means of mass education, and the means of mass employment and production.

But even in the advanced democracies—the modernized countries which allow and encourage competition among elites for mass support—there are forces that work against governmental responsiveness: centralization, bureaucratization, the polarization of interests, and powerful concentrations of private power. Modernization creates large, unwieldy, and rigidified bureaucratic organizations in government, business, education, and health—bureaucratic organizations driving to promote their own self-interest, easily ignoring the interests of their clients and members of the public. Modernization generates a large number of dependency relationships; we become dependent on people and organizations that are large scale, remote, and that deal with too many people or too many kinds of people, organizations that often have to protect themselves against attack and abuse by generating impersonal rules and distance. Modernization creates many interests, the possibility of new identities, new interest groups, but also new forms of social conflict and polarization and new kinds of incompatible demands. The modern city typically has groups demanding freedom to explore new and different life-styles—life-styles that others in the community find outrageous, immoral, and worthy of, not toleration, but suppression. More traditional rural communities have greater consensus over public morality than more anonymous, cosmopolitan centers that are open to many more stimuli and pressures for change.

But even so, the more advanced the society, the more its government is likely to develop the capacity to respond to a wide variety of demands; to reform and shake up its bureaucracies, both public and private; to build some consensus among its myriad subcultures; to give numerous groups—territorially and functionally based—some measure of responsive self-government. Modernization shifts the balance of power within nations from rural to urban elites; from those working in agriculture to those working in modern industry, commerce, and services; from landowning elites to the urban middle classes. These power shifts create the basis for the responsiveness of government to urban need in the form of the modern positive or welfare state.

3-4 MODERNIZATION AND EFFECTIVENESS

The best single predictor of effectiveness in urban government is the distribution of world income. The fact that the lowest 50% of the world's population receives less than 10% of world income, while the highest 20% receives 55% and the highest 10% receives 30%—and the gap is increasing all the time—has obvious consequences for the scope and effectiveness of urban government. The best rough predictor of health, safety, and welfare in a city is the rank of the country in which it is located in Table 3-2. That table shows the ratio between a country's share of world GNP and its share of world population. Sweden's share of world GNP is five and one-half times larger than its share of world population. In contrast, Laos has only about 1/25 the GNP that its population would entitle it to.

In the mid-1970s, an international survey was carried out in sixty countries, representing nearly two-thirds of the world's population—excluding the communist nations—by members of the Gallup International Research Institutes (sponsored by the Charles F. Kettering Foundation).[4] The survey makes possible the first direct comparison of satisfaction with performance across national boundaries. People in the various regions were asked, among other things, how satisfied they were with various aspects of their lives. The results for the various regions of the world are shown in Table 3-3. (Note that some of the regions included nations at very different levels of development; the Far East average includes both India and Japan. The Japanese satisfaction levels are much higher than the Indian. Note also that these are not restricted to urban areas.)

Table 3-2   Rank, by Country, of Shares in World GNP as Compared to Shares in World Population

Rank		Ratio of World GNP to World Population	Rank		Ratio of World GNP to World Population
1.	Sweden	5.539	26.	Singapore	1.571
2.	Switzerland	5.369	27.	Bulgaria	1.463
3.	United States	4.978	28.	Greece	1.432
4.	West Germany	4.477	29.	Ireland	1.410
5.	Canada	4.491	30.	Argentina	1.122
6.	Belgium	4.475	31.	Romania	1.058
7.	Norway	4.373	32.	Iran	1.055
8.	Denmark	4.278	33.	South Africa	1.032
9.	Netherlands	4.147	34.	Portugal	1.009
10.	France	3.829	35.	Hungary	.938
11.	Finland	3.724	36.	Poland	.881
12.	Austria	3.349	37.	Yugoslavia	.740
13.	Japan	2.820	38.	Mexico	.719
14.	Australia	2.813	39.	Panama	.651
15.	Britain	2.662	40.	Iraq	.644
16.	Czechoslovakia	2.654	41.	Uruguay	.605
17.	Libya	2.635	42.	Taiwan	.588
18.	Saudi Arabia	2.364	43.	Turkey	.585
19.	Soviet Union	2.170	44.	Peru	.578
20.	New Zealand	2.115	45.	Ivory Coast	.496
21.	East Germany	1.993	46.	Brazil	.484
22.	Italy	1.781	47.	Tunisia	.477
23.	Israel	1.693	48.	Lebanon	.466
24.	Venezuela	1.592	49.	Algeria	.455
25.	Spain	1.588	50.	Malaysia	.439

Table 3-2   Rank, by Country, of Shares in World GNP as
             Compared to Shares in World Population (continued)

Rank		Ratio of World GNP to World Population	Rank		Ratio of World GNP to World Population
51.	Ecuador	.413	73.	Congo	.118
52.	Zambia	.368	74.	Madagascar	.115
53.	South Korea	.366	75.	Haiti	.113
54.	Paraguay	.339	76.	Pakistan	.092
55.	Syria	.335	77.	Zaire	.092
56.	Chile	.327	78.	Tanzania	.091
57.	Cuba	.323	79.	Uganda	.081
58.	Albania	.302	80.	India	.081
59.	Colombia	.298	81.	Sudan	.074
60.	El Salvador	.297	82.	Cambodia	.073
61.	Morocco	.267	83.	Nepal	.072
62.	Nigeria	.258	84.	Burma	.066
63.	Jordan	.246	85.	Bangladesh	.063
64.	Ghana	.240	86.	Ethiopia	.062
65.	Philippines	.234	87.	Guinea	.054
66.	Thailand	.229	88.	Afghanistan	.053
67.	Bolivia	.211	89.	Niger	.052
68.	North Korea	.201	90.	Mali	.049
69.	China	.174	91.	Chad	.0396
70.	Egypt	.164	92.	Laos	.036
71.	Kenya	.125	93.	Rhodesia	.025
72.	Indonesia	.119			

Source: Calculated from *Reader's Digest Almanac and Yearbook* 1977, pp. 484-486.

Table 3-3   International Satisfaction with Performance: Results of the
             Gallup International Survey

Percentage of Respondents Who Are "Highly Satisfied" with Various Aspects of Their Lives					
	North America	Western Europe	Latin America	Sub-Sahara Africa	East Asia
Your family life	73	64	60	18	18
Your present health	63	51	48	33	18
Your leisure time	58	48	51	30	13
Your housing	55	49	37	14	14
Your work	49	40	22	7	7
Your community	47	42	38	17	13
Your standards of living	46	35	36	5	8
Your education—for work	40	28	26	6	6
Your education—for life	36	25	32	4	4
Life in nation today	36	29	38	18	12

Source: George H. Gallup, "Human Needs and Satisfactions: A Global Survey," *Public Opinion Quarterly,* Winter 1976-77, Vol. 40, No. 4, pp. 459-467 at p. 467.

One of the major preliminary findings of the survey was that the basic deter-minant of satisfaction with performance was economics. George Gallup writes:

Although one probably could find isolated places in the world where the in-habitants are very poor but happy, this study failed to discover any area that met this test. The nations with the highest per capita income almost invariably top every test of psychological well-being and satisfaction in major aspects of life. People in industrialized nations, compared with those who live in the developing nations, find their lives more interesting, worry less, and would like fewer changes. They are also more satisfied with their family life, their jobs, their community, their education, and with themselves.

Gallup noted, however, that people in the Third World believe that their lot will improve with time—and, in fact, they are relatively more optimistic in this re-spect than those living in the industrialized nations.[5]

That urban government performance—whether measured in terms of objec-tive indicators or satisfaction surveys—is highest in the more modern countries is not surprising since high-performance government first emerged in the industrializ-ing cities of Western Europe and North America during the nineteenth century. From these centers of innovation, urban technology spread throughout the Western world and into parts of the non-Western world through colonialism and cultural diffusion. Just as the West led the way in the development of modern industry, commerce, and agriculture, it led the way in the development of "urbanism" as a way of life based on modern science (for example, in public health), modern forms of social organization (for example, municipal service bureaucracies), and modern concepts of mass welfare.

Economic development in the West—the growth of industry and commerce—stimulated the growth of cities and provided urban governments with the means to pay for an ever-widening and expanding range of services. The cities of the indus-trial West degenerated into agglomerations of filth, pestilence, and disorder, but gradually programs were shaped to improve conditions of health, safety, and wel-fare—programs that differentiate the cities of the developed nations from those of the poorer nations.

Nineteenth-century British, French, German, and American cities led the way in developing the public services that made living and working together in large agglomerations relatively safe and comfortable. During the nineteenth century, British cities developed modern forms of police protection, slum clearance, poor relief, public baths, parks, and water supply. In Germany, cities became known for their schools, employment bureaus, electric street railways, public markets, and municipal savings banks. American cities led the way in developing street railways, electric street lighting, public libraries, and public schools. Paris was in the vanguard with regard to fire protection, public health, street paving, and city planning.[6]

Economic development—the growth of industry and commerce—provided government with the wherewithal to improve the conditions of health, safety, and welfare. Economic development, coupled with public policy, gradually overcame some of the adverse side effects of modernization—slums, industrial diseases, un-employment, and malnutrition.

Thus in the cities of the modernized nations, one expects to find not only urban government with integrity and responsiveness, but also:

dwellings provided with potable running water, sunlight, elevators, central heating, private bathrooms and toilets, separate kitchens, electricity, sturdy construction, inhabited by a single household, and no more than one person per room:

neighborhoods with schools, parks, playgrounds, nurseries, and modern shopping facilities; clinics; well-lit, well-paved, well-cleansed streets and arterial highways; well-maintained rapid transit or a diffused ownership of private automobiles; sewer, electricity, and drainage lines serving all dwellings; well-maintained public buildings and grounds;

districts and entire urban areas with public libraries, museums, recreation facilities, hospitals; expressways and transit systems; a range of mass media; a broad series of relatively effective service and regulatory agencies.

But to provide services and facilities characteristic of the cities of the rich nations requires among other things, heavy investment of capital and heavy operating costs. For this reason, we can probably assume that the high per-capita spending levels characteristic of the rich nations correlates with a high level of urban performance. Only the urban government of a wealthy country can afford to install and maintain costly and complex services; only in the wealthier countries is there public insistence on such services and the organizational tightness and social discipline to keep them running at top performance levels.

Modernization tends to create safe, healthy, affluent and well-governed cities. It tends to produce strong and effective national and subnational governments with the capabilities of formulating and implementing the range of complex, sophisticated programs needed to make the urban system function reasonably well. It tends to produce educated, law-abiding citizens able to do their part in making programs effective in health, transportation, education, recreation, social welfare, planning, and taxation. Without citizen cooperation, few urban programs can be successful. The success of health programs depends on people with high personal standards of hygiene and an appreciation of the requirements, limitations, and benefits of modern medicine. Successful education depends on a population with a sense of the limitations, requirements, and benefits of learning. The same applies to programs in such areas as taxation, traffic, litter and crime control—the basic ingredient is a modernized public that is willing, not only to provide political and financial support for programs in health, education, pollution and crime, but also to take the necessary personal actions in their private behavior.

Effective urban performance also depends on feedback from an informed and demanding citizenry. Without criticism from the public, ineffective programs cannot be identified, improved, or eliminated. Without a reactive public, modern urban bureaucracies can become self-serving, self-aggrandizing interest groups. Only the interaction of participant citizens with professionalized bureaucracy can produce strong and effective local urban government capable of adapting national and subnational policies to local needs and realities.

But modernization is only a moderately good predictor and explainer of urban government effectiveness. The reason is twofold: performance is better than one might expect in some developing modernized countries and worse than one might expect in some advanced countries.

"Overperformance" in the Third World can occur, first of all, because the urban areas in the Third World are areas of privilege. Low national per-capita GNP can quite easily result from averaging some urban affluence with massive and desperate rural poverty. The strong drive of rural peasantries throughout the Third World to get to the big city rests exactly upon this contrast in development levels. The differential between nations in their per-capita GNPs may exaggerate the differences between their urban segments. Second, in the poorer countries, the quality of life for the urban elites (the elite within the elite) may be extremely high—much higher, in fact, than for most urbanities in the wealthy countries. The urban elites in the poorer countries not only have access to the comforts and benefits of modern technology (either locally or by jet), they also enjoy large amounts of personal service—paradoxically, the scarcest commodity in the modern, "service" economy.

Conversely, one can find considerable "underperformance" in the advanced world. One reason is that modernization solves some problems of urban existence, only to create others. Affluence creates high-quality medical care; it also permits too much drinking, smoking, eating, and driving. Affluence means mass consumption, but also the wasteful use of resources and massive problems in disposing of waste. Affluence lengthens life but also weakens the family, and, thus, helps to create the problems of old age. Traditional societies have few old people and they are taken care of by their families. Modern society has many senior citizens, but they are less able (and less willing) to depend on their families for support. Modern cities thus need greater system capabilities than do less modern cities.

In the same way, cities in rich countries may have more crime, pollution, and social disorganization than cities in poorer countries. There is less crime in some Asian and African cities than in many cities of the advanced world. Cities in less modernized societies have stronger informal social controls over behavior and are thus able to inhibit deviant social behavior much more effectively than advanced cities, which have to rely on law and bureaucracy to enforce community norms.

Underperformance in the advanced world can occur also because modernization is a highly uneven process: some individuals, families, and localities in modern societies are usually left out of the mainstream of advancement. Per-capita income figures deceptively provide an average for the widely varying incomes of different families and regions. In every advanced country there are wealthy and depressed regions and inequalities among individuals in income, education, and skills. One of the major tasks of government in advanced countries is to help out those localities and people left behind in the development process; for without strong action, development tends to sharpen rather than reduce the gap between the mainstream "haves" and the minority "have-nots."

Urban governments in the advanced world may thus suffer from lack of resources because of their location in a poor locality or region; they may suffer (like New York City) from the mismatch of their resources with the burdens of providing for a large nonaffluent, nonproductive population. Though the countries with high GNP per capita constitute a privileged minority in the world of nations, they still lack the resources to provide all the school rooms, hospital beds, or apartments that are needed. They often lack trained personnel in all fields (for example, health) where they are needed. And they lack the resources to cope with rising service needs and service costs. Rising expectations and standards, rising salaries and other costs of producing services, and expanding service clienteles put a strain on the finances of even the wealthiest countries. Since all the high GNP countries are democracies, what government can provide is determined by what the taxpayers are willing and able to pay. In all advanced countries, there are limits to taxpayer tolerance and periodic taxpayer revolts, whether the latter take the form of defeats on bond issues or voting for taxpayer protest parties. In all the advanced countries, consequently, there are basic struggles over priorities, over the relative scope of the public and private sector and over the allocation of public sector funds. Consequently, modernization does not guarantee that wealthy countries will prefer schools over race tracks, hospitals over sailboats, or milk over alcohol.

PERFORMANCE IN THE ADVANCED INDUSTRIAL DEMOCRACIES

4

4-1 PERFORMANCE DIFFERENCES
IN THE ADVANCED WORLD

Modernization produces similar, but not identical urban performance. Knowing the per-capita GNP of a country, we can predict fairly accurately the level of integrity, responsiveness, and effectiveness in that country's urban governments. GNP also provides a fairly accurate prediction of the dysfunctions in urban life that we are likely to find—dysfunctions that modernization also tends to produce everywhere. Advanced countries have affluent, middle-class cities, serviced by bureaucratic organizations capable of performing a range of sophisticated functions; they also have pollution, congestion, and social conflict.

But, however similar they are in resources and problems, the cities of the advanced world are otherwise quite diverse in quality of life. Table 4-1 groups some major cities of the world in a rank order based on the level of national economic development. If modernization (represented by per-capita GNP) really predicted performance, we would expect to find similar performance at each level and better performance at each successive level. But a glance back to Chapter 2 will show that cities at the same level of development do not necessarily have the same performance characteristics, nor are the wealthier cities necessarily superior cities in all respects to less wealthy cities. Modernization (urbanization, industrialization, economic development, secularization, restratification) is compatible with very different kinds of city life since it occurs in such different social, political, and historical contexts. There are striking differences between the communist and noncommunist cities at the same levels of economic development. There are also striking differences, even within the group of capitalist democracies. The correlation between modernization and the quality of urban life is only moderately high.

Table 4-1   Predicting Urban Performance, Using per-Capita GNP (1975)

High per-Capita GNP
(High Urban Performance?)

    Kuwait City
    Stockholm   Zürich   Geneva   Göteborg   Bern
    NEW YORK   CHICAGO   LOS ANGELES
    Copenhagen   Cologne   Oslo   Montreal   Amsterdam   Brussels
    Helsinki   Paris   Vienna
    Prague   Tokyo   Tripoli   Sydney
    Auckland   London   East Berlin   Moscow
    Athens   Dublin   Rome   Caracas   Singapore   Tel Aviv
    Budapest   Mexico City   Buenos Aires   Belgrade   Panama City   Warsaw
                                 Lisbon   Johannesburg   Sofia
    Montevideo
    Lima
    Algiers   São Paulo   Managua

Low per-Capita GNP
(Low Urban Performance?)

    Quito
    Tirana   Asunción   Lusaka   Santiago (Chile)   Havana   Damascus
    Monrovia   Bogotá
    La Paz   Lagos   Manila   Casablanca   Accra
    Dakar   Peking   Cairo
    Dacca   Kinshasa   Kampala   Karachi   Calcutta
    Kabul   Mogadiscio   Addis Ababa   Ventiane   Conakry   Rangoon

Modernization produces the same kinds of urban problems, but some advanced countries have been able to cope with those problems—to mitigate the dysfunctions of modernization—more than others. American cities, in particular, do not reflect in the quality of their life—public or private—the high level of American achievements in business, science, education, and technology.

Foreign visitors are often shocked by their first glimpse of American urbanism. Richard Llewelyn-Davies, the distinguished British planner, has written:

My reactions on first arriving in an American city were perhaps typical of the reaction that European visitors to America often feel. The inner slum area of an American city, through which I drove between the airport and my downtown hotel, shocked me deeply. For most Europeans it is hardly believable that a society as wealthy as America could tolerate the physical squalor of the inner-city slums, let alone accept the human degradation that they represent. Of course, the more sophisticated visitor will have read of American urban problems, but the first exposure to their reality is astonishing. [1]

Many Americans have made the same point. Robert Heilbroner has written, for example:

> *In no large city in the United States do we find a concern for the living habitat comparable to that commonly found in the cities of such nations as the Netherlands, Switzerland, or the countries of Scandinavia. . . . To match the squalor or the worst of the American habitat one must descend to the middle range of the underdeveloped lands. These are, I repeat, "impressionistic" statements, for which quantitative documentation is lacking, but I do not think they will be challenged on that account.* [2]

Daniel Patrick Moynihan states bluntly:

> *It can be said with fair assurance that mass poverty and squalor, of the kind that may be encountered in almost any large American city, simply cannot be found in comparable cities in Europe, or Canada, or Japan.* [3]

Actually the picture of American urban performance is mixed, with strengths as well as weaknesses. In some ways, American city performance is superior to the norm; in some ways, it is inferior. Table 4-2 gives a rough summary of the performance record of American cities.

Table 4-3 is based mostly on hard, objective social indicators. Actually according to the recent international opinion survey by Gallup International, Americans tend to be more pleased with their urban surroundings than the people in any other country except Canada. [4] Americans tend to be satisfied with their housing and their public services, irrespective of race or ethnicity. In a 1975 opinion survey,

Table 4-2   The Performance Record of American Cities

We can summarize the comparative performance of American cities as follows:

Comparative High Performance	*Comparative Poor Performance*
High standard of living	Personal and property safety
Relative absence of status differences	Infant health care
Public works and facilities	Municipal corruption
Cost of living	Family breakdown, drug addiction
Regulation of traffic and pollution	Racial inequalities
Some forms of social disorganization (for example, suicide)	Conditions of the poor and minorities
Moderate taxation	Unemployment
Services and amenities for middle and upper income groups	
Shopping facilities	
Citizen participation	
Due process and protection of individual rights	

Table 4-3   Satisfaction with Performance in American Metropolitan Areas (1974)

	All	Negro	Spanish
Overall Opinion of Neighborhood			
Excellent	35.3	13.2	20.3
Good	44.6	40.0	47.9
Fair	9.3	35.8	24.5
Poor	3.3	10.2	7.2
Adequate public transportation	60.1	78.3	69.6
Adequate schools	79.3	77.6	79.4
Adequate shopping	87.6	78.8	89.7
Adequate police protection	85.9	76.9	81.8
Adequate fire protection	91.7	88.0	89.3
Adequate hospitals and health clinics	86.3	84.7	83.3

Source: Bureau of the Census, *Annual Housing Survey: 1975 (Part B, Indicators of Housing and Neighborhood Quality)* (Washington: 1977), pp. 1-42.

the United States Department of Housing and Urban Development found that though blacks and Latinos gave lower ratings to their neighborhoods than other people, there were no vast differences in the ratings given to various public services.[5] (See Table 4-3.)

Nonetheless, as noted in Chapter 2, the objective record of American cities with respect to safety, health, corruption, drug addiction, and other forms of social and individual breakdown is far below what one would expect in the wealthiest nation of the world. Why should this be so? It is not possible to offer here any detailed or comprehensive explanation of the underperformance of American cities: too many types of performance are involved and relatively little work has been done that moves beyond impressionistic comparisons to precise measurements and systematic explanation. In this chapter we can only point to factors that account for the performance variance that we know to exist, even if only impressionistically.

Major determinants of performance seem to us to be the following:

1. the pattern of values;
2. the pattern of social cleavage;
3. the pattern of politics;
4. the pattern of government;
5. the pattern of urban bureaucracy;
6. the pattern of urban policy;
7. the pattern of urban development;
8. the pattern of private sector performance;
9. the nature of performance itself.

4-2 EXPLAINING THE MIXED RECORD
OF AMERICAN CITIES

THE PATTERN OF NATIONAL VALUES

Basic to an understanding of the mixed record of American cities is a knowledge of widely held values in American society—values that affect the response of the American people to the challenges of urbanization. The key values seem to be those affecting authority, local control, mobility, rurality, capitalism, abundance, inequality, and American "exceptionalism."

Authority vs. Freedom: The Permissive Society Americans have historically been highly ambivalent about authority, believing, on the one hand, in the need for law, order, and stable government, and, on the other, in government as a source of evil restriction rather than as a source of good. Government officials have been objects of suspicion rather than deference. "Checks and balances" have been idealized rather than the majesty of the strong state. The ideal has been to minimize the discretion of government so as to maximize the discretion of private individuals and society. That government is considered best which governs least and is most permissive of individual development, entrepreneurship, and mobility. Fear that government power will be abused and misused has been greater than fear that government power will be *un*used. Government is not usually seen as the guardian of a shared collective interest. The consequence is that government in American cities has not been a powerful agent in attacking social problems, regulating interests, or ensuring individual conformity with community norms.

Government in the other advanced nations, particularly those in Western Europe, has been seen more positively as the embodiment of and guardian of the public interest, with the right and duty of ensuring conformity to that interest. There is greater public acceptance of the need for strong authority, even on the part of the revolutionary parties. Government officials have much higher prestige; they are more willingly given authority over individuals and interest groups. Thus, as Dean Rugg notes,

> *In most European countries the government is involved to so considerable an extent in the lives of the citizens that a public environment can be said to exist alongside the private one. What is meant by the concept of a public environment? The average urban resident in Europe is accustomed to controls in the public interest. . . . The public has come to expect [these controls] and often demands [them]. Examples of such control are frequent denials of petitions for zoning change, when the change may affect the public interest, and restrictions on sprawl of land uses owing to public costs for the infrastructure. In other words, the public interest (the majority) in densely populated Europe is often emphasized while in the United States a tendency exists to protect private interests (the minority) particularly if stimulation of private initiative is involved.*[6]

The practical consequences are that American urban bureaucracies—police, planning, health, and education—have fewer powers than their counterparts in other countries: private misbehavior is less feared than public misbehavior.

Central vs. Local Authority   Decentralized institutions for urban government rest upon strong American belief in the superiority of local to central authority. That central government is best, Americans tend to believe, which is most permissive of *local* development, initiative, and distinctiveness. Government at the grassroots is less distrusted than remote government in the state or national capital. Traditionally, the central government in Washington has been seen as having no direct authority over, or responsibility for, urban or local affairs. Even the state governments, with their constitutional responsibility for most domestic government, have been seen as properly working through locally elected officials, even for the implementation of state policy.

In other advanced nations, there has been greater acceptance of strong central government. The major strands of ideology have tended to favor centralism over localism. Conservatism in other countries has been centralist because of monarchical traditions, the aristocratic prestige of the central bureaucracy, and conservative preference for strong authority. The parties of the left have tended to be equally centralist, seeing in strong central government the engine to promote and defend social change and revolution. Localism has been identified with parochialism, backwardness, and incompetence; centralism, with professionalism, paternalism, national prestige and power, and rapid social change.

Stability vs. Mobility   Many contrasts between European and American cities derive from attitudes concerning mobility: the need and desirability of changing residence. As Coppa notes, Americans have always been nomads who equate geographic mobility with freedom, social mobility, and economic opportunity.[7] In the settlement of the country, land here has been a commodity to be exploited and then deserted for something better. American urbanites have something of the same throwaway, disposable attitude toward their houses and neighborhoods: something to be enjoyed fully, but temporarily.

Coppa writes:

> *Most urbanites in Europe do not equate mobility with success as do so many Americans who have no appreciation of dwelling for generations in the same neighborhood, perhaps the same house. To mobile Americans, programmed to move into bigger if not better houses, this would be tantamount to stagnation. To the European it is stability, and it offers the solace of living and dying among relatives and friends in the place one was born rather than being surrounded by strangers in a more prestigious area. When a man spends his entire life in one neighborhood he develops a far deeper attachment to his community and has a greater stake in its preservation. This situation, multiplied many times, helps to account for the care that Europeans lavish upon their cities.[8]*

Residential turnover has important consequences for performance:

1. There is less attachment to neighborhood and community and less feeling that public regulation is needed to preserve their physical and social characteristics.
2. Buildings and land are seen primarily as commodities rather than permanent elements.
3. Residences tend to be built of less permanent materials such as wood, rather than brick, stone, or concrete. This means a far greater fire hazard for American residences. Even buildings made of permanent materials in American cities are torn down after short use on the basis of real-estate market calculations.
4. City development follows the logic of the real-estate market rather than the design of a deliberate public policy for development.
5. Suburban sprawl, with what some regard as its wasteful use of land and capital, is designed to maximize mobility opportunities—opportunities for people constantly to "move up" by moving.
6. Mobility is seen as a constitutional right, implying freedom from personal registration and rejection of policies that would direct, restrict, or interfere with population movement.[9] Freedom of movement confers certain advantages on criminals, family deserters, and illegal aliens.
7. Mobility pressures are a source of social, particularly ethnic and racial, conflict.
8. Mobility also means the possibility to escape from deteriorating conditions: conditions can be allowed to deteriorate precisely because many people are free to move on and up. In contrast, Rugg has noted, "Europeans are generally quite vocal in their support of good maintenance for a public urban environment since they lack the means of mobility to escape the more objectionable areas."[10]
9. Mobility is seen within a differential spatial and temporal context: "The American has got used to moving over large distances. He almost has a feeling as if space is endless and he is always on the move in time as well as in space."[11]

Urban vs. Rural Values Antiurbanism in American culture has long worked against the building of socially and physically attractive cities. From Jefferson onward, American thought has opposed and seen cities as unhealthy, unclean, unfriendly, dangerous, radical, corrupt, alien, artificial, exploitative, dehumanizing, elitist, mob-ridden, materialistic, atheistic, and unnatural and seen rural localities and small towns as healthy, wholesome, egalitarian, moderate, spiritual, virtuous, hardworking, friendly, safe, productive, natural, and 100% American. Small town life has been the ideal; big city life, the necessary evil.

Cities in other cultures have been more esteemed: as the residences of the rich, the nobility, the high clergy; as the symbols of national grandeur and prosperity; as monuments to major moments in national history; and as major artistic and spiritual legacies of the national past. American cities have been accepted as commercial and industrial necessities and treated as commercial and industrial objects—convenient or, at least, necessary places for production and distribution to be developed in terms of market place rationality. (Indicative perhaps of American attitudes toward the city is the fact that in France there are 2.3 real estate salesmen and brokers per 10,000 people; in the United States, there are 8.6.) Cities in Europe and Latin America, in contrast, have been treated as centers of civilization—cultural, aristocratic, cosmopolitan, leisure-oriented—in contrast to rural areas identified with peasants, grinding labor, and dirt.

Antiurbanism has led the United States to exalt suburbanism as a way of combining big city conveniences with the ideal rural or small town life-style. Antiurbanism has meant a weak constituency for careful planning and development, and it has meant a lack of sympathy for or awareness of, urban problems, as well as a lag in the development of vitally needed urban services. Central cities in the United States could be left to decay because decay affects only "selfish" downtown real estate owners and the "undeserving" urban poor; decay has little emotional or symbolic cost to suburbanites or people in small towns. The suburban sprawl characteristic of American cities results from an effort to create endless numbers of "small towns" that ruralize the city so as to make it acceptable.

Where attitudes are prourban, there is less decay at the core. The core is not for the poor, but the rich; it has historical, artistic, and social importance—an importance that public policy must actively support and protect. Typically, slums in the prourban countries are in the surrounding suburbs, not in the center.

In the wealthier prourban countries, such as in Scandinavia, there is wide support for planned development. Cities grow under the strict control of the authorities. Frequently, new growth is directed toward and restricted to land purchased in advance and serviced by the government. The aim is preservation of the core and compact, high-quality urban, rather than low-density suburban development. Typically, in wealthier prourban countries, people accept high-rise living in contrast to the single-family dwellings with yards (green, and "un-urban"), which people in the countries idealizing country life insist on. Typically, also, in the wealthier prourban countries, there is a visible demarcation between the city and the surrounding area—a demarcation that comes from the fact that only compact development is permitted. In antiurban countries, cities blend into the countryside with gradually declining development densities; development tends to be the "scatteration" that results from the uncoordinated initiatives of a multitude of private suburban developers (and the acquiescence of the public planning authorities). Scatteration and sprawl result from the desire (and ability) of antiurbanites to obtain the benefits of urbanism while escaping some of the costs.

Rejection of big city life and the search to recreate small town life in the city underlie the fierce resistance in most American metropolitan areas to proposals to merge the "small town" suburbs into a single, large governmental entity. The desire to recapture small town values sustains the fragmentation of local government in American urbanized areas.[12]

One should not, however, overstate the extent of antiurbanism in American values. American urban history must be understood not only in terms of antiurbanism, but also in terms of "boosterism" and even deep affection for one's city, especially as it competes with other places. Americans have often taken considerable pride in their cities and committed a lot of time and resources to making their cities attractive and pleasant places in which to live.

Equality and Inequality   Crucial in shaping urban performance are our ambivalent feelings about equality—political, economic, legal, and social. Americans have combined an abstract belief in human equality ("all men are created equal") with the practice of slavery and, later, racial supremacy; a belief in social equality with the practice of discrimination against ethnic, religious, and regional minorities; a belief in equal opportunity with the practice of sharply unequal rewards and results.

This is not to say that egalitarian beliefs have served only to mask inegalitarian practices and have had no egalitarian consequences: for, in fact, egalitarianism accounts for the advent of mass democracy far earlier in American cities than in any other advanced countries; it accounts for the advent of mass education, including mass higher education, far earlier than elsewhere; it accounts for the great weight given by politicians to public opinion in shaping and legitimizing policies; and it accounts for the powerful egalitarian movement in recent times to reduce inequalities between rich and poor, black and white, older and newer immigrants, and men and women.

Conversely, the belief that inequality is natural, necessary, and legitimate has sanctioned the social-economic contrasts between the urban ghettos and the suburbs, impeded the movement to raise the status of minorities, particularly racial minorities, and legitimated strong differences between and within urban centers in public services.

In systems with stronger class differences, the reaction to social inequality has been more radical. People have rejected the existing society as basically unjust. They have seen the need for collective action to carry out drastic social reform. And they have insisted that government act to redress social grievances. Support for social welfare also, paradoxically, has come from those people with the highest status. Aristocratic groups, with traditions of noblesse oblige, have helped to compensate for the defects of unbridled capitalism in ways that American business elites did not. In the other advanced societies, the demand for policies to aid the working class and the poor stemmed from powerful egalitarian movements, on the one hand, and powerful paternalistic conservative groups, on the other.

Collectivism vs. Individualism   American concepts of equality have, thus, never provided the basis for a mass socialistic movement on behalf of working class, poor, or minority groups. In all classes people have tended to believe that: social problems should be solved primarily by individuals through their own efforts; individuals should be self-reliant and help themselves; individuals should be free to make the most of their property rights and economic bargaining power; individuals should advance through their own efforts rather than collectively as a mass movement.

Scarcity vs. Abundance   Socialism might have had more adherents in the United States had there been a sense of limited opportunities, horizons, resources, and possibilities. But Americans, as David Potter noted, are a "people of plenty."[13] Much in American culture reflects abundance: land, natural resources, energy, consumer goods, and houses. Opportunities are seen as plentiful, with more than enough to go around. With so much land, everyone should have a piece of his own. There is consequently little need for careful regulation of resource utilization; scarcity is un-American. The future is expanding opportunity and greater plenty; saving is un-American. Easy credit is practically a constitutional right.

The consequences for urban performance have been both positive and negative. Optimism about resources brought the development of the richest economy and the largest affluent mass society in the world. Resources *have* been developed. Negatively, there has been a waste of land and capital and perhaps an overutilization of nonrenewable resources. It has been difficult to plan more compact patterns of development—using less capital, land, and energy—because there has not been the sense of scarcity one finds in older, more densely populated nations.

Capitalism vs. Socialism   Americans have a unique faith in, and preference for, capitalistic solutions to urban problems. They much prefer to rely on the market to satisfy urban needs and preferences than to rely on government. Capitalism in their minds is associated with mass affluence, consumer choice, and individual opportunity. Socialism is associated with forced equality and government interference in private life. In most other advanced nations, socialism is viewed more positively and capitalism less positively. In most other countries, socialism is seen as a humanitarian movement to raise the masses to affluence or at least decency; capitalism is seen as a system with defects requiring radical reform. Socialist, Communist, and Labor parties provide a strong constituency for urban welfare programs and for urban planning. But they build upon traditions of public activism and control that predate the emergence of strong Leftist movements: in most of Europe and Japan, even before the emergence of the Left, there were conservative-bureaucratic traditions that legitimized paternalistic welfare programs and strict developmental control.[14]

Thus, in most of the other advanced countries, both conservative and socialist attitudes about property rights and the economy favor a large measure of collectivism. The laissez faire, procapitalist sector of thought is weak.

The consequences for urban performance have been crucial. Socialist cities or cities with strong Socialist Parties at the national level have generally been more concerned with ameliorating the conditions of poor people and the working class. They have built large amounts of public housing; given the more collectivist orientation of the people, public housing does not have the stigma of charity that it often has in American cities. Nor do public health care programs suffer from the "handout" stigma attached to them in the United States. Socialism appeals to people in the other advanced societies as a means of collectively "moving up"—advancing the welfare of whole classes of the underprivileged.

In American cities, people prefer to "move up" as individuals or as families rather than as members of a social class. The proper role of government is to promote individual, rather than collective, advancement. Social democracy is seen as the product of innumerable individual successes, rather than as the success of a collective movement. Social democracy is also seen as the result of satisfying individual preferences through consumer sovereignty rather than as satisfying class preferences on a collective basis. European socialists tend to reject consumer choice in favor of choice by the political and planning elite—an elite responsible for defining, identifying, and providing for the major needs of society.

The capitalistic, individualistic, privatistic bias of American thought accounts for some of the dysfunctions of American cities. Reliance on the market and faith in consumer sovereignty mean that the distribution of income is crucial in allocating all kinds of urban goods and bads. Low income means being forced to live in substandard housing in unsafe neighborhoods, with poor schools, and poor employment prospects. Low income means thinking of oneself (and being thought of) as "worthless" and a "failure."

Privatism means a *relatively* low level of taxation and therefore relative inability to use the public sector to mitigate some of the disastrous effects of low income. But privatism also accounts for positive aspects of American cities: the wide distribution of single-family home ownership and of the automobile—the two most important status symbols in the world. Individualistic privatism has been based on, and has reinforced, the absence of strong class divisions in American society. Mass affluence has blurred class differences even further. Privatism and the private enterprise system (stimulated, subsidized, and regulated by the public sector) have generated an affluent society for most Americans.

American "Exceptionalism"   A major source of policy innovation in a country is the example of other countries. Countries borrow policies, institutions, and programs from each other, just as cities and states borrow ideas from each other within each country. Lagging development of social policies in the United States derives from the fact that the United States, unlike other advanced nations, seldom looks abroad for policy inspiration. For most of our history, we Americans have considered our country an exception to the general rules, and we have rejected the examples of the Western European nations—however enlightened and progressive—as essentially irrelevant models. We have tended to believe in the superiority of our institutions and programs (if not necessarily of our luxury cars) and have been suspicious of foreign institutions and programs. Thus, social programs originating in other advanced nations, such as Germany, Sweden, France, or Britain, have either never been copied or have been introduced only after long dispute and delay. Resistance to foreign imports in policy—particularly in the social area—stems from national pride, but even more from the success of national political and economic institutions. Nations are more prone to imitate others when their institutions have failed or collapsed. Success is a reactionary force in policy development.

THE PATTERN OF SOCIAL CLEAVAGE

Perhaps the most distinctive characteristic of American cities and the factor most responsible for their performance levels is their social heterogeneity. Unlike most cities in the advanced world, American cities have multiracial, multireligious, and multinational populations.

Although this fact has contributed to the richness, diversity, and fun of American urban life, it has also contributed to the dysfunctions of American cities. Social diversity has meant a rather low level of social integration in the national society and in regional and local communities: separate races, religions, and nationalities have come to share values and mutual respect only gradually and incompletely. This has meant a lower sense of social solidarity in confronting community problems and agreeing on community norms. Urban groups—at least the needy—have tended to be members of ethnic or racial minorities, regarded with suspicion and contempt by the majoritarian "Wasps" (White "Anglo-Saxon" Protestants). Thus, in the nineteenth century, city needs were seen as those of foreign immigrants, speaking strange languages, behaving in crude, peasant-like ways, swayed by unscrupulous politicians and other "nefarious" interests, such as the Democratic party, the Catholic church, the liquor lobby, and gangsters. Nativism—hostility to foreigners and Catholics—played a major role in preserving rural and small town domination over state and national government and delaying governmental response to urban needs and demands. Immigrants in cities might need welfare, but they had to get aid from private charity or the political machine; they were newcomers, after all, with no great claims on long established groups; they had voluntarily decided to come to these shores and could leave any time they wished.

In the twentieth century, the negative coupling of "urban" with "foreign" gradually has been replaced with the equally negative coupling of "urban" with "black." Even the formerly disadvantaged ethnics find it hard to sympathize with the needs of the urban poor when the latter seem predominantly to belong to a race traditionally felt to be inferior. In a context of Social Darwinism, the plight of the urban blacks is seen as definitive proof of racial inferiority and of the inability of blacks to compete with other members of society. Poverty is seen as the result of individual and racial failure.

Ethnic, religious, and racial diversity creates difficulties for urban performance:

1. There is less consensus on cultural values and norms, less collective ability to act, less mutual sympathy and problem recognition. If racial, religious, or ethnic minorities are relegated to lower statuses in the city (less prestigious neighborhoods, jobs, schools, churches), then the middle classes may have less sympathy for their plight simply because of their physical, linguistic, or cultural distance.

2. For the new incoming groups, there are often sharp problems of adjusting to new circumstances—finding a place in a new society. Migrating groups may encounter discrimination, unemployment, low-status occupations, and school problems—especially when their cultural or social background is very different from that of groups already established in the city. Typically, the same low-status districts in American cities display high crime, poverty, and social disorganization rates as various ethnic groups move through them and, eventually, on to better neighborhoods. Crime becomes one way of adjusting to discrimination and the lack of opportunity in a land which preaches the virtues and necessity of "success."

3. The task of maintaining peaceful coexistence among potentially warring national, religious, and racial groups may be quite difficult: the city may become the turf for severe, even violent, intergroup conflict.

4. There is apt to be less consensus among the various groups on what the law is and how it should be enforced. Some groups may want strict enforcement of vice and temperance laws, whereas others may see no harm in a little gambling, wine, beer, or pot.

By and large, American cities have successfully integrated people from various classes, ethnic groups, religions, and regions, who manage to coexist rather peacefully despite differences in background, interests, and policy orientation.[15] Establishing detente among religious groups is no easy matter (cf., Belfast), nor is interethnic tolerance easily achieved (cf., Brussels or Montreal). Integrating the members of different races has proved to be a much more difficult task, given visible differences between the races and historic differences in status. Many of the worst aspects of American urban performance are legacies of slavery, racial oppression, and the racial caste system.

The importance of race in American urban politics can hardly be exaggerated. In 1960, 12% of the American urban population was nonwhite; 18% of the central city population and 4.5% of the suburban ("urban fringe") population. By 1970, nonwhites constituted 14% of the urban population: 22% of the central cities, but only 6% of the suburban population. By 1970, one-third or more of the people in 25 major American cities, including Atlanta, Baltimore, Chicago, Cleveland, Detroit, New Orleans, Newark, Oakland, Philadelphia, Richmond, St. Louis, and Washington, D.C., were black.

Racially mixed cities have lower performance than racially homogeneous cities because the normal interracial relationship is one of superordination and subordination, rather than equality. In a mixed situation, some racial groups are usually considered inferior and suffer from many forms of discrimination. Racially subordinate groups tend to get the worst jobs, unemployment, housing, schools, and to suffer the worst crime and health rates. Historically, it has been easier to establish a measure of equality among different classes, even among different religious and nationality groups, than among different races.

Other cities of the advanced world have either no racial problems or have less severe ones than we do. Nonwhite populations under European control were located in overseas colonies, which have since become independent; decolonization removed the necessity for interracial coexistence. Relatively few former colonials were allowed to move to the metropole after independence. In every case, the former colonial power erected immigration barriers to prevent mass migration. In parallel fashion, Australian cities have no racial problems because of the historic "White Australia" immigration policy. And certainly South Africa is no example of superior ability to build viable multiracial cities. The situation in the European cities would be radically different if the people of their former colonies were free to migrate to the metropole.

West European cities do, on the other hand, have problems integrating sometimes large numbers of foreign workers into the community. Foreign workers suffer from many of the same disabilities in European cities that minorities suffer from in American cities: poor housing, discrimination, and social hostility. But unlike minority groups in the United States, they are not citizens; they have no civil rights to assert and defend. They are theoretically only temporary residents and can therefore be deported at the government's pleasure. Moreover, their service needs are low since many of them are single men, without families. This means a relatively low burden of children and old people to be taken care of by the community. As foreign workers are allowed to bring in their families and become more or less permanent members of the community, more serious problems of integration—social, financial, and political—are emerging.[16]

Part of the performance pattern in American cities derives from their multiethnic character and part from their multiracial character. Part also derives from their class structure—their division into strata with widely differing income, education, occupational status, and (especially) wealth. Americans believe in equal opportunity and rough social equality, but they also believe, as we have seen, in the legitimacy of sharply differing income and wealth. Just as the high performance of American cities derives from the generous American share in world income (only Sweden and Switzerland have proportionately larger shares), high performance for middle- and upper-class American urbanites derives from their generous share of the American national income. Many aspects of poor performance in American cities derive from the inadequate access to urban necessities and amenities possessed by lower-class groups. (The majority of the American urban poor, it should be remembered, are white, not black.) Some of these contrasts are brought out in Table 4-4, contrasting conditions within the city of Los Angeles between affluent Malibu-Pacific Palisades and the Watts district of historic memory.

All cities in the advanced industrial democracies have class inequalities—contrasts between rich and poor or between high and low occupational status groups. Poverty—relative and absolute—can be found in all of these cities. But,

Table 4-4   Malibu vs. Watts: Performance Contrasts in an American City

	Malibu-Pacific Palisades	Watts
Median family income	$18,939	$4,942
Percentage of families in poverty	3	43
Percentage of old-age poverty	8	34
Percentage of non-high school graduates (25 years or older)	13	70
Percentage of high-school dropouts (16-21)	3	22
Percentage of families receiving welfare	2	37
Average month prenatal care begins	2.4	3.5
Average age of mother at first birth	25.3	18.4
Infant mortality rate per 100,000	23.6	28.0
Births to mothers with 4+ children	4.5	22.9
Gonorrhea rate/100	0.8	8.3
Syphilis rate/100	.06	1.18
Tuberculosis/100	.01	.20
Hepatitis/100	.18	.34
Narcotics arrests/100 (people 14 to 44)	2.5	4.6
Death rate/100 (25 to 44 years old)	0.1	0.8
Total number of fires, 1973-1974	93	1194
Percentage of preventable fires	39	99
6th-grade reading scores median	75	13
Percentage of unsound structures	1	15-24
Persons per square mile	1072	23,479
Birthrate/100 females (15 to 44)	4.6	13.3
Murder rate/100,000	4.2	43.4
Rape rate/100,000	23.0	155.5
Aggravated assault/100,000	124.6	1271.2
Muggings/100,000	104.7	539.3
Robberies/100,000	253.9	1138.3
Burglaries/100,000	1713	3661
Public library circulation/person	8.4	0.5

Source: Calculated from various volumes of *The State of the City 1975* published by Community Analysis Bureau, Office of the Mayor, City of Los Angeles.

somehow, in the other advanced countries—or rather the more socially progressive ones—class inequality and poverty do not create the massive slums, squalor, and social disorganization so prominent in American cities. In the absence of research on comparative urban poverty, it is hard to say why this is so; but some hypotheses can be offered:

1. the large scale of our cities and therefore the scale of the concentrations of poor people;
2. a more unequal distribution of income in American cities, with perhaps the lowest 20% of the people receiving an unusually small share of total urban income;
3. a greater degree of class segregation within the city and metropolitan area, with less intermixing of income and status groups than in other cities;
4. the identification of poverty with racial and ethnic minority groups with perhaps some stereotyping of all minority group members as poor and all minority group ghettos as poverty areas;
5. the correlation in American cities between poverty, crime, drug addiction, and other forms of social disorganization;
6. the centrality of many American slums as compared to the suburban location of slums in other countries;
7. and finally, the sleazy appearance of American slums as compared to the more picturesque slums of other advanced countries.

These are hypotheses, not findings. It should also be kept in mind that American urban poverty in some ways is not worse than urban poverty in other countries. In terms of housing and possessions, poor people in the United States might be considered, in many advanced countries, not poor at all. Table 4-5 compares the living conditions of blacks of various American cities with the total populations (not just workers, poor people, or foreign workers) in some major cities in the advanced democracies. The comparisons are not totally unfavorable to the performance record of American urbanism.

The combination of race and poverty in American cities makes the poverty and race problems doubly difficult to handle since the difficulties may be additive or even multiplicative. However, a Canadian study of urban poverty has observed that in one way, the American combination of race and poverty problems is positive: the poor, normally very disparate and difficult to mobilize for political action, can more easily be mobilized as a racial action group. Blacks are highly active as a group—much more active than most low-income groups; in responding to black demands for equality, American society may also help the poor in general.[17]

THE PATTERN OF URBAN POLITICS:
PARTIES, ELECTIONS, AND PRESSURE GROUPS

Patterns of values and patterns of social cleavage, however, only affect the scope of policy when they are articulated and organized for political purposes. There are major differences between American cities and European cities in the way that values and interests are articulated. In European-type systems, political parties play the dominant role in urban representation and policymaking; in American cities, the dominant role tends to be played by the urban bureaucracies, interest groups, and the voters.

Table 4-5 Comparative Living Conditions for Blacks in American Cities and General Populations in Other Cities

City	Infant mortality	Percentage with private bath/shower	Percentage with private toilet	Percentage owner occupancy	Percentage with telephone	Percentage with at least one auto	Persons/room	Percentage of dwellings with over one person/room
Black CHICAGO	37.3	96	96	28	74	52	0.64	19
Black NEW YORK	38.4	96	97	20	68	31	0.66	18
Black LOS ANGELES		98	98	38	81	74	0.56	16
Black NEW ORLEANS	38.5	97	98	30	75	45	0.74	28
Black PHILADELPHIA	39.4	98	98	49	76	45	0.56	11
Black DETROIT	30.8	98	98	52	81	63	0.55	12
Bonn	18.5	76	85	24	69	70	0.63	–
London	17.0	80	80	43	62		0.62	7
Copenhagen	16.0	57	90	19	62	39	0.57	14
Hamburg	22.0	70	83	17	58	51	0.67	
Geneva	25.0	92	100	2	84	88 (est.)	0.90	22
Vienna	22.0	60	75	8	69	38	1.10	
Zürich	18.0	85	100	7	94	69 (est.)	0.80	15
Stockholm	14.0	82	97		90	60	0.69	
Paris	13.0	48	63	25	36	52		
Bologna	36.5	89	98	35			0.87	
Amsterdam	14.0	66	94	6				
Tokyo	16.0	49	22	39	75	24	1.08	
East Berlin	21.0	59	80	43	35 (est.)	21	1.05	
West Berlin	26.0	67	84	8	41		0.67	
Birmingham, England	21.0	87	80	42		42	0.62	10

Source: For non-United States cities, R. Fried, *World Handbook of Cities* (various chapters); for United States black communities, United States Bureau of the Census, *Census of Housing: 1970 General Housing Characteristics: Final Report HC(1)-A1: United States Summary*; United States Department of Health, Education, and Welfare, Public Health Service, *Vital Statistics of the United States 1971* (Rockville, Md.: National Center for Health Statistics, 1974).

The relative unimportance of political parties in American urban government is, of course, ironic since for most of the nineteenth and early twentieth centuries American urban government and party government were synonymous. American cities were known throughout the world precisely because party bosses and machines ran them. One of the major aims of reformers around the turn of the century was precisely to rid American cities of these notorious characters and institutions. In this attempt they were generally successful. In city after city, nonpartisan forms of government were adopted: party labels were removed from the ballot; overt party roles in election campaigns and policy making were discouraged. City employees were given civil service protection and no longer obligated to pay a share of their salaries to the party or to work for the party at election time. Legislation was passed to minimize partisan discrimination in the award of contracts. Eventually about two-thirds of the cities and towns of the country became nonpartisan—at least formally. (In some cases, like "nonpartisan" Chicago, parties continued to play a dominant, if behind-the-scenes role in elections and government.)

In Europe, political machines and bosses on the American pattern never became common although the preconditions were there: extremely rapid city growth; the development of large, urban, dependent populations needing forms of protection and help; and business interests needing favorable decisions on land use, factory conditions, fire, building, and food inspection, and contracts. Strong party organizations were created and strong party leaders did emerge, sometimes to dominate European cities for decades, but they lacked the reliance on local patronage and the corruption of the classic American model.

European cities did not develop machines and bosses for many reasons. There is much tighter central government control and supervision over local government, impeding partisan and corrupt use of local government powers. In more centralized systems, people wanting assistance or favors tend to turn to the national politicians, and national bureaucrats; the latter, rather than local politicians, have tended, if anyone, to have patronage to dispense. Then, too, under national government legislation, local employees were given civil service protection, eliminating the possibility of using local government jobs as "spoils for the victor."

The pattern of social interests and cleavages to be represented has also been important. In European cities, the major clashes were those between ideologies, and between religious (and antireligious) groups, each seeking separate and distinctive representation in the political process. The only natural form of party system in such cities is a multiparty system (based usually on proportional representation or PR) in which each social, ideological, or religious subculture has its own party. It is harder to organize a machine when no party mobilizes majority support.

Then, too, the mass base for the classic machine was lacking. Immigrants to European cities were peasants moving from villages to cities in the same country—not, as they were in American cities, immigrants from foreign countries with easily obtained voting rights and the willingness to exchange votes for badly needed assistance from the machine. Immigrants to European cities were less likely to be given voting rights since universal and equal male suffrage did not exist in most countries until after 1900.[18] (To be sure, immigrants to European cities may have had less

Table 4-6   Party Representation on City Councils in Some Major Cities Abroad

		Seats
Stockholm City Council	Moderate Unity party	23
(1973)	Center party	15
	Liberal party	12
	Social Democrats	42
	Left party-Communists	9
		101
Oslo City Council	Högern Conservatives	31
(1971)	Christian People's	5
	Center party	2
	Left	3
	Labor party	35
	Socialist People's	7
	Communists	1
	Ecology party	1
		85
Zürich City Council	Peasants & Business	5
(1970)	Christian Social	15
	Protestant People's	12
	Liberals	26
	Social Democrats	41
	Independents	26
		125
Amsterdam City Council	Liberals	8
(1974)	Christian Democrats	7
	Democrats	1
	Radicals	3
	Pacifist Socialists	2
	Labor	17
	Communists	7
		45

need of assistance from a machine, given the earlier development in Europe of publicly sponsored social services.)

Nor, at the other end of the social spectrum, were conditions favorable to the emergence of machine bosses based on patronage and corruption. Most European cities had old and established social elites with a standing in the community based on aristocratic origins rather than on business success. Most European cities were located in monarchies with a definite and overt pyramid of social prestige. Public servants had the prestige of working for the monarch; the prestige of royal service also attached to service in local government, where the official or civil servant often had higher standing than the local businessman seeking favors or protection. In societies where status derived from birth rather than achieved wealth and income and where the capitalist had less prestige than the nobleman or city notable, there was little legitimate role for the unholy coalition of political bosses and businessmen

Table 4-6   Party Representation on City Councils in Some Major Cities Abroad (continued)

		Seats
Cologne City Council (1972)	Social Democrats	37
	Liberals	4
	Christian Democrats	26
		67
Vienna City Council (1973)	Socialists	66
	Catholics	31
	Liberals	3
		100
Tokyo Metropolitan Assembly (1963)	Liberal-Democrats (conservative)	51
	Komei (Buddhists)	26
	Social Democrats	2
	Communists	24
	Socialists	20
	Others	2
		125
Manchester (England) Metro District Council (1973)	Labor party	59
	Conservatives	40
Greater Manchester Metropolitan County Council (1973)	Labor	69
	Conservatives	23
	Liberals	13
	Independents	1
Birmingham (England) Metro District Council (1973)	Labor	73
	Conservatives	44
	Liberals	9

denounced by Lincoln Steffens as "The Shame of the Cities." City politics was a source of honor, rather than profit. The pressures and values of a feudal civilization, unlike those of a business civilization, made it implausible to think of city government as just another way of making money.

Finally, we might mention the form of city government. In addition to tight central control, European cities also featured a simplicity of structure not to be found in American cities. In European cities, local authority is concentrated in the hands of the city council and the city executive supported by the council majority. There are none of the checks and balances, divided authority, innumerable commissions and boards, or mutually independent elective executives that normally characterize American urban government. If, as has been asserted, the machine and boss emerged in American cities to provide some unity in these congeries of separate and independent authorities, the same necessity did not exist in Europe, where city government authority was monopolized by the council and the executive elected by it or appointed by the government.

The role and power of the voter in European cities has likewise been much less important than in American cities. The role of the voter in Europe has been to choose a city councilman.[19] The American city voter is allowed to choose not only a councilman, but dozens of other officials: representatives to the board of education, mayors, judges, city attorneys, comptrollers, and city councilmen (all in addition to choosing large numbers of state legislative and executive officials and four national level officials). In addition, the American city voter is allowed to decide many basic matters directly in referenda. Thus, the American voter has had more to exchange with a party organization and boss than a European voter.

A glance at Table 4-6 will reveal another major difference between American and European urban politics. Not only do European city councils have multiparty systems, but in all of them there is a powerful Leftist contingent—Socialist, Communist, or Labor.

In most advanced nations, industrialization created powerful socialist and communist movements based on strong shared resentment of social and economic inequality. A powerful socialist movement never developed in the United States for a variety of reasons.[20] Social resentment was mitigated by the high and rising standard of living of most American workers; by the influx of successively "inferior" ethnic and racial groups; by the lack of marked social differences among the classes; by the high rate or presumedly high rate of individual mobility up the ladder of success. Organizing the working class for political purposes was impeded by the ethnic, religious, and racial cleavages within the working class and by interclass consensus on basic institutions of constitutional democracy and capitalism.

The institutions of federalism, moreover, encouraged labor to act as a pressure group rather than as a political party; for state legislatures had authority over many basic aspects of working-class life, and state legislators were more amenable to proposals for social reform from politically neutral labor leaders than they would have been to those from a separate labor political party. Creating a labor party—in the absence of proportional representation and given the minority status of American labor in the electorate—would have been a self-defeating political strategy, particularly since American voters—of whatever class—had such strong loyalties to the two existing political parties. The Republicans and Democrats, moreover, have had the disconcerting habit of stealing all the popular planks from the platforms of radical parties.

Still a third difference in the political "input" side between the American and European cities concerns the power of pressure or interest groups. If parties tend to be weak in American urban politics—at least as policymakers—the same cannot be said for pressure groups of various kinds. P. J. Madgwick notes (from a British perspective) in *American City Politics* that

> there is . . . *more political activity in American cities than in British cities. Pressure groups are more active as well as more open. . . . There are more signs in American cities of reformist groups and amateur insurgency. The number and comparative vigor of some civic groups quite outshine the activi-*

ties of Britain's rate[tax]-payers, tenants and parents' associations, and civic societies. Britain lacks both the open, participant tradition of American politics and the specific challenge of referenda and elective ad hoc boards. In the face of so much political activity, American cities necessarily pursue a politics of accommodation and bargaining, leavened by political and administrative leadership. The result is a system which ranges from agitation and inertia to dynamism and power.[21]

Another major difference between European and American cities in the input side of urban politics concerns the electorate and its policy making role. As we have noted, the American electorate is given vast direct authority to make policy for American cities, deciding, for example, such things as the issuance of bonds for streets, sewers, and schools; the reorganization of city government; the salary and pensions of city employees; the adoption of programs in such fields as urban renewal, public housing, fluoridation, or the civil rights of homosexuals. Only Swiss cities accord similar authority on voters to decide municipal policy or structure. Most other cities in the advanced word give *no* direct voice to the voter on questions of civic importance.

But though the American electorate has a uniquely strong voice in making urban government policy, it is not as representative of the adult urban community as it might be. The proportion of adults voting in American cities tends to be much lower than that in many European and Japanese cities. Table 4-7 suggests (but does not prove) that this is so; it must be remembered that there are much higher proportions of adults in some European cities than in American cities. Table 4-7 uses the total population rather than the adult population to measure the extent of voter turn out.[22]

Thus, we have certain basic differences in the political input side between American and European cities—differences summarized in Table 4-8.

What is the impact of systems of political organization on comparative performance?

Reformers have long argued that parties are inherently an antiliberal force, a force conducive to dishonesty and political discrimination in urban government. With this argument, American urban government was made "nonpartisan," the assumption being that corruption in urban government stemmed from the needs and appetites of party bosses and cohorts. The Progressives also argued that a strong direct voice for the people through the initiative, referendum, and recall would also be a powerful check on the domination of urban government by special interests. The city manager scheme, moreover, would provide administration by an impartial, "nonpolitical" executive rather than an elected politician as mayor.

But is nonpartisan city government more impartial and honest than partisan city government? There is a rough historical correlation between party system and probity in the American context. Parties were quite strong in American cities, as was corruption; there is much less corruption today than there used to be and parties are weaker. Likewise, there seems to be worse corruption today in those

Table 4-7   Citizen Participation: Percentage of the Population That
Actually Votes in Local General Elections

Percentage of Total Population Voting in Local General Election	City	Country	Date
13.6	PHOENIX	USA	1975
13.6	MILWAUKEE	USA	1976
19.0	ALBUQUERQUE	USA	1977
19.5	Geneva	Switzerland	1971
20.9	OMAHA	USA	1975
22.4	NEWARK	USA	1974
22.5	Lausanne	Switzerland	1973
23.1	ATLANTA	USA	1977
23.6	Birmingham	England	1973
22.7	Vancouver	Canada	1976
26.9	London	England	1973
28.0	Liverpool	England	1977
28.6	Leeds	England	1977
28.6	MEMPHIS	USA	1975
30.0	Lyon	France	1977
31.6	Edmonton	Canada	1974
31.6	Leicester	England	1977
33.2	Berne	Switzerland	1976
34.7	Utrecht	Netherlands	1970
35.8	Paris	France	1977
36.6	PROVIDENCE	USA	1976
36.6	Stuttgart	West Germany	1971
37.2	Copenhagen	Denmark	1974
37.2	Rotterdam	Netherlands	1970
38.7	Bordeaux	France	1977
40.0	Nagoya	Japan	1977

American cities with relatively strong party systems. Nonetheless, it may be that we are dealing here not with cause and effect, but with the joint effect of some other variable. Parties and corruption may be strong in communities where the materialist ethos (public administration as the extension of business by other means) is particularly strong.[23]

But evidence from Europe suggests that in a different cultural context—one with less stress on individualist materialism (money) and more stress on class ideology (status)—strong parties can successfully combine with honest and impartial administration. In the same cultural context, it should be noted that there is much less corruption, not only in municipal government, but in the labor movement as well.

Are systems with explicit representation of the working class and the poor more responsive to those groups? Is the plight of the American poor compounded by the lack of specific representation by a Socialist, Communist or Labor party? As

Table 4-7   Citizen Participation: Percentage of the Population That Actually Votes in Local General Elections (continued)

Percentage of Total Population Voting in Local General Election	City	Country	Date
40.3	Lille	France	1977
40.3	Munich	West Germany	1972
40.6	The Hague	Netherlands	1970
41.3	Cologne	West Germany	1969
42.4	Amsterdam	Netherlands	1970
43.9	Brisbane	Australia	1970
44.7	Essen	West Germany	1969
44.7	Bonn	West Germany	1969
44.7	Yokohama	Japan	1976
45.2	Düsseldorf	West Germany	1969
46.2	Dortmund	West Germany	1969
47.1	Tokyo-to	Japan	1975
49.0	Palermo	Italy	1970
49.2	Nuremberg	West Germany	1972
51.0	Salzburg	Austria	1972
52.0	Frankfurt	West Germany	1972
52.3	Naples	Italy	1970
54.7	Helsinki	Finland	1972
55.6	Oslo	Norway	1971
56.9	Hamburg	West Germany	1970
57.3	Hannover	West Germany	1972
58.5	Linz	Austria	1973
59.4	Vienna	Austria	1973
60.4	Innsbruck	Austria	1971

Source: R. Fried, *World Handbook of Cities,* Ch. 9.

far as representation of the working class as such goes, the answer is not clear. One might argue that the underdevelopment of American social policy is proof of the political weakness of the working class and poor in the United States.[24] One could also point to the bloody history of the American Labor movement and the fierce resistance of the employers, aided by government, to unionization as further evidence. Then, too, if the urban political machine was based on working-class votes, the demise of the machines may mean a decline in urban government responsiveness to the working class.

However, it is not clear that American political and social institutions have been less responsive to working-class people than the systems in other advanced nations. The demise of the urban political machine was, in itself, partly the result of the fact that under the New Deal, the favors of political machines—distributed arbitrarily—were converted into services distributed impartially on the basis of general rules. The demise of the machine, moreover, was the demise of an organiza-

Table 4-8 Major Differences in Political Organization between American and European Cities

American Cities	European Cities
Usually weak parties	Strong parties
Weak socialist representation	Strong socialist contingent
One or two or no party control	Multiparty control
Powerful interest groups	Weak interest groups
Powerful voters	Relatively weak voters
Pluralistic decision making	Majoritarian or consensual decision making

tion devoted not only to the interests of working-class constituents but also to the interests of merchants, contractors, transit companies, and utilities—those who had not votes, but money to contribute to the machine's stock of incentives.

On the other hand, creation of nonpartisan electoral systems probably has meant reduced influence for the lower-income groups, workers, and minorities—people who, with less education, need party labels in order to recognize political friends and enemies. With less class pressure on them to vote, low-income groups may need the solicitations of party workers to realize their political potential. Where there are ideologically oriented working-class parties, with a sizeable share of the electorate, there may be greater motivation and determination to promote the interests of workers and poor people than where politics is dominated by pragmatic parties or personalistic organizations. Comparative studies in American cities show that city governments have been more responsive to lower-income groups—built more public housing, for example—in cities with relatively strong party organizations. Turnout is higher in such cities as is, presumably, the influence of those less apt to vote—people with less wealth, education, and status.[25]

However, it should be remembered that there may be a conflict between responsiveness to the labor movement and the working class and responsiveness to the poor and minorities. To some extent, responsiveness to one set of interests may automatically mean unresponsiveness to the other. Working-class voters have not always been sympathetic to the welfare needs of the poor or to the demands of minority groups for access to labor unions, housing, jobs, and good schools.[26] Working-class voters have often been more concerned—at least at the local level—with keeping taxes down than with enlarging the scope of urban services. Though working-class ethnics have been more sympathetic to black demands than many other whites, there still has been obvious friction between racial minorities and neighboring working-class people.[27] Thus, responsiveness to working-class demands and minority demands have represented something of a zero-sum game in American urban politics. How strictly a working-class party (as opposed to the more composite Democrats) might have responded to the demands of minority groups for greater access to urban goods (and greater freedom from urban bads) is problematical.

Then, too, it must be remembered that in the United States, the working classes' sense of differentiation from the rest of society has been weak. This has presumably been the result of a responsive social system. For a long time, moreover, the lack of social legislation was actually a matter of preference on the part of the American Labor movement; until the 1930s, organized labor actually opposed social insurance and health insurance.[28] In some ways, the Democratic party has functioned unofficially as the American equivalent of a European or Commonwealth social democratic party—one that has to operate in an unusually capitalistic civilization.[29] It is highly likely that the American Socialist or even Communist parties would have thrived only if the American working class developed the degree of alienation that developed in the societies with more advanced social legislation. Seymour M. Lipset is probably correct when he argues that the lack of a mass anticapitalist movement in the United States is the sign, partly of the responsiveness of the American political system (the early grant of suffrage and free public education), and partly of the responsiveness of American social and economic institutions (the wide and early diffusion of status symbols).[30]

On the other hand, one can argue that the presence in European cities of Leftist parties has not necessarily meant greater responsiveness to working class, poor, or ethnic-racial minority interests. On a national level, the presence of powerful Communist parties has meant—at least until recently—the neutralization of the left, the relegation of Leftist voters and parties to the status of pariahs. Moreover, even the more respectable Socialist parties have revised traditional programs calling for drastic social revolution in favor of more moderate programs—programs not terribly dissimilar from those of American liberal democrats. Communists and socialists alike, given the logic of democratic competition, have modified programs in order to win middle-class votes, often, in the process, arriving at the endorsement of rather conservative policies.[31]

It should also be noted that European socialists and communists do not derive from a populistic tradition. More often than not, run by middle-class intellectuals, European Socialist and Communist parties have what seem to be (from an American perspective) elitist conceptions of responsiveness. In the eyes of many socialists and communists, ordinary workers and poor people have relatively poor awareness of their true interests and need to be given enlightened leadership. The result is that, in many European cities governed by Social Democratic or Communist parties, there have been eruptions of groups in working-class neighborhoods, revolting against the "enlightened" policies of their socialist or communist city governments.[32] Socialist and Communist parties seem as prone to becoming prisoners of and advocates for professional municipal bureaucracies—parts of the community power structure—as their more populistic counterparts in American cities.

THE PATTERN OF GOVERNMENT

Advanced industrial democracies have similar institutions for urban government. In all of them, constitutional democracy means some local self-government, control, and democracy. But few advanced countries give as much authority over local affairs to local officials and electorates as does the United States. Jacques Servan-Schreiber, a French political leader, writes in *The American Challenge.*[33]

> We find . . . the confidence of the [American] society in its citizens—in the authority delegated to local government to administer everyday aspects of life and to make decisions in the fields of city planning, health, and educa-tion—decision-making powers our central government [in France] would be terrified to put into the hands of [locally] elected officials.

The localistic ethos in American political culture is reflected in the decen-tralized nature of American urban government. Urban government in America, more than in other advanced industrial democracies is *local* urban government. State and federal governments intervene in urban affairs less often and less directly than they do in other advanced nations. Local officials in the United States are sub-ject to less inspection and control than they are in other countries. The central con-trols imposed on New York City during its financial emergency by the federal and state governments are exceptional in the American context, but normal in those of Western Europe, Canada, and Japan. In those other countries, local officials are more closely dependent on national authorities for advice, supervision, and approval.

In addition, in the other advanced nations, many more services are directly performed by state or central governments. In Sweden, for example, cities are policed by national policemen and in West Germany, by state policemen. In Canada, the Royal Canadian Mounted Police provides law enforcement for many cities; in other cities, policing is provided by provincial (that is, state) police forces.

We should not overstate the decentralization of urban government even in the United States. Local governments in American law are treated as the creatures of state government, exercising only such authority as is expressly given to them by state governments. Local governments can be created or abolished by the state governments; unlike state governments, they have no independent constitutional existence (apart from their status in state constitutions). What American city governments can borrow or tax is determined by state legislation or by state consti-tutions. State legislatures must pass enabling legislation before cities in the state can participate in federal programs, such as urban renewal or public housing. Moreover, much of what city governments do is dictated by what they are required to do by state law: many functions are mandated, that is, they must be performed under law.[34]

The dependence of American urban government is financial as well as legal. In 1974, 38% of the general revenues of American city governments came from state and federal grants. In 1960, grants accounted for only one-fifth of city reve-nues. By 1974 intergovernmental grants made up 43% of general revenues for the 48 largest cities (48% for New York City).[35]

However, legal and financial dependencies notwithstanding, American urban governments are still more autonomous than their counterparts in other countries. American urban governments are also more complex in their institutions. The authority to make a collective decision tends to be much more dispersed than in other countries. In most advanced nations, authority to make a collective decision is given to an elected city council and a city executive elected by that council. All other city officials are appointed by, and derive their authority from, the city council or executive. There are no independently elected city officials, such as city attorneys or comptrollers, or independently elected boards, such as boards of education. In other advanced nations, the rule is to concentrate policy making authority in the council and executive authority in the executive. In American cities, authority is sliced up among many mutually independent officials—some elected, some appointed, some civil service—and a large slice of authority is apportioned to the voters, who not only elect many officials, but also vote on policies, including tax rates and the issuance of bonds.

Except in those relatively few cities where powerful political machines exist, there is little unified authority in American urban government: Instead, one typically finds bargaining and infighting between councils, commissions, mayors, managers, boards, and bureaucrats. To take public action locally requires more than simply mobilizing a party majority on the council, as in most advanced societies; it entails the more difficult task of mobilizing a cross-institutional coalition involving councilmen, commissioners, judges, bureaucrats, the media, the courts, and even the voters. American urban government is, consequently, not action-oriented.

Still a third differentiating factor in the pattern of government is the fragmentation of control over, and within, each urbanized area in the United States. Each metropolitan area is governed by many independent governments—some general in function, some specific. In addition to local governments with general functions, there are special districts for functions such as education, air pollution, highways and bridges, ports, water supply, public transportation, and regional planning. The Chicago metropolitan area has 1172 local governments; Philadelphia, 852; Pittsburgh, 698; and New York, 531. The average number of governments in an American metropolitan area is eighty-six.[36] Similar fragmentation has often occurred in other advanced nations, but in many of them, higher levels of government have imposed some measure of amalgamation.[37] Only in the United States does amalgamation into unified metropolitan government require a vote of the local people concerned—a vote that is almost invariably negative. Elsewhere, consolidation has been carried out by national or state fiat—without local voting—and has provided for unified metropolitan government in such cities as Toronto, London, Bordeaux, Strasbourg, Birmingham (England), Stockholm, Copenhagen, Lyon, and Montreal.

How do structural differences affect performance? Which works better: decentralized fragmentation or centralized unity? There is probably greater liberalism in the centralized-unitary systems than in the decentralized-fragmented systems. In the United States, as well as in most advanced nations, centralizing impulses favor honesty, due process, and impartiality in urban government. There is less corruption in the more centralized systems: concentrated power at the center and in the cities has made for more governmental integrity and due process than one finds in American cities. Police corruption, for example, seems to vary inversely with centralization, at least in the advanced democracies. Thus, in his studies of corruption in American cities, John Gardiner pinpointed as a main cause of local corruption the lack of state supervision.[38]

Decentralized fragmentation is designed to maximize responsiveness, even at the expense of liberalism and effectiveness. Allowing every subcommunity its independence, multiplying elective authorities, and requiring popular votes on major issues should mean more responsiveness than in centralized-unitary systems with fewer independent centers of power and a restricted role for the voters. However, the decentralized-fragmented model tends to be biased in favor of locally dominant majorities; taxpaying groups; and groups able to secede from the central city, move out into the suburbs, and establish their own enclaves. Centralized systems have probably been more responsive to lower-class and minority groups—groups less able to win local elections, requiring some redistribution of wealth from rich to poor, and without access to the suburban way of life.

There is also greater all-around effectiveness in managing urban problems in the more centralized systems. More centralized, less fragmented systems have been more action-oriented and less stymied by divided authority and veto groups. They have done more and done it earlier on behalf of the underprivileged. One reason is finance. Reliance on decentralized government to solve urban problems means reliance on local finance. But local taxation tends to be regressive; its incidence is highly visible and particularly painful. There is greater taxpayer resistance in decentralized systems, and, thus, less public money becomes available to government to compensate for the inequality created by the social and economic system.

Central governments deal with many urban problems much more effectively than local governments: they have greater financial resources; they operate over broader areas; and they deal more easily with the crucial variables affecting urban performance, such as inflation, unemployment, interregional migration of people and industry, immigration from abroad, transportation networks, and rural development. Centrally run services have greater prestige and are less easily intimidated by powerful interests, including organized crime.

Centralized systems are also more uniform in the quality of their services. Decentralization means that each locality produces only the services it is willing and able to perform. This means that one gets variation (or inequality) in provision for the poor on the order of four or five to one among American cities.[39] (See Table 4-9.) Moreover, decentralization tends to discourage the development of services, in that service expansion may raise taxes and, thus, drive out taxpayers.

Decentralization may also contribute to the lack of safety in American cities. More centralized law enforcement systems, endowed with stronger policing powers, could undoubtedly make a more effective war on crime, particularly organized crime. Replacement of the 17,000 separate law enforcement agencies in this country with fifty highly prestigious state police forces, supported by an expanded and strengthened national law enforcement apparatus, could undoubtedly provide better policing of our cities. Certainly standards of performance have been higher in state and national law enforcement than in median local law enforcement. But fear of

Table 4-9   Comparative Assistance to the Poor in American Cities (1970)

Less than $100 per Family per Month	$100-199 per Family per Month	$200 or More per Family per Month
Jackson, Miss. ($56)	Dallas ($118)	Los Angeles ($222)
New Orleans ($96)	Miami ($104)	New York ($240)
Birmingham ($59)	Indianapolis ($155)	Chicago ($242)
Charleston, S.C. ($77)	St. Louis ($114)	Boston ($271)
	Atlanta ($103)	Philadelphia ($256)
	Houston ($124)	Honolulu ($298)
	Cleveland ($172)	Detroit ($213)
		Newark ($280)
		Milwaukee ($273)
		Minneapolis ($272)
		Seattle ($228)

Source: Bureau of the Census, *County and City Data Book 1972* (Washington, D.C.: United States Government Printing Office, 1973), col. 76.

concentrated power—the fear that state or national police forces would be difficult to control—seems to justify the tradeoff of effectiveness for responsiveness and democratic control.[40]

THE PATTERN OF URBAN BUREAUCRACY

Can the relative insecurity of American cities be blamed on poor police and fire protection services? Is poor administration of health services or urban planning services responsible for comparative poor performance in health planning? Are the housing authorities responsible for slum housing and the social services responsible for poverty? Can the public schools be blamed for comparative lack of educational achievement?

American municipal bureaucracies have long been infamous for incompetence, instability, and corruption. Their major function was to serve the electoral interests of the political machine. Reformers, comparing American and European governments around the turn of the century, noted a crucial difference: European cities were governed by professionalized bureaucracies, American cities by party hacks. Since the turn of the century, the picture has changed considerably. Civil service rather than the party "spoils system" is the rule in American municipal administration. But the poor reputation of municipal administrators (and governmental administrators generally) has lasted, severely impeding the development of adequate programs for cities. The public has simply been unwilling to trust vast powers or sums of money in the hands of corrupt, partisan, or incompetent bureaucracies.

American municipal bureaucracies are now generally as honest, skilled, and professionalized as those in other advanced countries—though there are (in this as in other things) significant variations from city to city and within each urbanized area.

They are certainly highly paid—more highly paid, it would appear—than the municipal bureaucracies elsewhere. One reason they are so highly paid is the decentralization of pay and fringe benefit negotiations. In most countries, municipal employee pay raises are decided in nation-wide collective bargaining. In the United States, municipal salaries, pensions, and other "perks" are determined locally—often in local referenda in which municipal employees themselves are active. Police and firemen's unions conduct political campaigns to secure voter approval for higher wages and pensions. Employee unions are big contributors to councilmanic and mayoral campaigns and are among the most powerful organized interest groups in American city politics. One result is the disproportionately higher share that personnel costs have in the operating expenses of American cities compared to other advanced cities. (See Table 2-32.)

Although American workers in the private sector may earn their high salaries through their productivity, the same may not be true for American public service workers. Productivity in the public sector is always harder to raise (because it involves production of services rather than physical production of goods) than in the private sector. It may be, though, that American public bureaucracies do earn their comparatively higher salaries by being more efficient than their counterparts abroad, though the evidence is slim. Comparing the "clearance" rate for crimes (the rate at which police manage to identify suspects for known crimes) between an American city—Los Angeles—and Stockholm, we find a record of greater achievement in the American city, as shown in Table 4-10. This suggests that the crime rate differential between American cities and other advanced cities might be even higher were it not for the professional excellence of American police departments. The same might be said for other American public services, particularly fire and health departments.

Table 4-10   Comparative Bureaucratic Effectiveness: Police Clearance
Rates[a] in Stockholm and Los Angeles

	Percentage of Crimes Cleared		
	Stockholm	*LOS ANGELES*	*United States*
	(1972)	(1975)	(1975)
Car thefts	10	16	15
Crimes against person	36	48	50
Crimes against property	13	22	19
Burglaries	5	22	18
Theft, including petty	12	25	20

[a]Clearance rates are the rates at which arrests are made for known crimes or at which the crimes are "solved" without arrest.

Sources: Swedish Official Statistics, Central Statistical Bureau, *Kriminalstatistik 1972-1973 Del 1 Polisstatistik* (Stockholm: SCB, 1976), p. 21; Statistical Abstract of the United States 1977, Table 269; Los Angeles Police Department, *Statistical Digest: 1975.*

Much in the quality of urban life does not depend on the quality of urban services and regulations—the quality of urban policy. Whether streets are clean, properties maintained, personal health conserved, skills and knowledge acquired, and persons and property respected depends more on private than public behavior. The performance of the private sector—of individuals, families, peer groups, churches, corporations, unions, and associations; of various economic markets; of social institutions—determines the need for and sets bounds to the effectiveness of the public sector. At any given time, what the public sector has to do is determined by the failures of the private sector; what the public sector *can* do—at least in the advanced democracies—is determined by what the private sector is willing and able to pay for.

In the United States, private sector success has minimized the public sector agenda. The failure of the private sector in spreading affluence has been considered minor, compared to its success. Living standards for most people have been high, and they have increased enough for most years to discourage the emergence of massive discontent. Public policy, to compensate for the adverse effects of the unequal distribution of income, has thus remained little more than embryonic. In a rural-minded society—one used to self-reliance and the security derived from growing one's own food—the public sector has had only grudging legitimacy. It has been hard for rural, small town, and, more recently, suburban America to understand the distress of America's cities and hard for it to support government action that would guarantee to all citizens basic minimal standards of health, safety, and welfare. Ethnic and religious hostilities, powerful private interests, antisocialism, fragmented authority, and a conservative, but powerful judiciary have concerted to block the emergence of, in Harold Wilensky's words, "government-protected minimum standards of income, nutrition, health, housing, and education, assured to every citizen as a political right, not a charity."[41]

Privatistic values and decentralized power have produced a lag in the kind of government action that might have prevented the mass squalor and social disorganization in urban America today. Privatism and decentralization have worked well for so many people that a tradition has not been established, as in so many other advanced nations, of using government as a necessary means of improving the quality of urban life.

National policies to aid the urban and rural distressed became acceptable only with the collapse of the private sector during the Depression. In 1933, decentralized privatism could not aid the one-quarter to one-third of the labor force receiving no income. Under the New Deal, the resources of government were finally brought into play against the forces undermining the quality of life for people in cities: unemployment, sickness, old age, disablement, and other sources of family poverty. But even with New Deal social policies—including the Social Security Act (1935), the National Housing Acts of 1934 and 1937, the National Labor Relations Act

(1935), and the Fair Labor Standards Act (1938)—unemployment remained high and the position of minorities remained marginal in the context of national development.

The Great Society programs of the 1960s marked a second major push to catch up with policy development in other advanced societies. Realities of urban poverty were suddenly recognized in the midst of the Affluent Society; patterns of racial supremacy were suddenly perceived by blacks and many whites as intolerable. Government action was seen as an indispensable means of giving a share of well-being to the poor and the minorities. Thus, 1964-1966 saw major breakthroughs in urban policy: food stamps (1964); the War on Poverty (1964); civil rights (1964, 1968); education (1965); housing (1965); medicare (1965); and voting rights (1965). In 1966, Robert C. Weaver became the first black to enter the cabinet and the first Secretary of Housing and Urban Development.

Unfortunately, government action to improve the conditions of the poor and minorities competed for resources with defense programs and programs to aid middle-class, suburban, and rural groups. A basically privatistic and decentralized cast of public policy remained, allowing private individuals and firms to seek their own interest and requiring less fortunate individuals and firms to acquire some ability to compete. The spirit of American public policy remained promotive and permissive rather than directive (except for defense spending). Government action came late—after the defects of private performance had produced a nearly unmanageable accumulation of urban "bads"—crime, disease, vandalism, and drug addiction.

Ironically, government action, when it came, was sometimes negative for the performance of central cities. Highway programs disrupted viable neighborhoods. Urban renewal programs destroyed low-rent housing. Minimum wage laws reduced the number of jobs. Public assistance laws weakened family structure. Zoning laws prevented the construction of housing for the poor minority groups in suburbs. Decentralized tax policies drove wealthy families and employers into the suburbs, partly by forcing central cities to raise taxes to high levels to cope with rising service needs and declining tax bases, and partly by providing massive hidden subsidies (through the deductability of mortgage interest and property taxes) to suburban homeowners. Permissive rules on municipal incorporation allowed industries to escape local taxation by incorporating into independent enclaves and allowed middle-class groups to create their own jurisdictions, free from the burdens and anxieties of the central cities.

And in some cases, even the expansion of the public sector has not been effective in combatting urban problems. High crime rates in American cities are not the result of our failure to put enough criminals in jail and prison. In France and Italy, sixty-two prisoners are incarcerated for every 100,000 people; in England and Wales, seventy-eight prisoners. In the United States, there are 202 prisoners per 100,000 people![42] But even with three times as many people locked up at any given time, American society is losing the war against crime.

Even where public action has been proved effective and positive, its scope in the United States has been limited—at least compared to that in other advanced countries. Other advanced countries have more adequate welfare policies (see Table 4-11); they make greater efforts to plan urban development; they build much more low-income housing (see Table 4-12); they provide more uniform performance levels in education to merge into larger metropolitan entities; they make more effort to improve conditions in backward rural areas; they give fewer tax advantages to the owners of single-family housing; and they make more successful efforts to ensure full employment for all their citizens. Political demands and expectations in other advanced countries make stronger government action possible and desirable.

The laissez faire political climate in the United States makes strong government action—by any level of government—difficult, if not impossible, except in the area of defense. A British city planner, aware of conditions in both British and American cities, concludes:

> *American cities have had little political will or ability to act . . . the practical skill and experience that grew from a history of consistent public action in England are simply not there. . . . A European finds . . . the argument ['that social action cannot reduce urban poverty and its attendant ills'] hard to swallow. Our experience seems to contradict them, and we believe that social welfare policies, based on redistributional taxation, are on the whole effective in preventing urban catastrophe. We do not accept that there must always be a very poor minority, nor that urban problems are permanently insoluble.*[43]

When the federal government or other governments overcome inertia and attempt to act on behalf of the poor and minorities, opposition and resistance by white, middle-class, ethnic, or working-class groups often forces the government to

Table 4-11   Comparative Social Security: Minimum Benefits in Some Major Cities (1973)

	Minimum Pension per Year		
	Single Person		*Married Couple*
London	$ 861	London	$1391
Paris	973	Paris	1459
CHICAGO	1014	CHICAGO	1521
Vienna	1182	Vienna	1690
Sydney	1542	Zürich	2372
Zürich	1582	Sydney	2690
Copenhagen	1809	Copenhagen	2724
Oslo	1862	Oslo	2891
Stockholm	1877	Stockholm	3040
Brussels	3175	Brussels	4233

Source: Union Bank of Switzerland, *Prices,* p. 40.

Table 4-12 Comparative Public Housing Effort (c. 1970)

			Public Housing Units per 1000 Residents				
Less than 5	5-14	15-24	25-34	35-44	55-64	75-84	85+
KANSAS CITY	HONOLULU	BOSTON	Geneva	Copenhagen	Naples	The Hague	Birmingham, England
HOUSTON	DENVER	BIRMINGHAM	NEWARK	Turin	Venice	Bologna	Sheffield
INDIANAPOLIS	DALLAS	Berne	Tokyo				Stockholm
LOS ANGELES	CINCINNATI	ATLANTA	Yokohama				Munich
MILWAUKEE	CHICAGO	Perth					Amsterdam
OKLAHOMA CITY	BUFFALO	Stockholm					London
OMAHA	Basel	Lausanne					Milan
PHOENIX	BALTIMORE	NEW ORLEANS					Rotterdam
SAN DIEGO	LOUISVILLE	PITTSBURGH					Vienna
Edmonton	MEMPHIS	Rome					Hong Kong
	MIAMI	Zurich					Bradford
	NEW YORK						
	PHILADELPHIA						
	PORTLAND						
	SAN FRANCISCO						
	SEATTLE						
	ST. LOUIS						
	WASHINGTON						
	Singapore						

Source: R. Fried, *World Handbook of Cities,* Ch. 6.

abandon its efforts. Government policies to disperse the poor and minorities into the suburbs have been adopted; efforts have been made to carry them out; but most of them have been abandoned in the face of fierce resistance. In a decentralized democracy, government lacks the strength to take on intensely entrenched majoritarian interests.

It is difficult for government, any government, to make up for the defects of performance in society and the economy. In other advanced nations, government action has been more readily accepted, but in some ways less needed, for family and neighborhood "government" have remained strong. In the United States, the burden on a relatively unprepared public sector has been unduly great, given the permissiveness, weakness, or even breakdown of the private institutions regulating behavior. Deficiencies in health, education, and safety in American cities must be blamed not only on governmental inaction and defects in the operations of the markets, but also on the declining ability of American families, churches, peer groups, and neighborhoods to mold behavior.

THE PATTERN OF URBAN DEVELOPMENT

A crucial and obvious difference between American cities and cities in other advanced nations is the age of the cities. Cities founded centuries ago in Western Europe have the advantageous legacy of more beautiful central cores (built slowly in accordance with aristocratic tastes), stronger civic pride (and, therefore, determination to regulate and guide development), and more prestigious centers (and, therefore, less willingness to tolerate central blight and decay). Cities with rich historic remains from the Middle Ages or even before; cities which incorporated (granted charters and independence) during the Middle Ages; cities that were the residences of kings, popes, princes, and bishops retain to this day a great sense of civic glory and tradition. This sense confers prestige on public service, both at the political and administrative levels and it inhibits corrupt behavior. It means greater elite and public support for planned development—development designed to preserve the prestigious central core of the city. There is also greater readiness of the middle and upper classes to reside in the historic center rather than desert to the suburbs. Inner districts remain vital centers of recreation, culture, tourism, and shopping. Medieval street plans do, of course, generate traffic congestion and housing tends to be poor in the older sections.

American cities are products of nineteenth-century commerce and industry. Together with the industrial centers of Europe (the cities seldom visited by tourists), they lack prestigious and aristocratic centers. After more than a century of commercial development and redevelopment, little remains of their historic heritage. Their central cores are characteristically called "Central Business Districts" rather than "Historic Centers." Their cores are seen as real estate, office space, skid rows, and ghettos, perhaps, more than as ensembles of theaters, opera houses, museums, and civic buildings.

But if we look at the age of housing, many American cities are older than European cities. (See Tables 4-13 and 4-14.) In terms of the average age of dwellings, Rome, Italy, is a much younger city than Buffalo, New York! The reason for this is the great expansion of many European cities in recent decades compared to the decline of American central cities. In this case, age confers more disadvantages than advantages; there is little venerability attached to the older housing in American cities.[44]

Another basic difference between European and American cities concerns the form of urban development. A preference for laissez faire market solutions to urban development problems has meant that American cities have developed with little planning and with little overall design. Spontaneous market forces have tended to produce the low-density, sprawling city.

In Western Europe, with its sense of scarcity and historical continuity and its greater acceptance of regulation in the collective interest, development has been more compact. Tight controls have been exercised over new urban growth. City governments, rather than private developers, have determined the pace and direction of city expansion. City governments have purchased land suitable for development and ensured that new construction was in districts which were not constructed or inhabited before the installation of necessary utilities and services. Care has been taken to ensure sufficient open, green space around residential developments. New developments have been linked with public transportation networks, the assumption being that despite the growing diffusion of automobiles, complete dependency on the auto is undesirable.

The urban sprawl characteristic of most American cities has drawbacks. The costs of bringing in utilities—water, sewage, electricity, gas, and telephone—to new districts is much higher than where development is compact. Valuable agricultural land may be unnecessarily converted to residential or commercial usage. A scattered development pattern forces people to rely on private means of transportation for commuting and shopping; those who cannot drive (the young and the old, the disabled, and the poor) find themselves cut off from the community. Sprawl creates many city centers—the polynucleated city. In such a city, adequate public transportation is difficult to maintain since points of arrival and departure are both so scattered. Poor people in the central city find it hard to get to jobs spread out around the city.

Low-density development permits a high degree of segregation based on class, race, and ethnicity: every social group with some mobility can establish its enclave in or next to the city. Those without mobility—the poor, the aged, and minority groups subjected to discrimination—are trapped in ghettos. Sprawl allows many to escape and ignore the plight of those caught in the central city trap.

In European cities, compact development around a central core has often meant socioeconomic segregation on a vertical rather than a horizontal basis: the same apartment buildings contain families of different income groups, with the least desirable walk-up and garret apartments occupied by low-income households.

Table 4-13 Comparative City Age: Percentages of pre-1950 Housing Units as of 1970

10-20%	30-40%	40-50%	50-60%	60-70%	70-80%	80-90%	90-100%
Rome	Cologne	ATLANTA	LOS ANGELES	NEW ORLEANS	BALTIMORE	CLEVELAND	BUFFALO
	DALLAS	Bonn	DENVER	BIRMINGHAM	Bordeaux	DETROIT	
	Hannover	Frankfurt	Dortmund	WASHINGTON	CHICAGO	NEWARK	
	HOUSTON	Helsinki	Essen	Amsterdam	CINCINNATI	ST. LOUIS	
	HONOLULU	Munich	Göteborg	The Hague	London	SAN FRANCISCO	
	SAN DIEGO	Nuremberg	Malmö	KANSAS CITY	MINNEAPOLIS	Paris	
		Venice	MIAMI	Lyon	NEW YORK	PITTSBURGH	
			Oslo	OAKLAND	PHILADELPHIA	PROVIDENCE	
			Rotterdam	SEATTLE			
			Stuttgart	Stockholm			
				Marseilles			
				Vienna			

Source: Fried, *World Handbook of Urban Cities,* Ch. 6.

Table 4-14   Comparative City Age: Year 100,000 Population Was Reached

Before 1800	1800-1825	1825-1850	1850-1875	1875-1900	1900-1925	1925-1950	1950-1975
London	Glasgow	Brussels	BUFFALO	Graz	Essen	Wellington	Salzburg
Paris	Manchester	Budapest	PITTSBURGH	WASHINGTON	Duisburg		
Peking	NEW YORK	Prague	Bordeaux	Catania	Helsinki		
Canton	Hamburg	Turin	Messina	DETROIT	Linz		
Constantinople	Liverpool	Sheffield	Belfast	Frankfurt	Bern		
Tokyo	Rio de Janeiro	BOSTON	Bologna	The Hague	Malmö		
Naples	Warsaw	BALTIMORE	Buenos Aires	Montevideo	OAKLAND		
Osaka	Leeds	Bangkok	CHICAGO	Stuttgart	ATLANTA		
Kyoto	Edinburgh	Bristol	Dresden	Lódź	PORTLAND, OREG.		
Cairo	PHILADELPHIA	NEW ORLEANS	Melbourne	Nuremberg	DENVER		
Moscow	Birmingham,	Florence	Munich	Oslo	SEATTLE		
Lisbon	England	Genoa	Nottingham	Toronto			
Vienna	Havana	CINCINNATI	Rotterdam	Athens			
"Leningrad"	Baghdad		ST. LOUIS	Göteborg			
Amsterdam	Marseilles		Stockholm	Dortmund			
Calcutta			Valencia	Utrecht			
Seoul			Hull	Zürich			
Bombay			Leipzig	Nice			

Table 4-14   Comparative City Age: Year 100,000 Population Was Reached (continued)

Before 1800	1800-1825	1825-1850	1850-1875	1875-1900	1900-1925	1925-1950	1950-1975
Berlin			Montreal	LOS ANGELES			
Madrid			SAN FRANCISCO	Booatá			
Dublin			Sydney	Geneva			
Rome			WASHINGTON, D.C.	Basel			
Venice			Graz	Brisbane			
Palermo			Bremen	Beirut			
Milan			CLEVELAND	Lima			
Mexico City			Toulouse	COLUMBUS			
Delhi			NEWARK	Nagasaki			
Madras				Trieste			
Barcelona				Le Havre			
Tunis				Algiers			
Lyon				Ibadan			
Copenhagen				MILWAUKEE			
Shanghai				JERSEY CITY			
				PROVIDENCE			
				TOLEDO			
				ST. PAUL			
				KANSAS CITY, MO.			
				MINNEAPOLIS			

Within the same buildings, blocks, and neighborhoods, one can see apartments of different size and quality and price. The result is a mixture of social classes within most urban districts rather than the socioeconomic segregation by district characteristic of American cities.

Then, too, in European cities, centripetal forces operate to preserve the central core from decay. Social mixture helps to preserve all districts from the kind of deterioration characteristic of the poorest sections of American cities.

But the compactness of European cities has its costs, too. Though most Europeans prefer single-family dwellings with gardens, few of them enjoy this luxury. Tight regulation of development drives land and housing prices too high to permit the construction of anything but multifamily dwellings. Then, too, continued dependence on a single central core means considerable traffic congestion; it also means that those unable to live near the center suffer problems of accessibility—problems less frequent in polynuclear cities. Compact cities may be nice for tourists to visit, but to most Americans, they are probably less liveable than cities built at lower densities.

THE MIXED ECONOMY

Radicals ascribe the poor performance of American cities to capitalism. Poor performance occurs because it is unimportant or even useful to the capitalists in control of the dominant economic institutions.[45] However, the problem with this explanation is that the capitalist mixed-economy produces different results in different countries. Capitalism generates little crime or disorganization in Western Europe, Japan, or Australia, but a great deal in America.

There is, to be sure, less interference with market forces in America than in Europe. One reason for this is surely the extraordinary performance of the American private enterprise system, which has provided more benefits for more people (and earlier) than any other system in the world. The American economy provides both high wages and relatively moderate living costs. One important element in living costs is the price of land, and land in the United States has been relatively cheap and abundant compared to land in the other advanced nations. Most Americans have been able (at least until the recent explosion in housing costs) to enjoy the luxury of single-family dwellings because of the relative cheapness and abundance of land for development and because of the wide availability of automobiles and highways.

The American economy offers perhaps the broadest range of consumer goods at some of the lowest prices in the world; it provides employment for large numbers of people at some of the highest wage rates in the world; it provides housing, which is far more spacious and well equipped and with more surrounding green space, than in most comparable cities in the world; and it provides large amounts of leisure for the enjoyment of urban and rural amenities.

But if the American economy has been unusually strong, it has also had weaknesses—weaknesses with consequences for the quality of American urban life. Reliance on market solutions has meant high unemployment, slums, poverty, and all their correlates. It has meant majority affluence and minority deprivation. It has also meant pollution and environmental degradation. It has meant differential access to the various qualities of urban life and differential freedom from the hazard and horrors of urban life.

THE NATURE OF HIGH PERFORMANCE

A final reason for the mixed performance of United States cities seems to be that all cities in the advanced world have some defects, some form of underperformance. Cities measuring high on all indicators or by all performance standards do not exist, even at the highest levels of development.

The wealthiest advanced country in the world is Sweden, and Swedish cities are as fine as can be found anywhere—widely and justly admired products of planning, enlightened social policy, and commitment to community welfare. Affluence is combined with a strong sense of obligation to the less fortunate. Yet, Swedish cities are not perfect. Housing is one of the sore points: despite massive governmental efforts, housing has been scarce. By American standards, Swedish dwellings are small. Until recently, many lacked standard items of housing amenity, such as private baths, toilets, or kitchens. Then, too, practically no single-family housing has been built, despite strong demand for that form of housing in Sweden (as in most other advanced nations).[46] There is little individual home ownership in Swedish cities.

Swedish cities also display some major forms of social disorganization: suicide, alcoholism, and illegitimacy. The suicide rate is ten times greater in Stockholm than in New York; the illegitimacy rate is more than two times greater; and the alcoholism rate (as measured by deaths from cirrhosis of the liver) twice as great. Although there is greater personal safety in Swedish cities than in American cities, some forms of crime (burglary and bank robbery) have become rather serious problems. Finally, one might note that the price of developed (that is, adequate) social services comes high: Swedish governments take double the amount of taxes from wage earners that American governments do (between 40% and 50% of gross earnings).

Swiss cities rival Swedish cities as examples of successful urbanism: prosperous, well ordered, and responsively governed. In some ways, Swiss cities are even better than Swedish cities—at least in terms of social disorganization (suicide, alcoholism, and illegitimacy). But here, too, there are deficiencies to record. Although Swiss city governments have been highly responsive to the electorate through the frequent and regular use of the popular referendum, only recently was the right to participate given to women. Women voted in elections for the first time in Geneva in 1961; Basel in 1968; and Zürich in 1969. The social conservatism that delayed the advent of female suffrage until the 1960s is also reflected in very strong traditional social controls over individual behavior: low crime rates are partly the result of what critics call the "village-small town" social atmosphere of Swiss cities.[47] Moreover, there has been much less planning of urban and regional development in

Switzerland than in Sweden, and a much greater disposition to give scope to private enterprise in industrial and residential development. The result has been greater sprawl than in Swedish cities, despite the extreme shortage of land in Switzerland. Environmental controls have been late to develop: a characteristic result is that swimming has been banned in Lake Geneva since 1965. The city of Basel has no facilities for sewage treatment; sewage is dumped directly into the Rhine.

Particularly sensitive is the situation of foreign workers in Swiss cities.[48] Since World War I, a sizeable proportion of the labor force in Swiss cities has consisted of foreigners. In 1970, foreign workers made up about one-third the labor force in Zürich and Basel and about two-thirds in Geneva! Foreign workers have performed the menial and manual labor which Swiss workers refuse to perform; they have filled the jobs with the lowest pay, poorest working conditions, least job security, and lowest social prestige. They have been subject to discrimination on the part of employers, unions, landlords, and other natives with whom they come into contact. They have suffered from and contributed to the severe Swiss housing shortage, high rentals, and overcrowded schools and hospitals. Many live in company supplied dormitories with four to eight men in a room, often sleeping in double-decker bunks. Their low position in Swiss society is analogous to that of minorities in American cities, except that they can be deported to their native lands at the will of the government. The hostility (albeit declining) of many of their Swiss neighbors is reflected in the outcome of national referenda held in 1970, 1974, and 1977, which called, in effect, for the expulsion of most foreign workers from the country. Forty-six percent of the country voted for expulsion in 1970, 34% in 1974, and 30% in 1977.[49]

There is similar resentment and mistreatment of foreign workers in all the other countries of Western Europe based on the lowly socioeconomic status of the workers and the cultural differences between Western Europe, on the one hand, and Southern Europe, North Africa, South Asia, and the West Indies, on the other. The problem of establishing equitable, nonexploitative, and peaceful relations among different racial, ethnic, and religious groups has been no more successfully solved in other advanced societies than in American cities.

We should also mention the fact that the cost of living in most respects is much higher in the other advanced industrial nations than in American cities. Food costs twice in Stockholm what it costs in New York, San Francisco, or Chicago, although rents tend to be lower. It takes a skilled worker three times longer to earn the price of a new car in Stockholm than in New York. (See Table 4-15.) The cost of living also tends to be higher in Swiss cities. (See Table 4-16.)

Though Australian cities lack the crime and appalling ghettos of United States cities, Americans tend to find them similar in "institutions, brand names, modes of dress, patterns of interpersonal communication."[50] They have more equally distributed affluence than American cities. On the other hand, Americans moving to Australian cities find problems to adjust to:[51]

lower wage scales, shortage and/or expense of consumer goods, loneliness, driving on the left, problems associated with shopping (different names for

Table 4-15   Comparative Living Costs: Weeks of Work for an
             Auto Mechanic to Buy a New Volkswagen (1973)

NEW YORK	13
CHICAGO	17
Montreal	19
Zürich	21
Geneva	24
Düsseldorf	27
Sydney	30
Tokyo	32
Paris	36
London	37
Stockholm	37
Amsterdam	38
Brussels	38
Milan	38
Vienna	38
Istanbul	289
Bogotá	743

Source: Union Bank of Switzerland, *Prices,* p. 30.

familiar items, different store hours), the absence of business contacts, the accent, the pace and laxity of work and business procedures, the absence of central heating in houses, the quality of service in public areas such as restaurants, some patterns of conversation, food, the general cost of living, and male (chauvinist) attitudes toward women.

Then, too, though residential contrasts in socioeconomic status in Australian cities are not as striking as in United States cities, they are still considerable. The following criticism of local government fragmentation in Sydney may sound familiar:[52]

Because local government authorities are varied—in population, history of settlement, financial capacity, governing machinery, the demand for their services, and their willingness to provide services—the local government services a person will have received have depended a great deal on where "home" is in Sydney. Is this inequitable? Those who emphasize pluralism, local democracy, and "self-help" for each region, irrespective of its comparative needs, demands, and resources, might regard this unevenness as reasonable. Others would emphasize the interdependence of modern urban systems and the need for everyone, particularly more vulnerable citizens, to be assured by government of a basic range of services, and regard the present system as unjust—a further confirmation of an increasingly socially stratified society, in contrast to Australian egalitarian ideology.

The dysfunctions of cities in other advanced countries are less well known than the dysfunctions of American cities. Other countries are more discreet about investigating and reporting such matters than we are. American statistics systematically compare performance variables for blacks and whites. It is hard to find comparable statistics in the other advanced countries which reveal the disparities between the rich and the poor, between foreign workers and natives, or between various religious or ethnic groups. Thus, although black-white inequalities are so justly publicized for American cities, equivalent inequalities in other societies (between, for example, French and non-French in Canadian cities; foreigners and natives in Swedish, West German, and Swiss cities; Flemish and Walloons in Belgian cities; or Protestants and Catholics in the towns of Northern Ireland) are seldom published.

CONCLUSIONS

Chapter 3 (on modernization) stressed the commonalities of performance among the cities in the developed world. This chapter stresses the differences among cities in the advanced industrial democracies. Perhaps it might be appropriate to ask at this point: Are the cities of the advanced world becoming more alike or more dissimilar? Or are the differences of today much like the differences of years past and likely, therefore, to persist into the future?

In favor of the persisting differences hypothesis, we can point to the early comparative urban government literature—from the period 1890 to 1925. During this period, the study of American urban government was less parochial than it is today. Urban government textbooks compared American city performance with European city performance almost as a matter of course. Comparisons resulted in the same mixed record presented in this chapter.

Critics condemned many of the same things:

1. The high crime rates:

    It is a rather doleful commentary upon the progress of American civilization that crimes of violence are relatively more numerous in the United States than in any other civilized country. The number of felonious homicides (including murder and manslaughter) is nearly ten thousand per annum. That is to say one person in every hundred thousand is done to death by pistol, blackjack, knife, or other deadly instrument each year. Likewise in burglaries and robberies the United States holds the world record.[53]

    (The murder rate in the 1970s, though double the rate in the 1950s, is about the same as in the 1920s.)

2. The high death rate from fire (but at the same time the excellence of the American system of fire fighting):

    The annual loss of life and property by fire in the United States is larger than that of all the European countries put together.... Chicago and Paris are cities of about the same rank; but the annual losses by fire in the former city exceed those of the latter four or five times over.

Table 4-16 Comparative Living Costs: Hours of Work to Purchase Goods and Services (1973)

	Shopping Basket	Women's Clothing	Men's Clothing	Services	Monthly Rent Modern 3-Room Apt.	Household Appliances
NEW YORK	10	12.3	29.8	5.75	79	108
SAN FRANCISCO	12.6	14	40	7.2	55	150
CHICAGO	11	19	32	7.5	93	115
Stockholm	22.5	18	46	10.5	42	160
Zürich	16.8	18	35.6	7.5	61	172
Geneva	17.6	20	40.25	8	78	187
Brussels	18.5	28.6	46.6	12.2	49	252
Amsterdam	18.5	20.6	40.5	10.6	48	182
Copenhagen	26.6	25.25	63.5	13.8	62	247
Düsseldorf	21.25	19	45.6	11.2	74	161
Helsinki	24.2	15.5	40.5	14	78	275
London	18.8	16	47	9.3	75	215
Milan	20.3	16	43	7.6	58	177
Montreal	11	14.6	40	7.4	39	155
Oslo	21	25.6	53	13.3	84	246
Paris	19.3	24.75	52	9.5	107	193
Sydney	12.75	17.8	41	8.8	74	274
Tokyo	25	12.5	58	10	188	334
Vienna	23.6	26.6	44.75	10.8	87	306

Source: Adapted from Union Bank of Switzerland, *Prices*, pp. 45-50.

But

In the organization of fire-fighting forces, in modernness of apparatus, and in the efficiency of fire-fighting methods, the United States is way ahead of all other countries. Yet, this superiority has not availed to keep fire losses within bounds. The great cities of Europe spend astonishingly little on the maintenance of their fire-protection services; their equipment and their methods are in some cases almost grotesquely out of date; nevertheless, they manage to keep fires from spreading and are reducing their losses year by year.[54]

3. The lack of professionalized urban bureaucracies:

In European cities the engineering work of the municipality is entrusted to a professional of high rank who holds his office without limit of time and is well protected from the pressure of political influence. This is true of British, French, German, and Italian cities alike. In these countries municipal engineering is a profession; men prepare for it, enter it young, and spend the active years of their lives in it. In American municipalities, on the other hand, political considerations often determine the selection of the city engineer and continue to influence his actions after appointment. The term of office is rarely more than four years and there is no assurance of reappointment. . . . The pay is rarely sufficient to attract high grade men; the emoluments of private practice are much larger. . . . The consequence is that men who have failed to make headway in the private practice of their profession often drift into the city's engineering service and sometimes to the top of it. Much of the unpardonable waste in municipal construction has been the outcome of poor designing, faulty specifications, loosely-drawn contracts, and slipshod inspection of work in progress—all of which hark back to the lack of skill, diligence, and integrity in the engineering department. It is an unfortunate fact in many American cities, but a fact nevertheless, that the engineer who stands true to the public interest as he sees it, and declines to let politics sway his professional judgment, eventually finds himself without political friends and incurs the risk of losing his place.[55]

4. The weakness of city planners:

In the United States the progress of city planning has been less rapid [than in Europe and South America], partly because the people as a whole are more tolerant of eyesores, and partly because Americans do not take enthusiastically to projects which extend over a long term of years. Another obstacle to the progress of replanning in American cities may be found in the relatively narrow powers which the municipal authorities possess and the extent to which even these narrow powers are divided among various officials. . . . Something may also be attributed to the lack of popular confidence in public officials and to the widespread feeling among businessmen that if these officials are given large sums of money to spend for public improvements they will waste a large fraction of it. City planning sometimes involves large contracts, and the tax-

payers have been justifiably reluctant to entrust the work, with the huge patronage involved, to the customary type of municipal politician.[56]

5. The lack of protection from social insecurity and lack of "provision for the unemployed and those in distress":

The individualism of the American city has retarded the development of social activities necessary to a well-ordered municipal life. Only within recent years have we begun to develop markets for the reduction of the cost of living, the intensive supervision of the health of the people, the protection of the public against false weights and measures, the supply of pure food and milk, and other measures of a similar sort. . . .

The German city has carried activities of this sort further than any cities in the world. Almost all cities own their own abattoirs, in which all meat sold within the city must be slaughtered. Markets are universally owned and have been for centuries. In addition, the German city has developed many agencies of a preventive sort for the protection of the workers. Among these are pawn-shops and savings banks, the loaning of money for the building of homes, employment agencies and lodging houses, as well as emergency work in hard times. In addition, the state provides insurance against sickness, disease, accident, and old age, while poor relief is administered by the community rather than through private agencies as a necessary part of a well-ordered administration. . . . No cities in the world have given as much thought and consideration to the protection of its people as have the cities of Germany.[57]

(Conditions of racial minorities in American cities were not criticized in those early days, partly because Negroes constituted only 6% of central city population in 1900 and 7% in 1920; 10% in 1940; 17% in 1960; and 20% in 1970. They constituted 9% of the total suburban population in 1900; this dropped to 5% in 1940 and has remained at 5% since then!)[58]

Urbanists of the early 1900s also found positive things to say about American cities:

1. Their democratic nature (responsiveness)[59]

The American city government is training great masses of people in the art of self-government. And this is one of the ends of government. With us suffrage is a personal right. It is extended to all men and in some States to all women as well. It is not a property or a tax-paying privilege as it is in Germany or England. Universal suffrage with an untrained foreign-born population still further complicates our problem, although it is not the cause of our failures, as many people assume.

We are building our democracy on men and are developing our cities on a human rather than a property basis. This has been a temporary burden. It has probably delayed efficiency. But it involves self-government and a sense of responsibility on the part of the voters. And the achievement of this itself is even more to be desired than efficiency.

2.   The excellence of some public services:[60]

Some city departments . . . are in advance of those of any in the world. Our fire departments have long been efficient. Fire apparatus and morale and training of men are generally of a high standard. Bad fires are not traceable to the fire department so much as to our building codes.

The free public library is distinctively an American institution. No country in the world has opened up branches and democratized the use of books and reading-rooms for circulation and research purposes as we. . . . Commissions come from Europe to study our libraries, just as commissions from this country go to England and Germany to study departments in which these countries are advanced. . . .

The public schools of America are fairly comparable with those of any country. With us education is on a democratic basis and it has the virtues and faults of its ideals. And viewed from this, the democratic standpoint, our schools are probably as efficient as those of any other country. . . . The appropriations for school buildings, for equipment, free school-books, gymnasiums, playgrounds, kindergartens, for the promotion of school hygiene, nurses, and health officers, are more generous and progressive than those of any other country unless it be Germany.

The playground, too, is an American idea. It had its birth in this country and here it has developed most rapidly. No other country has utilized it as an educational and social force as have we. Nor has any other country made as generous provision for parks as have the cities of America . . .

When we consider that the schools, fire, library, and park departments involve approximately one half of the city's expenditure, it is evident that the American city is not all bad. And in some activities it is in advance of the world.

3.   Despite the tenements, there is a comparatively better quality of American housing:[61]

Probably the worst housing conditions are those of England and Germany. . . . In Berlin nearly one third of the people live in dwellings in which each room contains five or more persons, while 80% of the working people in the larger towns are said to live in cellars, attics, and tenements unsuited to the maintenance of a proper family life. . . . The German city is confronted with a housing problem far more serious than our own.

Comparative statistics suggest that the level of affluence was much higher, at least by some measures, in American cities than in European cities. In the 1920s, for example, American cities led the world in the diffusion of the private auto, as shown in Table 4-17.

Table 4-17   Comparative Motorization in the 1920s

	Persons per Private Auto (1927)
LOS ANGELES (1923)	2.9
CLEVELAND	4
COLUMBUS, OHIO	4
Ottawa	8
Paris	27
Stockholm	31
Geneva	35
Copenhagen	41
Prague	81
Rome	91
Buenos Aires	105
Cairo	117
Berlin	126
Dresden	132
Frankfurt	137
Munich	141
Amsterdam	141
Bucharest	152
Budapest	178
Vienna	664
Osaka	701
Ahmedabad	849

Source: (Calculated from Institut International de Statistique, *Statistique Internationale des Grandes Villes, 1931* (The Hague: Stockum, 1931), pp. 190-215.)

But, if there is continuity in the performance differences over time, there is also some convergence. Frequently noted (and often regretted) is the actual or supposed Americanization of European cities. Americanization is taken to mean several kinds of things: the diffusion of automobiles, supermarkets, and fast-food chains; the development of suburbs; the spread of domestic appliances; the expansion of higher educational opportunity and the development of socially mixed secondary schools; the spread of housing with private plumbing and central heating—the various features of the "soft life" as lived in American cities. Americanization may mean the growing presence of racial and ethnic minorities in many European cities and the resulting challenge to the adjustive powers of formerly homogeneous urban communities. Less positively, European cities may becoming Americanized in terms of growing air pollution, crime and juvenile delinquency, narcotics addiction rates, welfare dependency, family breakdown, unrest in municipal services, and crisis in health care delivery systems.

Less noted is the fact that American cities are being "Europeanized." American cities are coming to experience a taste of the centralized control and dependency on higher levels of government that has always been a fact of life in Europe,

Canada, and Australia. Then, too, traditional laissez faire policies have given way to a vast expansion of the public sector. Public social welfare expenditures in 1960 accounted for 38% of government spending at all levels; by 1975, they amounted to 58%. Social welfare expenditures by all American governments tripled between 1960 and 1974, rising (in 1974-1975 dollars) from $485 in 1960 to $1319. In 1965, 400,000 Americans received food stamps; in 1974, 13,600,000. In 1960, 3,100,000 people received public assistance to families with dependent children; in 1975, 11,400,000. In 1960, no Americans were enrolled in Medicare (hospital and medical insurance); by 1975, over 23,000,000 people participated in that program.[62] The policies and practices of American government have undoubtedly become more comparable to those of the social democracies. Finally, the growing price of land and housing together with the energy crisis may be inducing a more scarcity based form of urban development: more compact development with more high-rise, less sprawl, and tighter controls. Perhaps most symbolically, even American urban transportation is becoming "Europeanized" into more public and more compact forms of travel.[63]

URBAN PERFORMANCE IN LESS DEVELOPED COUNTRIES

5

Logically, there should be no problem of urban performance in the Third World; with less developed, less modernized societies, the Third World should have few cities. Urbanization, we tend to assume, is an integral part of modernization. If a country is modern, it has cities; with cities, therefore, there must be modern politics and economics. Since we associate modernization with the concentration of people in cities, we would expect urban problems to be a minor factor in the government policies of developing countries, compared with policies for the agricultural areas.

But, even if we find cities in the Third World, this should mean progress, not crisis. Urbanization should not be a problem, but a solution to the problem of underdevelopment. Urbanization should mean modernization, and both imply an evolution from subsistence agriculture to industry, from personalistic politics to the politics of parties and interest group politics, from familial relationships to impersonal (secondary) associations, and from rural poverty and illiteracy to urban advancement in comfort and status.

Actually, such expectations are founded in the experience of the advanced countries rather than extrapolated from the experiences of the developing countries. Current thinking about urban problems in the developing areas is both less ethnocentric and less optimistic. It is not so certain that, in looking at the consequences of urbanization and the growth of big cities in the new nations, we can expect cities in the developing world to be like those in the West. It is now argued that urbanization and city life in developing areas have distinctive cultural and historical attributes which differentiate both the non-Western experience and its consequences from the Western. What we are learning is that urbanization can have different causes, forms, and consequences in different contexts.[1]

Many countries in the world, in fact, are more urbanized than modernized. They have more people coming into and living in their cities than their level of economic development would indicate as "normal." Many of these cases of over-urbanization or hyperurbanization are to be found in Latin America and the Middle East—regions in which rapid urban growth is occurring without a commensurate growth in urban industrial employment. Thus, the resources are not available to cope with the financial costs of the urbanization process. Cities in many developing areas are growing not so much because of the "pull" of factory jobs (as in the West) as because of the "push" from an overcrowded, feudalistic, impoverished, and isolated countryside.

Not only can urbanization in the Third World not be equated with modernization, it may actually work against it. Urbanization may not be a measure of progress towards political, economic, or social development; it may, in fact, retard development. As population moves into the cities, the need and demand for costly urban infrastructure and services vastly increases. Rural populations expect and get little service, rudimentary facilities, and few amenities and comforts. City residents—new and old—however, have greater needs and expectations. Political pressures build up, forcing governments to spend money on public health, education, housing, markets, water, electricity, and roads—objects that have only an indirect impact on economic development—compared to direct capital investment in industry or agriculture. Thus, it is argued that urbanization diverts investment funds from the most productive uses.[2]

Urbanization may also not necessarily be a sign of progress towards political development—the development of a stable, effective, and responsive political system. In the West, urbanization was part of the process that created the bases for modern constitutionalism. The urban middle classes (the "bourgeoisie," meaning literally, "city-dwellers"), with wealth and status derived from commerce, industry, and the professions, were the principal political forces behind the establishment of regimes based on limited government, the rule of law, and impartial administration. Later the urban working-class movement became the major force in spreading the rights won by the bourgeoisie to all citizens, irrespective of status and income. But urbanization in the Third World is creating cities without either a strong, liberal middle class or a strongly egalitarian proletariat. In many Third World cities, the middle class is either weak, alien, authoritarian, and/or part of the ruling oligarchy. The industrial proletariat is either nonexistent, part of a government controlled labor movement, or nationalistic rather than egalitarian. A large lumpen proletariat, however, does exist of people without steady employment or legal means of support; thus urbanization in the Third World does not necessarily create the social bases for a modern political system.[3]

However, even in the less urbanized countries of the Third World, the urban segment carries a weight disproportionate to its numbers and, with this, a capacity to create an "urban crisis" in predominantly rural societies. Most of the new nations in Africa have less than one-tenth of their populations in cities, and yet, in many of them, there is serious concern with urban problems. In these countries, many of which have per-capita GNP's of less than $100 per year, the major problem is often to ensure a sufficient food supply to ward off urban famine. A decline in agricultural production drives people from the land, but also threatens city dwellers with starvation.

Just how important are the urban problems of the Third World in the overall picture of urban performance in the world? It is difficult to answer precisely if only for the fact that the category of Third World cities is not itself precisely definable. In general, by "Third World city," we mean a city located in the poorer, noncommunist countries. But there is no obvious cutoff point between rich and poor cities or countries. There are several ways in which one can measure development or modernization, and each measure can produce a scale with many gradations. Most countries in the world are neither as advanced as the United States or Northern Europe nor as underdeveloped as many countries in Africa and Asia, but fall somewhere in between. Whether they are classified as being in the Third World depends somewhat on the arbitrary decision of the classifier.

The United Nations classifies the nations of the world—communist and non-communist—into "more developed" and "less developed."[4] Table 5-1 shows the growing importance of the urban population of the "less developed countries" (LDCs) in the total picture of world urbanism. United Nations experts estimate that by 1980, about half of the world's urban population will be located in the LDCs as compared to only one-quarter in 1920. It is clear from United Nations' projections that Third World urbanism is growing—and at an explosive rate.

Of the approximately 1700 urban areas in the world with 100,000 or more people, roughly one-quarter are located in the less developed noncommunist countries, that is, countries with less than $800 per-capita GNP: about 100 in Africa, about 150 in Latin America, and about 200 in Asia and the Middle East.[5] The non-

Table 5-1   The Urban Importance of the LDCs

Less Developed Countries	1920	1940	1960	1980
Percentage of total world population	64	64	67	72
Percentage of world population living in urban areas with 20,000 people	26	30	41	51
Percentage of world big city population (500,000+)	13	19	37	48
Percentage of multimillion city population (2.5 million+)	0	9	31	47

Source: Calculated from United Nations, *1970 Report on the World Social Situation* (New York: United Nations, 1971), p. 153.

communist Third World, even though it has half the population of the world, has only one-quarter of the world's major cities. (The advanced democracies have less than 19% of the world's population, but they have one-half of the world's major cities.)

The category of "Third World city" is imprecise not only because there is no sharp demarcation between rich and poor countries and cities, but also because "Third World" conditions are to be found not only in Africa, Asia, and Latin America, but also in Europe and North America. The people living in the *bidonvilles* ("tin-can cities") around Paris, the *baracche* around Rome, the *coree* around Milan do not live that differently from those living in the *favelas* of Rio or the *ranchos* of Caracas—or, for that matter, in the "Hoovervilles" in most American cities during the Depression. Foreign workers in Europe—the Algerians, Turks, Portuguese, and Italians living in France, Switzerland, or West Germany—and the minorities in American ghettos and *barrios* have housing, health, employment, and discrimination problems that are not that different from the problems of poor urbanites in the Third World.

Conversely, Third World is not synonymous with Asia, Africa, and Latin America since Asia has some countries considered more, rather than less, developed (Japan and Israel), as does Latin America (Chile, Argentina, and Uruguay—according to the United Nations, at least).

Nor is the Third World city synonymous with the so-called "preindustrial" city. A frequently used typology today classifies cities according to their position in a developmental hierarchy as preindustrial or industrial.[6] In industrial cities, urban growth is associated with increasing employment opportunities in industry, attachment to an urban way of life distinct from rural folkways, rationalistic tendencies, and achievement-oriented norms. Preindustrial cities are opposite in values— dependent, traditional, and ascriptive. Unfortunately, by this reckoning, all the world's cities before the nineteenth century as well as contemporary cities in parts of Asia, Africa, Southern Europe, and Latin America fall into the same preindustrial category. We are little helped in predicting performance when pre-Columbian Chichen Itza, seventeenth-century Paris, and contemporary Yoruba mudtowns are placed in the same class.[7] The preindustrial-industrial sequence assumes that the course of industrial-urban development will radiate, following the path taken by the United States and Western Europe; in fact, there may be a wide range of responses to the introduction of advanced technology in cities.

In this chapter, we shall be dealing with the cities that lie in the countries which are noncommunist and which have less share in world GNP than their share in world population—cities where the major constraint on performance is mass poverty.

5-2 INTEGRITY IN THIRD WORLD CITIES

Urbanization—if tied to modernization—can mean the development of city governments which operate with a high degree of lawfulness, due process, honesty, impartiality, and respect for human rights. In the West, notions of constitutionalism (limited government), the rule of law, the independence of the judiciary, civic equality, individual rights, and the public nature of governmental office emerged simultaneously with the development of a modern capitalism. Principles of due process in government were often institutionalized before massive urbanization. Urbanization in the West took place within the framework of well-established national systems of constitutional government.

Western principles of government spread throughout the world under colonial administrations and indirectly through cultural diffusion. Modern notions of government—national and local—were brought to Latin America by the Spanish and Portuguese; to Africa by the British, Dutch, French, Italians, Portuguese, and Germans; to Asia by the British, French, Dutch, and Americans; and to North America by the British and French.

But the diffusion and institutionalization into the daily practice of government of legalitarian ideas and practices has been uneven. Premodern norms and practices persist around the world, even within the more developed democracies. It is difficult to "constitutionalize" urban government in the advanced world, but it is even more difficult in the less developed countries.

Most Third World cities are governed by authoritarian regimes—either military or party dictatorships. The failure to establish limited government at the local level is just part of the failure in most new nations to establish constitutional systems at the national level. Military and party dictatorships do not tolerate the institutions needed for government integrity: strong and independent courts, representative assemblies, opposition political parties, a free press, and private watchdog interest groups. It is difficult to keep government within bounds without strong outside checks on performance—checks that tend to be lacking in most Third World countries. The lack of checks on urban government bureaucracies reproduces the same lack of checks on national government bureaucracies.

Then, too, the absence of external checks is not counterbalanced by strong internal checks within the urban bureaucracies. Officials in Third World cities do not generally see public office as a public trust. Oftentimes, they see in an office a form of private property to be used for maximum personal or group advantage. Authority is seen as a means for extorting bribes. The law, together with abundant rules and regulations, is seen as a means of holding up action until proper payment is made. In the advanced world, bribery is perhaps most frequently employed to prevent the law from being enforced. In Third World cities, bribery is usually required to secure the normal performance of duty.[8]

Even the military, which often justifies coups by the need to drive corrupt civilians from power, does not provide an example of impartial, strictly disciplined, lawful administration once it is in office. As Eric Nordlinger writes:[9]

> *Military governments are on the whole no less corrupt and self-serving than civilian ones. It has even been said that African praetorians are more corrupt and self-indulgent than their civilian predecessors; and as much so as their Latin American counterparts. . . . Once they have the opportunity to do so as*

> *governors, soldiers are just as likely as civilians to enrich themselves through legal, quasi-legal, and illegal means. . . .*

Certainly many African cities have been terrorized by lawless bands of soldiers. The military dictatorship of Idi Amin or the military juntas operating in Greece, Chile, Argentina, and Brazil have been among the most flagrant violators of human rights.

To be sure, the political culture in most developing countries is not conducive to limited, honest government. Ordinary people often demand, or are used to, various forms of arbitrary and corrupt official behavior. Members of the public feel that there are no dishonest officials, only disloyal ones—ones who refuse to share their "profits" with friends, relatives, followers, and clients. They expect officials to be generous, moreover, because officials are more fortunate than those without some public office. Relations between officials and members of the public are personalistic: payments and services are treated as personal favors from the official, given as a person rather than as a member of a party or government agency. Personal bonds of obligation are seen as much more important than abstract legal relationships. It is generally assumed that poorly paid officials cannot live on their salaries alone, but must be given additional compensation by members of the public requiring some decision.[10]

Norms of political culture are sustained by a highly rigid and hierarchical social structure: one which places the official at vast social remove from ordinary members of the public. Officials, instead of dealing with educated middle-class equals, deal mostly with people who are vastly inferior and poorly educated. Thus, the normal relationship is one between patron and client, or between the dispenser of favors and the humble petitioner. The social structure reinforces discriminatory decision making when the city's population is divided into mutually antagonistic racial, linguistic, caste, or tribal groups; in such "poly-communal" cities, there may be considerable support for discrimination and even violence against minority group members.[11]

Sometimes one form of integrity—due process—is suspended in order to fight corruption. Periodically in Third World countries, strong-arm methods are adopted in order to repress corruption; paradoxically, this was the case in India in 1975-1976 when the opposition was jailed, the legislative and judicial organs intimidated, and the press muzzled—all in the name of allowing the executive unfettered ability to stamp out corruption. (The end result may be to allow one set of corrupt officials to displace another.)

Arbitrary government is also, paradoxically, caused by growing modernization, particularly in those Third World countries that have competitive political systems. In traditional societies, people support authority because of its inborn, inherited right to rule. Once people cease to believe in the divine right of the "gentle folk" to rule them, traditional authority must be replaced by authority of a different kind: either the authority of a transcendent personality (charisma); the authority of law (a constitution); or authority based on gratitude for favors and services rendered. Arbitrary and corrupt government, particularly in the competitive or semicompetitive Third World countries, can be the result of politicians' efforts to build networks of support based on patronage in societies with no other basis of authority. The urban political machine is a classic mechanism for building loyalty and support for a political system in societies where petty favors and services still have more meaning and value for the mass of the people than the principles of "good government."

It has been argued that corruption and a favoritistic administration may be more justified in Third World cities than in the advanced world.[12] Corrupt, or at least favoritistic and personalistic, administration is a vital way of building support for the regime in nations where traditional authority has largely disappeared (at least in the cities) without being replaced by the authority of impersonal law. Just as urban political machines assimilated millions of immigrants into the American political system during the nineteenth and early twentieth centuries by providing them with all kinds of services and immunities—legal and not-so-legal—politicians in Third World cities are attempting to ease the adjustment problems of migrants today by dispensing much the same kinds of favors. Third World urban politicians, much like the city bosses of nineteenth-century America, seek to build support by making "particularistic" deals with individuals and neighborhoods rather than by making universal rules and general policies.

Aprodicio Laquian notes:[13]

> *The persistence of these [particularistic] fragments is frustrating to many Western planners and administrators, whose rational comprehensive plans, zoning laws, merit bureaucracies, and objective criteria of excellent performance are undermined by particularism.*
>
> *Instead of condemning fragmentation, however, it should be seen in the light of the developmental goals aspired to in the developing countries. By doing this, it is seen that while it is, indeed, detrimental to administrative efforts to provide effective and efficient services to the urban government, its impact on the goal of arousing popular participation and involvement in political affairs is distinctly salutary. The more intimate traditional unit of the neighborhood makes for a more viable political community. The more direct relevance of political affairs to the personal interests and fortunes of people results in deeper involvement. The fact that one facet of Third World urbanization tends to frustrate one set of goals and achieve another raises anew the question of what is developmental.*

Although it may be necessary to sacrifice honesty and impartiality for responsiveness in Third World cities, there are limits on how far this can go. In Third World cities, there is a constituency for "good government": there are many people with a strong dislike of corrupt, arbitrary, and lawless behavior. The military would not, after all, justify coups on grounds of morality if there were not widespread support for the "Western" code of official behavior. The growing professional classes—doctors, lawyers, engineers, accountants, and teachers—are an important liberalizing force, as are some student groups and, perhaps, the foreign press. Third World countries tend to have dictatorial or oligarchical regimes, but these regimes tend to be unstable. One reason for this is the fact that in most Third World countries there are significant forces working for lawful, limited government.

The checks on urban government in Third World countries tend, in any event, to be greater than those in the totalitarian countries. There is usually some opposition, some freedom of the press, some judicial independence, some concept of legal limitations on government authority, or some pressure to conform to notions of the rule of law and due process. As we shall see, these elements of integrity tend to disappear under communism.

5-3 RESPONSIVENESS IN THIRD WORLD CITIES

Urbanization without modernization should be explosive. Driven by overpopulation, soil depletion, and a desire for a better, less isolated life, migrants are streaming into Third World cities en masse. They leave the village, with its strong social ties, tightly enforced mores, familiarity, easygoing ways, and low expectations for a city filled with strangers, among whom there are few, if any, common ties or common mores. In the city, jobs are difficult, even impossible, to find. Housing and food are expensive. The only available shelter may be sleeping on sidewalks, in railway stations, under bridges, or in the shacks of a shantytown. In the shantytown, conditions are horrendous. Shacks have leaking roofs and dirt floors. There is no running water, no electricity, no toilets, no bath. Seven or eight people may live and sleep in the same room. The streets are narrow, unpaved, and filled with garbage and sewage. There is no protection (in the form of storm drains or solid housing) against flooding. More often than not, the shacks are built on land belonging to the city or some absentee owner. Those who build them or rent them live in perpetual fear of being ousted by the lawful property owners. Public authorities periodically send in bulldozers to drive squatters from their precarious settlements.

Lack of sanitation means that disease is endemic. As Charles Abrams wrote:[14]

> *Absence of a system for removing excrement from living areas continually exposes the healthy to the contaminated wastes of the ill and the disease carrier. In the crowded urban communities that have mushroomed in recent years, such pollution is accepted as part of the way of life. For example, in Lagos, Nigeria, out of 4759 schoolchildren whose stools were examined, 85 percent were infected with parasites, roundworm and hookworm being the most common forms. Dysentery and diarrhea accounted for 10.1 percent of all the deaths in 1960. In the same year, 54.5 percent of all deaths in Nigeria's capital city occurred among children under five years of age. ...*

In the rural area, there is little contact with modern ideas or modern affluence. Migration to densely packed urban settlements brings exposure to both. Migrants now see how the other half lives; their sense of both absolute and relative deprivation grows. They come to expect basic public services—schools, hospitals, utilities, transport—services which are nonexistent or in short supply. They, moreover, find themselves transferred from rural strongholds of conservatism into the hotbeds of urban radicalism. Political extremism of left and right flourishes in contexts where the status quo has few defenders.

The social basis of the Third World city is also explosive. The migrants who come from rural areas—because of scarce housing, poverty, and transportation costs—tend to be young males, more easily mobilized for political riots than shaped into a trained, effective labor force. They come from homogeneous villages into an urban "community" composed of numerous, mutually hostile, suspicious and warring subcommunities—subcommunities that often make incompatible, symbolic demands on government. Even for those long established within the city, the educational system produces numbers of radicalized students with poor job prospects—another source of violence and political extremism.

On the input side of government, then, in Third World cities one finds a growing demand for jobs, services and improvements; for radical change; and for symbolic recognition. Facing these demands are authoritarian officials with little tolerance for demand-making pressures, or criticism—whether practical or radical; and large-scale urban bureaucracies absolutely incapable of meeting more than a small share of the service demands placed upon them, professionally indifferent to the perpetual "crisis" conditions in the city, and resentful of the "destructive" criticism from the *lumpen intellighentsia.*[15]

In modernized politics, the strains of urbanization are mediated through organized interest groups, political parties, and the articulation of interests through the free press. Elected politicians exert pressures on government bureaucracies to meet public demands. Community resources, supplemented by regional or national resources, can be mobilized to meet most demands. Demands for radical change are uncommon. People from various subcultures normally manage to coexist on the basis of mutual tolerance. There is a vast urban middle class to act as a buffer between rich and poor and to exert pressure for high performance on the urban bureaucracies. In Third World cities, however, we do not find interest groups, competing parties, a free press, surplus financial resources, a large middle-class buffer, or competent, minimally responsive bureaucracies. We should, therefore, expect to find cycles of repression and revolt rather than the routinized responsiveness of the advanced democracies, but we do not.

In fact, there is less turbulence in Third World cities than one might expect.[16] Despite horrendous conditions, despite explosive population growth, and despite enormous performance gaps, Third World cities have not become ungovernable centers of political turmoil.

One reason is that migration and urban poverty do not radicalize most people. The view of the migrant and the shantytown dweller as alienated, uprooted, desperate, and violence prone is vastly oversimplified, as is the view of rural-urban migration as inherently destructive of political stability.

It is all too easy for an outside observer to project his or her own performance criteria on people with different perceptions, values, expectations, and priorities.

This is easy for a foreign observer, but just as easy for a "native" outsider. Shanti Tigri writes about Indian cities:[17]

> *Growing slums, worsening sanitary conditions, lowering living standards, and unemployment concentrate misery visibly, not in inaccessible villages, but in areas which are the habitat of writers, social reformers, artists, poets, teachers, religious preachers, humane societies, dreamers, city planners, sociologists, journalists, and economists.*

An outsider is particularly likely to overrate appearances and to stress the need for visible, physical improvements. Migrants and squatters may be far more interested in finding steady jobs, increasing their income, and getting their children educated than in moving to better housing or to a neighborhood with better services. Wayne Cornelius has discovered, for example, that among migrants to Mexico City, income, employment, education, and certified title to one's land are top priority items of personal concern—much more important than housing, services, or even health.[18] Throughout the Third World, the urban poor attach less priority to housing quality than to security of title to their land and basic community services, like water, sewerage systems, and paved streets. Actually, as Cornelius found in Mexico City, priorities may differ from settlement to settlement within the same city, depending on the age and stage of development of the settlement.

Second, migrants do not necessarily consider government responsible for solving all their problems. Among the Mexico City migrants interviewed by Cornelius, for example, people did not consider the government responsible for "providing economic help to those in need, providing employment, [or] redistributing wealth" ("trying to even out the differences between the rich and poor classes in Mexico"). But "they overwhelmingly perceived the government as responsible for providing most kinds of community-related services and improvements."[19] Studies in other Latin American cities show that even here there are differences. Migrants in Lima, Peru, tended much more than migrants to Mexico City to believe that the prime responsibility for solving community problems lay with the community itself through self-help rather than with the government. There is a smaller responsiveness gap when people do not politicize their needs, that is, expect government to do something. Urbanization is supposed to politicize personal needs—make people expect more from government than they did in rural areas—but clearly there are limits to this "revolution of rising expectations."

One of the things limiting the politicization of needs into demands is, in fact, the "ruralization" of the city—the transfer of rural ties, institutions, expectations, and customs to the city. Migration to the city is supposed to be a disruptive experience, tearing a person away from the close familarity of the village and thrusting him or her into a remote, impersonal, and strange urban environment. But in practice, rural migrants frequently succeed in transferring their village into the city, together with all psychological, moral, and material props the village can provide. Major cushions against personal breakdown in the urban environment and major means of adjustment to harsh new conditions are family and neighborhood social networks, often transferred from the village.

Help in adjusting to city life is provided not only by friends, relatives, and neighbors, but also, in some of the more competitive or semicompetitive political systems, by local political leaders. In Tammany Hall fashion, local political leaders become the patrons of the new migrants and of neighborhood improvement associations by acting as middlemen between the migrant and the government. Some Third World political regimes discourage demand making by doing little in response to demands. Others actually encourage migrants and squatter groups to bring their problems to party and government officials for paternalistic assistance. Thus, expectations and aspirations are often shaped by the government itself: governmental responsiveness encourages further demand making. Reaction to governmental inaction or indifference may be not radicalization, but (at worst) resignation and (at best) self-help.

Migrants often organize peaceful delegations to present petitions for action to the authorities rather than organize protests or demonstrations. Migrants are often deferential rather than defiant towards the authorities. They feel awkward as "foreign" newcomers to the city; they feel that the authorities are more inclined to act in response to petitions rather than to threats; as squatters on someone else's land, their position is precarious. The government, after all, may repress defiant protest with violence.[20]

It is important to note that migrants typically present limited demands (that is, requests), involving specific community improvements. It is as difficult to mobilize the urban poor in Third World cities as in American cities on behalf of generalized reform, not to mention revolutionary change. Specific needs, rather than system change, are the core demands—demands which government and party officials, in turn, can tolerate and accommodate without disturbance to the existing distribution of power, wealth, and status.

Regimes can encourage demand making or discourage it. The reaction to discouragement on the part of the urban poor is likely to be not rebelliousness, resentment, and violent extremism, but rather depoliticization. Unresponsive government officials and party officials come to be seen not as unresponsive but as simply irrelevant in the pursuit of survival.

When national governments are not unresponsive, they often go to the other extreme and favor the urban areas or one big city over all other localities in the country. Cities may have considerable power in national politics and receive a disproportionate share of governmental benefits. In several countries, one big city has a large share of the national population. This is very common in Latin America: Buenos Aires has 19% of the national population, Montevideo (33%), Caracas (21%), Asunción (18%), Guatemala City (13%), San Jose (12%). It can also be found in Africa: Tunis (17%), Brazzaville (29%), Libreville (21%), Tripoli (23%), and Dakar (15%). One city often has more than half of a country's total urban population; this is the case of Nairobi, Kampala, Dakar, Singapore, Colombo, Katmandu, Beirut, San Jose, Kingston, Panama City, Buenos Aires, La Paz, Asunción, and Montevideo.[21]

National governments in the poorer countries have frequently been accused of overallocating resources either to the largest city or to cities generally, at the expense of other cities or the rural hinterland. Government policy is seen as being responsible, at least in part, for the drastic differences in living conditions between the leading city (or cities) and the rest of the country. For it is true that however bad conditions may be in Mexico City, Caracas, Jakarta, Manila, or Cairo, they are considerably better than in most other parts of Mexico, Venezuela, Indonesia, the Philippines, or Egypt.

One large city can dominate a nation's political, social, and economic life. It may be the national political capital; the center of publishing and communications; or the hub of finance, commerce, and industry. It may lie at the center of national and international traffic or be the site of the leading schools and universities. It may house the headquarters of all important national or international organizations or have the best medical facilities and personnel. It may be the major destination for foreign and domestic tourists and be considered the national showcase—a visible symbol of national identity and progress. It may even be where rich agricultural landowners spend much of their time and money. Largest cities are—for these reasons—usually the focus of rural-urban migration and the locus of urban growth and development.

In many Third World countries, political life turns on a struggle for national resources between the cities (or The City) and the countryside. The urban interest often wins out in the competition for power and benefits because it has immediate and strong political pressure, even in a rural country. Government investments in the big city are politically profitable because they are so visible. Private investments in the big city are economically profitable because opportunities there are better known, some infrastructure already exists, and investment there is less risky than in other places.[22] Accordingly, governments anxious to promote economic growth respond to demands from the big city for infrastructure (ports, roads, and plants).

Then, too, governments anxious to promote political stability (rather than economic growth) try to avoid riots based on deteriorating living conditions—disorders that are deeply embarrassing and dangerous when they occur at the center of the national stage. Urban groups, as it happens, have a greater capacity to blackmail their national governments than rural groups whose protest is less easily organized, more difficult to cover by the media, and, thus, more easily ignored. Exaggerated responsiveness to the big city also occurs because the government considers the growth of that city "inevitable" and prefers to adjust government policy to growth rather than adjust growth to the needs of government policy. Mass migration to the big city may be accepted fatalistically and may even be seen as the opportunity for a politically profitable exchange of investment in return for a mass base of political support.

Nonetheless, the rural areas offer an alternative base of support: one that provides larger masses of people, and one that can be motivated by hatred for, and resentment of, the big city and its privileges. There may be more political profit in spreading ("scattering") investments around the country than in concentrating them in the one big city, particularly since, in many countries, the big city is the stronghold of opposition to the current regime. Rural areas have political resources, to be sure, and, thus, there is nothing inevitable about the outcome of the urban-rural fight for political predominance.

5-4 COMPARATIVE EFFECTIVENESS IN THIRD WORLD CITIES

By most performance indicators, the cities of the Third World perform badly. It is not that they have problems that are unique. As Robert Sadove has remarked: [23]

> *Almost every major city in the world has slums, unemployment, housing shortages, inadequate transport systems, and congestion of people and traffic. And every major metropolitan area is increasing in size. These are the liabilities of urban living everywhere. [The difference] lies in relative magnitudes. Greater population increases, lower per capita income, fewer capital resources, greater unemployment, and less developed urban infrastructure characterize the cities of the developing world.*
>
> *The magnitude of these problems compared with the paucity of available resources to deal with them demonstrates that the developing urban world faces a situation radically different from that of cities in the developing countries.*

Symbol and indicator of the performance differences between the rich and poor countries is the extent to which governments have lost control of the urban development process. In the rich countries, cities grow in accordance with laws and regulations on building, zoning, and subdivisions; few dwellings are built without a permit and on land to which the builder has no title. Dwellings cannot be occupied without a certificate of occupancy—a certificate that is not given when basic facilities are lacking. In the Third World cities, the bulk of development continues to take place illegally; most dwellings are constructed without permit on land that belongs to someone else. Dwellings are occupied even though the most basic facilities (water and sanitation) may be lacking. If sovereignty means control over territory, such sovereignty no longer seems to exist in the cities of the Third World.

Thus, when West Europeans build New Towns, they do not confront the situation that occurred at the Brazilian new town, Brasília, in which, as of 1962, 41% of the population lived in unplanned settlements as compared to 59% in the planned settlements! [24]

The mushrooming growth of squatter settlements, uncontrolled settlements, or spontaneous settlements—by whatever name they may be known—widens the urban performance gap between rich and poor countries. Such settlements constitute a form of urbanization without urbanism—cities without the basic elements that distinguish the urban from the rural way of life: paving, sanitation, electricity, running water; dwellings made with concrete, bricks, wood, or stone; or dwellings with wooden, stone, or concrete floors.

Typical might be the shantytowns of Tijuana, Mexico, across the border from San Diego, California. Tijuana is perhaps the fastest growing city in the world. In a 1966 report (things have been improved somewhat since then), conditions were described as follows:

Fifty percent of the people in the city lack running water, electricity, washing machines, sinks, comfortable beds, decent furniture, floors, roofs that don't leak—the things Americans take for granted. The vast majority here do not have telephones or television. They have no paved sidewalks, no paved streets. Hundreds of families with 6 to 12 children boast a single wage earner who is lucky to earn $1 or $1.50 a day. They're crowded in primitive one-room shacks with no indoor toilets. They don't even have outhouses. The poor people of Tijuana live in slums that rank with the worst in the world, that rival Rio's incredible favelas and the refugee hovels hugging the hills of Hong Kong.

Dusty, shack-cluttered streets stand out starkly on Tijuana's many hills that rise abruptly from the lush, manicured farms on the outskirts of San Diego. Row after row of makeshift shanties climbing the hills were thrown together out of scrap lumber, out of the termite-infested timbers that were trucked here from Southern California—and sold as housing material. The poor people of Tijuana are dressed in castaway clothes shipped in from San Diego, Los Angeles and San Francisco. Old shirts, dress pants, dresses and blouses sell for as little as five cents, a dime or a quarter . . . When it rains, scores of shacks stuck to steep canyon slopes collapse and are carried off in flood waters. Tijuana's 35 firemen spend most of their nights going to cardboard and frame shacks accidentally set ablaze by candles or kerosene lamps, sole source of light in most homes. Yet, still the people flock to Tijuana . . . for this is the frontier, the land of opportunity.[25]

The conditions of the people who live in Calcutta in *bustees* are even more extreme:

More than 57 percent of multi-member families live in no more than one room. Of these families, over one half have 30 square feet or less per family member. Only 7 percent of the city's families live in separate flats or houses, 45 percent have no electricity, 36 percent cook in the living room, and 78 percent have no separate kitchen. . . . Educational facilities are provided for little more than fifty percent of the children of school-going age. Thus, a very large proportion of the city's children never receive formal education. . . . The number of cholera cases alone ranges between 5,800 and 9,200 a year. . . . Nearly one third of the city's families have no water tap at all (and must use street taps from which no more than some ten gallons per head per day can be drawn), and almost two-thirds share taps with other families. The same proportion of families are without a bath and must use street taps and hydrants, the latter providing only unfiltered water. . . . The sanitary removal of human wastes from continuous daily contact with people is now being provided for much less than 40 percent of the people of the area. . . . Most of the roads outside of certain elite areas are potholed and strewn with garbage, and many of them are patched up only on the eve of a municipal election. Lighting is either lacking or extremely poor. . . . Only ten percent of multi-member families have at least one privy for their own use, and twelve percent have no access to any privy at all. It is not surprising to find that many side streets are used as public lavatories. . . . Cows and buffaloes live all over the city.[26]

Observing Calcutta, a correspondent for the *New York Times* writes, "It is easy to understand why pronouncements about a 'final breakdown' fail to jolt anyone into action in Calcutta, for it takes a cruel and restless imagination to grasp the concept of a breakdown any more final than the one with which the city is already confronted."[27]

Two points should be stressed about performance in Third World cities. One is that conditions in the spontaneous settlements are not uniformly bad. Actually, squatter cities—just like regular cities and suburbs—come in all sizes, shapes, and varieties. They range greatly in the class of people who have built them and who inhabit them, in their facilities, in the quality of housing, and in the quality of neighborhood life. At one extreme might be a spontaneous settlement in Mexico City, *Colonia Militar,* which, in Wayne Cornelius' description, "originated as a highly organized, swiftly executed [land] invasion led by army officers employed at a nearby military installation."

The initial invasion group met frequently over a two-year period prior to occupation of the land formerly the site of a commercial sand-mining operation. During the organizational period as well as subsequent to the invasion, access to the settlement was carefully restricted to exclude 'undesirables,' defined either as persons with criminal records or those lacking sufficient income to build a permanent dwelling and improve their property within a relatively short period of time. The selective recruitment of settlers, as well as much careful attention devoted to street layout and grading, sanitation, the installation of regular electrical service (at the expense of the settlers), and the building of a school and a church were intended to give the settlement an appearance of order and permanence, thus reducing the danger of eviction by the government. But an even more important factor explaining the absence of serious eviction attempts during the first eight years following the invasion was the presence of large numbers of public employees—army officers and enlisted men, lower-level bureaucrats, teachers, and policemen—who had taken up residence in the settlement.[28]

Some squatter settlements in the Third World are inhabited by lower-middle-class people with considerable concern for, and ability to do something about, the quality of life in the settlement, including securing benign government attention. There are probably many more settlements—those inhabited by the poor—which have some facilities; housing built of semipermanent or permanent materials; and only some ability to negotiate with government for improvements.

Beneath these—what Laquian calls "the slums of hope"—are what he calls the "slums of despair": horrendous places with high rates of crime, of personal and family breakdown, and of unemployment and underemployment; total or nearly total lack of potable water, paved streets, sewerage and drainage, street lights, and electricity; absent or nearly absent public services such as police and fire protection, mail delivery, health clinics, schools, markets, and bus lines; housing made of mud, cardboard, tin cans, with dirt floors and six or seven people living in a single room; and, perhaps most gravely, little community cohesion, organization, or leadership.[29]

But we must remember that, in some ways, performance may not be lower in the Third World cities than in the cities of the advanced world. Third World slums in some ways are better than slums in the advanced world: they are not, like American urban ghettos, centers of decline, decay, and disorganization—but are often centers of growth and optimism about the future. Third World cities—in both the legal and irregular sections—often have less crime than advanced cities. There is often much to admire and much to be charmed by in Third World cities, including the more relaxed pace of life, the traditional crafts, and the quality of interpersonal relations. Certainly for the elites, as we have said, Third World cities have much to offer in the way of old and new amenities.

Nonetheless, for many nonelites in Third World cities, life is neither relaxed or charming, but "brutish, nasty, and short." As the Gallup International Survey suggests (see p. 79), people in the poorer countries lead anxious, worried lives; they have fewer satisfactions; they worry less about the cost of living than getting enough food; and they live in physical surroundings of sometimes indescribable squalor. Why is this so?

RURAL UNDERDEVELOPMENT

One reason why nations receive a share of world income inferior to that of their population is the extreme poverty of their rural areas. Low national income—in predominantly agricultural nations—derives from extremely low productivity in the countryside: people on the land produce little more than they consume. Low productivity in the rural areas of theThird World is accompanied by high birth rates, poor education and training, poor nutrition and health, isolation from the outside, little leisure, low incomes, and few services (for example, electricity). As J. S. Forrester has stressed, urban performance is a function of rural performance: "The over-all condition or urban life for any particular economic class or population cannot be appreciably better or worse than that of the remainder of the country to and from which people may come."[30]

Paradoxically, even "improvements" in the countryside can further depress rural conditions: mechanization reduces the need for labor, and migration of young people to the cities leaves the rural areas to the sick and old, the women and children. A further paradox is that although the improvements in the urban areas—even rapid economic growth—provide added resources, they also stimulate heavy migration from the less fortunate areas.

Another cause of poor performance in Third World cities is the explosive rate of population growth—a growth based both on heavy migration and on heavy rates of natural increase (that is, excess of births over deaths). The cities of the West during their period of most rapid expansion never matched today's Third World cities in expansion rates. One reason was that they grew largely from migration; the rate of natural increase in the cities was held down by extreme death rates. The cities of the Third World are not the death traps that the cities of the West were in the nineteenth century. Modern public health and medicine—the modern means of "death control"—are highly effective, even in Third World cities, in reducing mortality rates.

Third World cities are characterized by extreme rates of natural increase. Table 5-2 starkly contrasts the LDC cities and European cities in the rate of natural increase—a contrast in growth rate that exists independently of internal migration rates (though it reflects them). Thus, even were the flood of rural migrants into Third World cities to cease entirely, those cities would still face an overwhelming task of providing enough housing, employment, and subsistence for their populations. A natural increase rate of 35% per year (the rate shown in Table 5-2 for Tripoli, Libya) means that a city will double its population every twenty years without further migration! In Third World cities there are typically at least twice as many births as deaths; in places like Seoul, Teheran, Bangkok, Baghdad, and Manila, there are more than five times as many births as deaths. In advanced cities, births barely outnumber deaths (about 1.7 to 1 in American cities); in Central and Northern European cities, like Vienna, West and East Berlin, Budapest, Hamburg, and Prague, there are far more deaths than births. There is *no* natural increase in any West German city![31]

Natural increase rates are likely to remain high in the Third World and low in the advanced world. The Gallup International Survey found that most people in the advanced countries were opposed to further population growth and thought that families should have, as an ideal, two children. In Africa, Latin America, and the Far East, there was general support for rapid population growth and the ideal family was considered the one with four or more children!

Migratory pressures on Third World cities are also intense. The Gallup Survey found intense desires on the part of Third World rural populations to move to the city. Although most people in the advanced world would prefer to live in small towns, villages, or rural areas, most rural dwellers in Africa, Latin America, and Asia want to come to the very largest cities. Although only 13% of the people in North America and 19% of the people in Western Europe prefer living in a city of 100,000 or more, 36% of the people in Latin America and 40% of the people in Sub-Saharan Africa would like to do so. Only in the Far East (India and Japan) did 17% of the people prefer the big city, most people preferring either the small town (10,000 to 100,000) or the rural area. In the United States, preference for big city living was

Table 5-2   Comparative City Growth:
             The Impact of Birth Rates

Natural Increase Rate (Births minus Deaths)
per 1000 Residents c. 1970

Manila, Philippines	+47.6
Recife, Brazil	42.0
Saigon, Vietnam	36.7
Tripoli, Libya	34.9
Bangkok, Thailand	33.6
Panama City, Panama	30.3
Mexico City, Mexico	28.5
Brasília, Brazil	26.5
Tunis, Tunisia	25.6
Madras, India	25.6
Accra, Ghana	21.6
Taipei, Taiwan	20.8
Quito, Ecuador	19.6
Cairo, United Arab Republic	19.3
Madrid, Spain	17.5
Naples, Italy	16.4
Hong Kong	15.8
Tokyo, Japan	14.3
Colombo, Sri Lanka	13.0
Dublin, Ireland	12.4
Edmonton, Canada	11.6
DETROIT	8.8
ATLANTA	8.7
Belgrade, Yugoslavia	7.7
NEW YORK	7.1
NEW ORLEANS	5.6
Lisbon, Portugal	4.3
London, England	4.2
Moscow, USSR	1.8
Zürich, Switzerland	−0.2
Budapest, Hungary	−0.4
Copenhagen, Denmark	−0.4
Brussels, Belgium	−2.3
Stockholm, Sweden	−2.6
East Berlin, GDR	−2.9
Prague, Czechoslovakia	−3.8
Hamburg, West Germany	−4.5
Vienna, Austria	−7.1
West Berlin, West Germany	−9.6

Source: R. Fried, *World Hanbook of Cities,* Ch. 12.

expressed by 13% of the people, as compared to 11% in France and Britain, 29% in Mexico, and 32% in Brazil.[32]

Thus, a large part of the growth of Third World cities is due to migration, as shown in Table 5-3.

High natural increase rates combine with high immigration rates to produce explosive growth rates in most cities of the Third World. (See Table 5-4.) The average increase rate of the urban population in Asia, Southern Europe, Africa, the Middle East, and Latin America in the period 1940-1960 was 4.2% for all cities above 20,000 people and 7.3% for cities above 100,000.[33] An annual growth rate of 4.2 means that a city doubles population in less than seventeen years; a growth rate of 7.3% means that a city doubles its population every ten years! Thus, not only is the Third World city growth rate extraordinary, it tends to be focused on the larger cities. To double the services of a city—its dwellings, water supply, electricity, street paving, schools, markets, police stations, clinics, hospitals, buses, sewers, and drains—every twenty years would strain the resources of the wealthiest cities; to double them every ten years is clearly beyond the capabilities of any city.[34] Thus the service gap in Third World cities is immediately related to the facts of demography.

Remarkably, in many, perhaps most, large cities in the Third World, the regular population—people living in regularly subdivided settlements—is growing rather slowly and even declining: the population explosion is occurring mostly in the uncontrolled squatter settlements. Between 1965 and 1970, the regular population of Ankara, Turkey, dropped from 519,000 to 500,000, while the uncontrolled settlements grew (at a rate of 10% per year!) from 460,000 to 750,000. Between 1952 and 1966, the regular population of Mexico City dropped from 2 million down to

Table 5-3   Comparative City Growth: The Impact of Migration

City	Period	Total Population Increase (Thousands)	Migrants as an Estimated Percentage of Total Population Increase
Abidjan	1955-1963	129	76
Bogotá	1956-1966	930	33
Bombay	1951-1961	1207	52
Caracas	1950-1960	587	54
	1960-1966	501	50
Jakarta	1961-1968	1528	59
Istanbul	1950-1960	672	68
	1960-1965	428	65
Lagos	1952-1962	393	75
Nairobi	1961-1969	162	50
São Paulo	1950-1960	2163	72
	1960-1967	2543	68
Seoul	1955-1965	1697	63
Taipei	1950-1960	396	40
	1960-1967	326	43

Source: *World Bank Operations,* p. 482.

Table 5-4   Comparative City Growth: The Impact of Birth Rates and Migration

Country	Estimated Percentage of Annual Growth Rate of Urban Centers, 1960-1970	Principal City	Annual Growth Rate of Principal City, 1960-1970
Botswana	3.3	Gaberones	N.A.
Burundi	7.2	Bujumbura	N.A.
Kenya	5.1	Nairobi	6.0
Tanzania	8.6	Dar es Salaam	9.0
Uganda	9.2	Kampala	9.2
Ethiopia	2.4	Addis Ababa	3.9
Lesotho	7.9	Maseru	N.A.
Malagasy	4.3	Tananarive	5.6
Malawi	10.1	Blantyre Limbe	N.A.
Mauritius	5.3	Port Louis	N.A.
Rwanda	8.3	Kigali	N.A.
Somalia	6.0	Mogadiscio	N.A.
Sudan	4.3	Khartoum	3.4
Swaziland	9.4	Mbabane	N.A.
Zaire	3.9	Kinshasa	10.0
Zambia	6.4	Lusaka	N.A.
Cameroon	6.8	Douala	4.0
Central African Republic	8.4	Bangui	N.A.
Chad	7.9	Fort Lamy	N.A.
Congo Peoples Republic	5.4	Brazzaville	4.0
Dahomey	6.0	Cotonou	N.A.
Gabon	6.5	Libreville	N.A.
Gambia	3.8	Bathurst	N.A.
Ghana	6.8	Accra	6.8
Guinea	6.6	Conakry	7.0
Ivory Coast	9.3	Abidjan	11.0
Liberia	10.4	Monrovia	—
Mali	5.7	Bamako	5.6
Mauritania	2.4	Nouakchott	—
Niger	2.4	Niamey	—
Nigeria	6.0	Lagos	—
Senegal	4.0	Dakar	6.0
Sierra Leone	3.8	Freetown	—
Togo	8.2	Lome	—
Upper Volta	5.1	Ouagadougou	—
British Solomon Islands	4.7	—	—
China (Taiwan)	4.1	Taipei	4.7
Fiji	3.9	—	—
Indonesia	4.2	Jakarta	4.7
Khmer	4.8	Phnom Penh	7.6
Korea, South	4.1	Seoul	8.0
Malaysia	5.9	Kuala Lumpur	4.0
Papua and New Guinea	7.3	—	—
Philippines	4.3	Manila	4.3

Table 5-4   Comparative City Growth: The Impact of Birth Rates and Migration (continued)

Country	Estimated Percentage of Annual Growth Rate of Urban Centers, 1960-1970	Principal City	Annual Growth Rate of Principal City, 1960-1970
Singapore	2.6	Singapore	2.6
Thailand	4.5	Bangkok	6.0
Afghanistan	2.3	Kabul	3.2
Ceylon	3.6	Colombo	2.8
India	2.9	Calcutta	1.8
Iran	4.8	Teheran	6
Nepal	8.0	Katmandu	7.9
Pakistan	4.3	Karachi	5.6
Cyprus	3.9	Nicosia	—
Egypt, United Arab Republic	4.0	Cairo	4.1
Finland	2.7	Helsinki	3.2
Greece	1.6	Athens	3.0
Iceland	2.7	Reykjavik	—
Iraq	4.0	Baghdad	4.4
Israel	3.7	Tel Aviv	3.0
Jordan	4.8	Amman	4.5
Lebanon	4.0	Beirut	3.4
Morocco	4.9	Casablanca	4.2
Portugal	1.7	Lisbon	1.2
Southern Yemen	4.2	—	—
Spain	1.7	Madrid	2.8
Syria	3.4	Damascus	2.4
Tunisia	3.2	Tunis	.8
Turkey	4.2	Istanbul	5.0
Yemen Arab Republic	5.9	—	—
Yugoslavia	4.8	Belgrade	3.7

1.8 million; the population of the uncontrolled settlements rose (at a rate of 11% per annum!) from 330,000 to 1,500,000. A similar drop and rise occurred in Caracas, Venezuela. Thus, it is easy to understand why 35% of Caracas' population resided in the squatter settlements by 1964; by 1966, the figure for Mexico City was 46%; by 1970, the figure for Ankara was 60%.[35]

Note that the rate of urbanization in the Third World is not much higher than it is in the advanced world or than it was in the industrial nations at the peak of their urban growth. Paradoxically, the cities of the Third World are growing at enormously faster rates than the cities of the advanced world, yet the rate of urbanization is not high. The reason for this paradox is that, if urbanization means a shift in the proportion of the total population in favor of urban areas, this shift is occurring only very slowly, despite impressive migration rates. Unlike the rural areas of the West during the nineteenth century (which emptied their populations into their own cities or cities overseas), the rural areas of the Third World are growing at ex-

Table 5-4 Comparative City Growth: The Impact of Birth Rates and Migration (continued)

Country	Estimated Percentage of Annual Growth Rate of Urban Centers, 1960-1970	Principal City	Annual Growth Rate of Principal City, 1960-1970
Costa Rica	4.6	San Jose	5.4
Dominican Republic	5.7	Santo Domingo	5.9
El Salvador	4.0	San Salvador	4.6
Guatemala	4.9	Guatemala City	5.0
Guyana	3.2	Georgetown	3.1
Honduras	5.2	Tegucigalpa	5.9
Jamaica	4.3	Kingston	5.0
Mexico	5.2	Mexico City	5.0
Nicaragua	4.6	Managua	5.9
Panama	4.4	Panama	4.9
Trinidad & Tobago	6.0	Port of Spain	—
Venezuela	5.6	Caracas	5.5
Argentina	2.4	Buenos Aires	3.0
Bolivia	2.4	La Paz	2.3
Brazil	4.6	São Paulo	6.4
Chile	3.4	Santiago	3.1
Colombia	5.0	Bogotá	7.0
Ecuador	4.7	Guayaquil	5.9
Paraguay	3.5	Asunción	3.6
Peru	3.3	Lima	5.1
Uruguay	2.9	Montevideo	4.7

Source: *World Bank Operations,* pp. 478-481.

tremely high rates. High birth rates and sharply declining death rates means that the rural areas are holding their own in the competition for shares of the total population.[36] Thus, in the Third World, we have rapid urban growth without urbanization, at least in one sense of the term!

Rapid immigration has negative consequences for performance, other than creating a huge unmet need for services. Rural migrants add to the pool of the un-skilled unemployed. Those who have difficulty in finding steady employment or in otherwise adjusting to their new urban environment account for much of the social disorganization in Third World cities: the "juvenile delinquency, drunkenness, murder, theft, and robbery." They provide raw materials for the "political demonstrations and rioting [that] dislocate traffic, trade, and production and result in the loss of property and sometimes even of life."[37]

While migrants in advanced cities face similar problems of adaptation, the pace of the migratory flow in the Third World is such that it magnifies adjustment problems. Given the poverty of most migrants, it is impossible for them to afford even minimum-quality, regular housing in an officially authorized subdivision. The result is the multiplication of squatter settlements around Third World cities that provide rent-free land. Then, too, coming from rural areas, migrants are apt to bring with them poor health habits, little family educational background, casual notions of public sanitation, and rural attitudes towards punctuality.

Although some of their characteristics generate community problems, other characteristics can be viewed positively. Migrants are often ambitious and skilled enough to build their own housing. They may have greater social solidarity than older residents and, thus, be able to cope with problems through informal arrangements. Coming from rural villages that are so much worse than the big city, their expectations are lower and they may cope more easily with hardships and deprivations than can their less rugged "city cousins." When, as is often the case, migrants come into the city expecting to stay only temporarily—until, say, enough money is earned to buy some farm land—they may also be less prone than long-term residents to be concerned about poor performance.

GOVERNMENTAL VARIABLES

Although in advanced nations there are strong and relatively stable political systems capable of formulating and implementing policies for cities, in the poorer countries urbanization is occurring without this framework of national loyalties, legitimate national government, and disciplined public administration. Political instability—frequent military coups and political upheavals—makes it difficult for government officials to plan ahead, implement plans, or pay much attention to anything except political survival. Because of the interpenetration of national and local levels of government, national instability has a strong local impact: national coups usually lead to massive purges of officials at the local level.

Second, governmental officials, national and local, may not be performance-oriented, oriented, that is, to the production of concrete improvement in conditions. Their energies may be absorbed in personal, factional, or ethnic rivalries. They may be more concerned with keeping the military happy through generous military expenditures than with the task of social and economic reform and improvement. In 1974, the developing countries spent 5.3% of their meager GNP on military expenditures, as compared to 5.8% in the more advanced countries.[38] Where the performance gap is so great, as it often is in the Third World, rulers may prefer to accent symbolic or foreign politics rather than domestic performance politics.

Third, the performance of local urban authorities tends to be rather poor, although the local officials often valiantly struggle to do their best despite political interference, the lack of public support, and the shortage of money and skills. Pressures towards centralization are very strong despite initial ideological bias in favor of decentralization and local autonomy in many of the new nations, particularly in the former British colonies.[39] Thus, central controls over local authorities have multiplied; ministers have to approve all contracts, appointments, dismissals; vital functions and key personnel have been transferred to or retained by central administrative agencies. Ministries and public corporations may come to do most of the vital work in urban government: preserving basic health and safety; building and designing public works and housing; planning; providing public transportation; and supplying water. One central government agency in Santiago, the capital, is responsible for constructing sidewalks in all the cities up and down the 2500-mile length of Chile![40]

Where the central government does not directly operate urban services, it often exercises penetrating controls, requiring local officials to secure central approval for all their major decisions: projects, budgets, personnel appointments and dismissals, contracts, and loans. Local councils, where elected councils are permitted, can be and often are dissolved by central action. When national governments themselves are either of recent origins or plagued with chronic instability, they are prone to regard local autonomy with suspicion—all the more so when professional talent is scarce and is concentrated at the national level.

The result is that urban government in the Third World tends to be virtually a branch of national government. The central government tends to raise and spend most of the money and employ most of the staffs responsible for urban government. Whereas in the more advanced countries, provincial and local authorities tend to raise and spend 20% to 50% of all government revenues and expenditures, in the developing areas, they tend to raise between zero and 15%. Where resources are scarce, central governments take the lion's share—sometimes to keep money out of the hands of unreliable or corrupt local officials, sometimes so as to have the money available for purposes of building support for the national regime.

Often inheriting the attitudes of the former colonial authorities, central governments tend to have little respect for local authorities and little disposition to grant them power or autonomy. The weakness of local urban governments is part of a general institutional weakness throughout society: urban local governments are weak much as trade unions, business firms, and professional associations are weak. Municipal enterprise is as difficult to stimulate as enterprise and development in other sectors of society.

But centralization—direct national operation of urban services and/or tight central control over local operations—does not always mean less corruption or greater effectiveness. National agencies are often afflicted by many of the same problems that debilitate lower levels of government: lack of money, lethargy, and lack of skills. Quite often centralization simply means endless delay before central authorities act on local projects. Central officials are much more removed than local officials from pressures for action and from responsibility for blunders. Quite typically, there is a division of labor between central and local officials which allows each level to blame the other for poor performance.

Fourth, Third World countries lack highly trained, professionalized urban bureaucracies. For example, comparative studies of education show that teachers in Third World countries tend to be much less well trained than teachers in the advanced countries. In a large-scale international survey of education on the same science test of the International Education Association, science *teachers* from a developing country scored below the average for secondary school *students* from advanced countries.[41]

Urban bureaucracies in the Third World are far more likely than those in advanced countries to be "welfare bureaucracies"—bureaucracies whose major function is to give employment rather than produce services. Typically, Third World bureaucracies are vastly overstaffed but underproductive since they are not performance-oriented. Pay scales are extremely low; this allows many people to be given jobs, but forces most of them either to moonlight or to accept illicit sources of income. The pace of activity is typically very slow. Periodic efforts to reduce corruption result in the proliferation of checks, counterchecks, controls, and clearances, the result of which is to bog action down in a morass of red tape—red tape that seldom eliminates corruption. Typical perhaps of most urban bureaucracies is the postal service: delivery tends to be slow; packages or letters with resale value do not get delivered; letters are delivered to the wrong addresses; and only the central districts are covered.

Fifth, there is obviously the question of finance—ability and willingness to raise the revenues necessary for high performance. To be sure, money isn't everything: quite different performance can be gotten from the same resources. Yet, finance does set basic parameters. Thus, for example, the developing countries have more than three-fourths of the world's children, but they spend only 8.6% of the world's education budget![42] (One result seems to be that it takes one-and-a-half years of school in developing areas to achieve the same results obtained in advanced countries in one year.)[43]

Obviously it is not possible to tax the people of Third World cities at the same pressure as in the richer cities: people at very low income levels need most of their income for bare necessities. But even so, tax pressure is often lower than it might be, given the institutional and cultural problems of taxation in low-income countries. Tax administrators tend to be inefficient and corruptible. There is widespread cultural approval of tax evasion. There are few giant industrial or commercial establishments (or workers) to tax, but rather more difficult categories: farmers, small retailers, and the casually employed and underemployed.[44] Since income is difficult to tax in poor countries, reliance is usually made on sales and property taxes, both of which tend to hit hardest the city's poorest families.

Sixth and finally, government bears some of the responsibility for poor urban performance through its policies, decisions, and actions, as well as through its nonpolicies, nondecisions, and inaction. Government may actually create poor conditions, as when soldiers or policemen commit, rather than prevent, robberies and murders.

Most of Uganda's robberies are attributed to undisciplined soldiers. When their pay is late, they help themselves to whatever they see in a shop and justify it by saying the shopowner was hoarding or overcharging. In Zaire, drunken soldiers who need beer money on Saturday night will set up impromptu roadblocks along the airport road and assess instant import duties *on valuables carried by visitors in taxicabs. A reporter paid $20 five times to get a portable typewriter into town. "I asked a Tanzanian official why they didn't give guns to the policemen here to cut down on crime," said an American in Dar es Salaam. "And he laughed. 'Give them guns,' he said, 'Who do you think are the biggest robbers?' "*[45]

Government also depresses conditions when, as in developing countries all over the world, it sends bulldozers into squatter settlements to destory the dwellings and drive people off—without providing some alternative shelter, except, perhaps, in some extremely remote new settlement.

Governments are often hostile to spontaneous settlements, and for a variety of reasons. *Bidonvilles, favelas,* and *ranchos* reflect poorly on the government's ability to exercise its sovereignty. Thousands of people are simply ignoring the law, property rights, and urban plans in order to construct their own "do-it-yourself" cities. Squatter settlements are often built near diplomatic or expensive residential districts and, thus, they are regarded as eyesores or as insults to the propertied elite. But there are other grounds—besides vanity—for opposing squatter settlements, including the fact that squatters frequently build chaotically, leaving no space for the future installation of roads, schools, markets, or stream embankments. They often build in such a way as to block access to unoccupied land that could be used for industry or additional residential settlement. Although squatter settlements have the advantage of providing cheap housing, they have the disadvantage of being located far from the centers of employment; thus, workers who settle in them have to spend some of the money they save in rent on transportation.

Squatter settlements tend to be low-density and remote from the center. Where (as in Hong Kong, for example) multistory dwellings are built nearer the center in more compact forms of development, workers are nearer the places of employment, shoppers can be nearer stores, and the necessary utilities and services can be brought in much more cheaply. Rich countries can afford suburban sprawl; poor countries cannot afford their largely uncontrolled form of suburban sprawl, nor can many of them imitate Hong Kong in a massive public housing program. Typically, they ask their city planners (or foreign consultants) to draw up plans for the regular and rational expansion of the city; the resulting plans are often based on the latest Western ideas on urban design and use the most enlightened Western standards for the quality of housing and neighborhoods. Such plans typically take little account of the illegal settlements that surround and engulf the legal city. Just as typically, such plans—while they serve to ingratiate international sources of financial aid—have little impact on actual development.

The major response of most Third World governments to the spread of squatter settlements—aside from periodic demolition and "paper planning"—is inaction, tempered by gradual recognition of the settlement's de facto, if not de jure, existence. Whether government gives title to the land and whether it brings in some services (seldom all) depends a good deal on the initiative of the squatter settlement leadership.[46] Governments mostly pursue a policy of "benign neglect" because they feel politically powerless to evict the settlers, once the settlements have been established. (The rule in some Mediterranean countries like Italy and Turkey is that once a dwelling is roofed, it cannot morally—at least—be demolished. Dwellings are frantically constructed in Turkish and Italian cities during the night so that by dawn, when the police arrive, the dwellings have their protective roofing.) Squatters may have little positive power to get facilities from governments, but they are often effectively organized for defensive purposes. Many politicians in the Third World build personal followings by becoming the defenders of squatter settlements and arranging for water or electricity to be brought in.

Another reason for governmental impotence in dealing with squatter settlements is the fact that Third World cities have fragmented government much like cities in the advanced world. Thus, Manila is governed by eight, mutually antagonistic authorities; Mexico City is divided up between the Federal District and its agencies and the municipalities of the State of Mexico; Buenos Aires is similarly split up between local, state, and federal authorities. Central city authorities often refuse to service squatter settlements that happen to fall into a neighboring jurisdiction: the rival governments often refuse to join in regional schemes to relocate squatters into more regular dwellings or settlements. Although most Third World governments are authoritarian rather than pluralistic, there is little effective power anywhere in the system to reorganize the government of major cities. The authoritarian structure consists of numerous feudal satrapies whose rivalries and mutual antagonisms allow them to be more easily dominated by the central elite.

Then, too, strong action to improve conditions in the uncontrolled settlements is impeded by the fact that much of national policy making is dominated by economists—professionals, who tend to take a dim view of investment in such unproductive things as housing and neighborhood improvement. Capital is scarce; providing decent housing and neighborhoods is prohibitively expensive; thus, the economic planners much prefer investments in agriculture, industry, and transportation. The building of housing and neighborhood improvement is left to the self-help efforts of the squatters.

Another factor inhibiting positive action by government to create better housing and neighborhoods is the political power of real estate interests. Third World cities typically contain large unoccupied tracts of land that are being held for speculative purposes. Real estate speculation is one of the most profitable forms of private investment—given the huge demand for urban land and rapid inflation. Property tends to be taxed at unrealistic rates, partly because of the power of landowners in national and local politics. Thus, land tends to be costly—too costly for government to purchase in order to provide cheap land—legal land—for the army of would-be urban settlers.[47]

Some Third World countries have attempted to stem the tide of illegal urbanism by pouring investments into other parts of the country and steering investments away from the major focus of migration. They seek to alleviate pressures on the big city or at least prevent them from getting worse by holding people on the land through the promotion of a few centers of growth to rival the big city. In few countries have attempts to reduce rural-urban migration been successful. Population growth in rural areas proceeds too rapidly for rural development schemes to have much of a chance. Migrants and investors still prefer the same big city location as before. The results of decentralization—of attempts to reduce the attractiveness of the big city—by diverting public funds from the big city to other parts of the country have been negative. Little development has occurred elsewhere, while the quality of life in the great urban center merely deteriorates.

The only leverage over performance that can be had is through birth control. Policies for "death control"—since they are culturally quite acceptable and rather easily applied—have been all too successful. Policies for "birth control"—since they are culturally unacceptable and applied only with difficulty—have not been successful. Population growth is still seen positively by too many people—by the masses of the people (seeking security) and by government elites (seeking national grandeur). But even a strong and effective population policy, if adopted, can bear fruit only in a generation. For the immediate decades, the die has been cast.

URBAN PERFORMANCE IN THE COMMUNIST WORLD

6

Modernization—the level of modernization (economic development) achieved—is the prime determinant of most forms of urban government performance. Next in importance is the *type* of modernization: whether urban development takes place under capitalist democracy, under communist, "proletarian" dictatorship, or some type in between. About one-quarter of the world's cities are developing under communism. Most of these cities are in the Soviet Union (222 metropolitan areas with more than 100,000 people) and China (139). The others are located in Eastern Europe (Yugoslavia 19; Poland 16; Romania 14; East Germany 11; Czechoslovakia 6; Bulgaria 6; Hungary 5; Albania 1); in Cuba (6); and in Asia (North Korea 9; Vietnam 9; Laos 1; Khmer Republic 1; Outer Mongolia 1).[1]

Cities under communism share a number of characteristics.[2]

- Political control is exercised by a hierarchical, disciplined, highly ideological political machine, the Communist party, which tolerates no rival competitor for power.
- There is total control (or attempted total control) by the party of all organizations in society, all units of production, all units of government, all associations, all media of communication, and all educational institutions. Resistance, dissent, or unauthorized criticism are not allowed.
- The function of the media is to implement party policy; only information about government, politics, and society that is likely to have the "correct" impact on public opinion is allowed to be published.
- Social and economic development is steered and controlled through central planning agencies that impose goals and resources on all institutions in government and society.
- Work is compulsory: good work is rewarded, low productivity is penalized.
- Property in land and the other major means of production (capital, resources, machinery) is vested in the state (that is, the party).

- Government organs—national, regional, and local—are dominated by the party.
- The state determines, in accordance with the central plan, the capital to be invested in any industry and in any locality. It decides, again according to the plan, the occupations people will be trained for, where they will live, the quality of their housing, and the kind of goods they can buy and at what prices.
- The state determines what is scientifically, religiously, and culturally "correct" for people to believe, and the party line defines "the public interest."
- Partisanship—adherence to the party line—is considered desirable and necessary in art, science, religion, sports, business, government, and justice.
- Great efforts are made to enlist active and enthusiastic mass participation in the execution of party decisions. Voluntary effort on the part of individuals, neighborhood groups, and mass organizations is used to administer many programs, including law enforcement and minor criminal justice.
- The division of labor among institutions (government, party, the military, public institutions, labor unions, and economic ministries) is kept confused so as to preserve the monopolistic control of the party.
- Public administration has a huge scope: public authorities are responsible for ministering to all social needs; planning and managing the economy; executing party orders in all spheres; stimulating and supervising any institutions outside the formal framework of government.
- The presumption is normally in favor of the rights of the State over the rights of individuals.
- The authority of the party rests upon its quasi-infallible knowledge of, and commitment to, the interests of humanity.
- The ultimate goal is a classless society based on material abundance and individual selflessness.

Under communism, urban government is, thus, part of the machinery to carry out the "party line." According to communist theory (at least of the Soviet variety), under the dictatorship of the proletariat, the conflicting class interests characteristic of capitalist society no longer exist. The Communist party represents the ruling proletariat; any other organization must, by definition, represent some foreign or domestic class enemy. Any newspaper, TV station, political group, labor group, religious group, group of authors, scientists, or artists that claim the right to make independent judgements about "truth" or "policy" and to resist acceptance of the party line must, by definition, be counterrevolutionary and working to restore the power of feudal landowners or the capitalist bourgeoisie.

Urban government is more important in communist cities than in western democratic cities because government performs so many functions—functions that are privately performed (or not performed at all) in the West. Party and government provide goods and services that are produced in the private sector in Western democratic cities. More significantly, party and government feel responsible for molding the entire social, intellectual, and moral life of the community, for creating new kinds of human beings, for changing mentalities derived from the bourgeois past, and for mobilizing intense enthusiasm for new programs in all spheres of life.

Communism is incompatible with most forms of governmental liberalism. Ideologically, communists reject the principles of due process as being, in their eyes, designed to protect the rights and interests of the bourgeoisie, rather than, as Westerners tend to think, the rights and interests of all. Law is seen as necessarily permitting some class or classes to rule and as being designed to further class interests and not as promoting and protecting individual rights, except of those controlling the means of production. Even when the proletariat comes to power, law continues to protect class interests, except that the proletariat is a class whose interests (in theory) coincide with that of the whole people. Law is not seen as a restraint on government, but as a coercive tool of the party-state in communism. The rights of the state have clear priority over individual rights.[3] Even more antagonistic to human rights is the systematic use or threat of terror as a means to hold power and to implement policy by repressing real, imagined, or pretended enemies of the regime. Terror is unpredictable repression: against opponents, against factional enemies, sometimes, at least in the past, simply against those who fail to perform. To be fully effective, terror must happen not only to the guilty but, potentially, to anyone, guilty or not. In this way a climate is created in which dissent stays within bounds.

It is hard for the communist elite to accept restrictions on its ability to act. The elite, while (in its own eyes) representing the hopes of humanity, is surrounded by numerous and powerful class enemies, both within and outside. Moreover, (again in its own eyes) it holds a monopoly on truth in all its forms. To curb the party's power or to limit the dictatorship of the proletariat, would permit subversive ideas and forces to threaten the liberation of humanity.

Urban government in communist systems takes place within a framework of constitutions, laws, and courts, but none of these institutions are designed to limit the action of government officials unless the party so determines. However, there are pressures within communist systems for some lawfulness, some rule of law, some conformity with constitutional guarantees of due process. The lawless terror of the Stalin period (1925-1953) in the Soviet Union was condemned at the highest levels by Stalin's successors, who moved to establish some measure of "socialist legality" in the operations of Soviet government. Most political prisoners were released from the concentration camps; the secret police lost much of its power; and greater independence was given to the courts in preventing and punishing illegal behavior, whether official or private. Dissenters are now sent to mental hospitals, rather than labor camps.

The official guardians of legal values in communist cities are the Procurators. Following the Soviet model, a network of centrally controlled procurators has been established in communist countries with sweeping powers over both government officials and citizens. In China, under the 1954 Constitution, the procurators have a number of impressive functions and powers:

1. To supervise the decisions, orders, and measures of local state organs to ensure their conformity with law, and to supervise persons working in organs of state and citizens to ensure observance of law;

2. To enquire into criminal cases, conduct public prosecution, and support public prosecution;

3. To supervise the investigatory activities of the investigatory organs in order to ensure their conformity with law;

4. To supervise the adjudicatory activities of the people's courts to ensure their conformity with law;

5. To supervise the execution of the judgments of criminal cases and the activities of the organs for reform-through-work to ensure their conformity with law; and

6. To exercise the right to prosecute or join in the prosecution of important civil cases involving the interests of the state and the people.[4]

Procurators offices are, under law, completely independent of any local organs, including party organs or secret police organs, and are strictly subordinate to the national procurator general. They cannot annul illegal decisions but they can request correction by a higher authority. In theory, no one can be arrested in China, the USSR, or in any communist bloc nation without the approval of the procurator (or a court decision).

Ironically, the Soviet procuracy was granted powers such as the above by the Constitution of 1936 (the "Stalin Constitution")—at the height of the lawless terror of the Great Purges. The procuracy was easily ignored by the dictator and his henchmen. Neither in the USSR nor in China does the procuracy prevent widespread arbitrary and illegal behavior by police, government officials, or party. The police, thus, function virtually unchecked in most communist systems. In the USSR, the procuracy investigates many complaints against the police each year, but according to one study, "the feeling is general among the Soviet population that the procuracy is not overenthusiastically fulfilling this function."[5] Despite liberalization, there are still sharp limits on individual rights in communist cities. What civil rights and political rights exist, only exist at the convenience of the party. In most of the communist countries, there are no popular traditions of civil and political freedom against which current behavior can be judged. Fighting city hall is difficult in the West, where protections for individual rights have a long (if checkered) history; in communist cities, the battle is a good deal more uneven.[6]

Lack of human rights in communist regimes is also related to the fact that such regimes have been established, for the most part, in countries without a strong individualist tradition. Such traditions diminish in intensity from East Germany eastward into Eastern Europe and practically disappear in the Asian communist systems. (Cuba may be a rather more Westernized communist system.) Western cultures tend to see freedom and due process in terms of the individual; non-Western cultures tend to see them in terms of the group or community. Cultures without the experience of Western Christianity; the Roman idea of the rule of law and independent courts of law to protect individual rights; the Western spirit of individual inquiry; or the development of a powerful capitalist middle class—all lack the ideals underpinning Western concern for "human rights."

The performance of communist cities is poor in terms of due process. Is it also bad in terms of governmental integrity? Does the absence of checks and balances mean widespread corruption? Does absolute power absolutely corrupt communist city administrators?

Much in the communist system of urban control is conducive to corruption. There is, first of all, the historical legacy of corruption. In most communist countries, with the exception of East Germany and Czechoslovakia, corruption is a native tradition. Corruption was endemic in Tsarist Russia and eastern Europe, and it reached fabulous levels in precommunist China, contributing significantly to the victory of the Reds.[7] In addition to national traditions, there are other predisposing factors, such as:

1. absence of external checks on behavior, secrecy, and the ability of officials to neutralize numerous internal checks and balances through the formation of "mutual-protection societies" among those who are supposed to check on ecah other's activities;
2. government control over most of the economy and extreme pressure on managers and workers to meet their production targets (at whatever cost in irregularity or illegality);
3. the extreme scarcity of goods and, therefore, the temptation to embezzle state property and divert state property into illicit production channels or activities;
4. the adoption of extremely unpopular policies, such as those in China requiring students to leave the cities for a life in the backward countryside;
5. the general propensity of officials and employees not to act unless given some special incentive ("bureaucratism"); and
6. the allocation of so many goods, services, privileges, and immunities—housing, jobs, residence permits, food, consumer goods, building land, electricity, gas, telephone service, the right to travel, the right to publish—by the personal decision of some government official rather than by impersonal market forces.

But these sources of corruption are countered by the puritanical pride and fervor of the party and by proliferating checks and counterchecks (those of the secret police, procuracy, finance ministry, economic planning agency, civil service agency, state control ministry, party control network, the judiciary, the informer network and even local elected deputies).[8]

Which of these sets of tendencies prevails? About Soviet cities, accounts vary. David Cattell writes about Leningrad:[9]

> *Given all the checks, particularly financial checks, corruption is not easy to carry out, and the puritanism of the ideology is still sufficiently strong that the practice is frowned on by society. The general impression held by Leningrad's citizens seems to be that the local administration is often bureaucratic but not corrupt. Nevertheless, a friend in the administrative process can be*

very helpful in getting things done. The citizen or lower government official who does not have blat *(influence) or who is not a member of the in-group is frustrated by negative answers and restricting regulations and finds that it is difficult, if not impossible, to get anywhere with the bureaucracy.*

But the picture, apart from the regular organs of government, according to Hedrick Smith in *The Russians,* is rather contrasting:[10]

parallel to the official economy . . . an entire, thriving counter-economy which handles an enormous volume of hidden trade that is indispensable for institutions as well as individuals. Practically any material or service can be arranged nalevo *["under the table"] —from renting a holiday cottage in the country, buying a raincoat or a pair of good shoes in a state store, getting a smart dress made by a good seamstress, transporting a sofa across town, having the plumbing fixed or sound-proofing installed on your apartment door, being treated by a good dentist, sending your children to a private playschool, arranging home consultation with a top-flight surgeon to erecting buildings and laying pipe in a collective farm.*

This counter-economy has become an integral part of the Soviet system, a built-in, permanent feature of Soviet society. It encompasses everything from petty bribing, black marketing, wholesale thieving from the state, and underground private manufacturing all the way up to a full-fledged Godfather operation which was exposed and led to the downfall of a high Communist party figure, a candidate member of the Politburo. It operates on an almost oriental scale and with a brazen normality that would undoubtedly incense the original Bolshevik revolutionaries. Yet, ordinary people take it for granted as an essential lubricant for the rigidities of the planned economy. What the elite get legally through their special stores and system of privileges, ordinary people are forced to seek illegally in the country's counter-economy

As a general rule, corruption levels (at least outside of East Germany and Czechoslovakia, with its Hapsburg Empire heritage) are below those of the prerevolutionary times in most communist cities. Communist party officials enjoy privileges and a higher standard of living, but are not known to make personal fortunes from their positions of absolute power. Communist officials in Asia, Eastern Europe, and Cuba are probably more honest and less extortionate than their predecessors and officials in neighboring countries. Given the closed nature of communist systems, however, we cannot be very sure.

Another form of integrity is impartiality, "equal protection," or the lack of official discrimination. Given the communist emphasis on social equality, we would expect that officials in communist cities would be scrupulous to treat all citizens and groups alike. Whereas in former regimes, discrimination based on class, race, ethnicity, or religion was probably the norm, such discrimination would have no place under communism, with its drive towards a classless society.

In practice, government in communist cities has engaged in some forms of official discrimination:

- against former members of the middle and upper classes, denied access to employment, education, housing, when not liquidated or imprisoned;
- against nonparty members: party members tend to be given immunity from arrest and to be given special privileges in housing and consumer goods; they are also given most responsible positions in society;
- against religious minorities: active religionists suffer. Jews, for example, are considered a nationality rather than a religious group; they must identify themselves as Jews on all official or semiofficial forms; they are barred from many professions; governments tend to discriminate against Jews on the basis of traditional Eastern European anti-Semitism.
- political dissenters are also subject to abuse, harassment, and discrimination.

Though the Soviet Union is a multinational, multiracial society, Soviet cities do not have large racial minorities or minority ghettos simply because the racial and nationality groups tend to stay in their traditional areas: Ukrainians in the Ukraine, Georgians in Georgia, etc. The nationality figures for Leningrad, the second largest Soviet city, are as follows:

Table 6-1   Percentage of Ethnic Minorities in Leningrad

Russians	89.0
Ukrainians	2.5
White Russians	1.6
Estonians	0.2
Latvians	0.1
Lithuanians	0.1
Jews	4.1
Tatars	0.8
Poles	0.3
Finns	0.1
Armenians	0.1
Georgians	0.1
Chuvachi	0.1
Others	1.0

Source: Statisticheskii Sbornik, *LENINGRAD I LENINGRADAS-KAYA OBLASTA V TSIFRAS* (Lenizdat, 1974), p. 19.

Even so, Soviet cities are not entirely free from the racial tensions common to American and British cities. A comparative study of police-minority group relations in American, British, and Soviet cities notes:[11]

The police, whether recruited locally or not, are perceived as representatives of "Great Russian chauvinism," if not imperialism. If the difference in a given city is between a largely European militsiya [police] force and an Asian popu-

lation (as in Tashkent or Alma Ata, for example), the confrontation may sometimes take on a racial overtone. . . . In [Central Asia,] militsiya senior officers appear still to be recruited almost exclusively from the European populations of the area (these officers rarely speak the native language but commonly insist that the natives speak Russian in any police transaction); this despite the current formal program to recruit nationality cadres into the upper levels of administrative organizations.

It should be noted, however, that the Soviet regime, though dominated by Russians, has made great effort to improve the condition of national minorities, attempting to Russify them by giving them access to better living conditions, education, cultural facilities, and economic opportunity.

The Chinese also have a minority nationality problem, but again the minorities do not live among the dominant Han people in the major urban centers of industry and commerce. As in the USSR, ethnic minorities—Tibetans, Mongols, Manchus, and Moslems—are scattered around the borderlands. Although the Chinese communists are working to improve the living conditions of the fity million non-Han peoples, there have been familiar sounding, official denunciations of Han chauvinism:[12]

the Han peremptorily taking over leadership positions in minority areas instead of working through local minority officials, discriminating against minorities in the hiring and promotion of personnel . . . and [allocating] resources. Chief blame [is] placed upon an admittedly widespread attitude among the Han that they were more advanced in all fields of human endeavor.

Since the fifties, Sinification has been the major policy, with an emphasis on nation-wide uniformity in laws, institutions, and literature.

A legal, in fact a deliberate, part of communist policy is discrimination in the allocation of material goods and comforts. Under capitalism, income differences produce differences in goods and comforts based on the operation of the labor market. Under communism, it is not the impersonal market, but government that allocates goods and comforts in accordance with income differences. Equalization of conditions may be the ultimate communist objective, but in existing communist cities, inequalities exist in accordance with the principle expressed in Article 12 of the Soviet Constitution.

Article 12: Work in the USSR is a duty and a matter of honor for every able-bodied citizen, in accordance with the principle: "He who does not work, neither shall he eat." The principle applied in the USSR is that of socialism: "From each according to his ability, to each according to his work."

Thus there are major social-economic inequalities in all communist cities.

- In North Korea, housing is divided into five types according to size and quality, and then allocated according to occupational responsibility. The lowest grade goes to general laborers and office workers; the highest grade goes to high government and party officials. Once an individual has been assigned quarters, he cannot move to better quarters unless he is promoted in occupational rank.[13]

• There are major inequalities in Soviet cities between districts built by major economic ministries and those under the jurisdiction of city soviets. Ministry districts often have much better housing, better facilities, better utilities, and better schools.[14]

Conditions in the suburbs in communist cities are often much worse than nearer the center, particularly if, as in the USSR and perhaps other communist countries, government policy is *not* to supply basic services to those who build their own private homes in the suburbs.[15] Table 6-2 shows the contrasts between central Budapest, Hungary, and the 44 surrounding communes (localities).

However, since there is probably greater social admixture in every district of communist cities than elsewhere, there is probably also greater interdistrict equality. Contrasts in living standards tend to be hidden rather than flaunted in communist cities.

6-2 RESPONSIVENESS IN COMMUNIST CITIES

By the standards of Western democracies, communist city governments are not responsive nor are they designed or expected to be. Responsiveness is defined in class terms: to Marxist-Leninists, governments differ only in terms of which class they are responsive to (that is, in whose interests they act). Since under communism, class conflict has supposedly been abolished and the proletariat has supposedly taken control, governments no longer need reconcile class conflicts or cater to the interests of the bourgeoisie. There is no class conflict and, therefore, no basis for either autonomous local governments, competing political parties and groups, or

Table 6-2   Inequalities in Communist Cities: the Case of Budapest

Percentage of Housing with	Central City—Suburban Inequality in a Communist City: Budapest, Hungary (1970)		
	Budapest	Suburbs (44 communes)	Metropolitan Area
Running water	91.1	24.4	82.0
Sewer connection	77.1	4.4	66.8
City gas	49.1	1.4	42.6
Telephone	26.9	0.0	
Persons per physician	227	2000	256
Persons per hospital bed	75	294	84
Percentage of population	85	15	100
Pupils/class (elementary)	37	45	38

Source: Calculated from La Documentation Francaise, *Notes et Études* No. 3886-3887 (May 14, 1972), p. 58.

autonomous associations such as trade unions. What distinct and legitimate interest would they represent? Since exploiting upper and middle classes has been eliminated, autonomous urban governments, parties, or groups could only represent counterrevolutionary interests hostile to the welfare of the proletariat, that is, the people.

The proletariat is presumed to dominate government through the Communist party; it is assumed that the party knows what policies are in the best interests of the proletariat and that it has the virtually unchallengeable right to set policy.

The basic authoritarian thrust of communism was expressed by Joseph Stalin in *Problems of Leninism* (1928):[16]

> *The Party cannot be a real party if it limits itself to registering what the masses of the working class feel and think. . . . The Party must stand at the head of the working class; it must see farther than the working class; it must lead the proletariat, and not follow in the tail of the spontaneous movement.*

If communist constitutions resembled Western constitutions by describing power relationships in the state, communist cities would be responsively governed. According to the Soviet, Chinese, Cuban, or East German constitutions, power is held at all levels by elected representatives of the people. The norms of "democratic centralism"—formulated by Lenin—underlie communist constitutionalism; they specify that local, regional, and national power is to be in the hands of elected deputies who can be recalled by the voters at any time. Executives at every level of government are elected by representative councils and are strictly accountable to them. To be sure, the principle of dual responsibility means that executives are accountable and subject to the orders not only of the assembly at the next highest level (this is the "centralism" in democratic centralism) but also to assemblies elected at their own level (the "democracy"). Even so, were assemblies and executives freely elected from top to bottom, undoubtedly even the highest level of government would have an incentive to be as responsive as possible to the voters.

In practice, however, assemblies—whether local, regional, or national—have no independent power. They are dominated by members of the communist party who designate those who can be elected by the people. Democratic centralism applies also to the party: elections from top to bottom, in practice, mean that each level is chosen by the level above. The top party elite selects those who are to run the party at lower levels; the party hierarchy, in turn, selects those who are to be elected to run the organs of government. The system provides maximum incentive for executives in government to be responsive to the party rather than to the local or regional elected government assembly and for executives at all levels to be responsive to those higher up in the party chain of command. There is little incentive to be responsive either to local elected assemblies or to the voters. Party organs repeatedly have to urge and order lower level officials to pay *some* attention to the needs and preferences of the voters.

Much in the structure and style of communist regimes works against responsiveness in urban government, at least as conceived in Western democratic terms:

- Elections are noncompetitive: elected officials need have no fear of not being re-elected; bureaucrats need not concern themselves with the electoral fate of their elected (nominal) superiors.
- The media of communication are controlled by the party and government. They cannot reflect independent inputs from the public unless the party or government wants such inputs published. The public has no independent sources of information (except direct experience).
- People are not free to organize pressure groups to influence city government: only organizations controlled by the party-government (whether labor unions, cultural groups, sports associations) are permitted to exist.
- The principles of "democratic centralism" formally subordinate responsiveness to local interests to responsiveness to higher-level interests. Urban governments are first and foremost "organs of state power."[17]
- The existence of the secret police, the pervasiveness of informers, and the recent history of terrorism discourage the open expression of criticism and the articulation of demands.
- Suppliers of basic urban services like local factories are subordinate to regional and central economic ministries. Even departments of the city government are closely tied to their counterparts at the regional and national level. Their responsiveness tends to be oriented upward in the chain of command.
- The dogmatic, "infallible" character of party rule—"the party knows best"— discourages the development or expression of independent, or particularly innovative, perspectives.
- Central economic planning means that the well-being and careers of local officials depend on pleasing superiors in the planning hierarchy rather than the local populations.
- Local officials are appointed by the party and are constantly transferred from post to post rather than locally selected.
- Policy emphasis on defense and industrial investment sharply reduces resources available to respond to demands for improvement in the quality of urban life.
- There is no consumer sovereignty with regard to the distribution of urban goods and bads. In Western cities, people (with some income) can choose the locality in which they wish to live on the basis of the package of services it offers and taxes it demands. Cities compete for taxpayers, that is, shares of national private income and capital. In communist cities, service levels are determined by central plans rather than by the distribution of private income, and individuals are not free to locate where they wish.

Although the spirit of communist politics and economics is elitist indifference to public opinion, communist regimes do strive for popularity through a scheme of limited, manipulated responsiveness. Unlike traditional dictatorships, communist regimes are far from wanting local government to be strictly and merely a bureaucratic arm of the State. Communist systems are concerned that local governing organs also serve the purpose of mobilizing mass support for the regime and mass participation in campaigns to transform and develop society. This is one of the reasons why communist regimes spend so much time and effort producing almost universal participation in local elections. This is also why the central party organs allow and encourage popular criticism of *local* performance.

Soviet citizens, for example, are allowed and even encouraged to complain about performance deficiencies to party and government organs. According to James Oliver, citizen complaints and demands:

> *cover nearly the entire range of activities under the jurisdiction of the city government apparatus. The citizens complain about the quality of new construction; request additional housing space; and complain about the slowness of housing repairs and their quality. They make demands concerning the quality, assortment, and availability of goods in stores and shops and the location of retail outlets and restaurants. They complain about the quality of service in retail outlets, restaurants, and consumer service facilities. They express their concern about health facilities, about poor street lighting, about unkept parks, about cultural facilities, and about the condition of streets and sidewalks. They complain about the behavior of officials, and they complain about the activities of their neighbors. The regime that has undertaken, with great pride and deliberate purpose, more activities than any in modern history is confronted with demands covering a wider range of subjects than any regime in history.*[18]

Encouraging people to present demands and complaints about local system performance gives lower officials an idea of deficiencies in their own performance; gives higher-level authorities a check on lower officials; deflects criticism from higher levels to lower levels; gives a vent to frustrations; and builds citizen support for the regime. Expression of demands is a positive sign, perhaps, that citizens have some expectation that demands are not only tolerated but have some chance of being met.

Some responsiveness in communist systems is provided by this system of controlled complaint. Responsiveness is also provided by the fact that—again, contrary to the image of communism as a monolithic military hierarchy—even in communist systems, some degree of local autonomy does exist. City governments, particularly in the larger cities, are given some discretion to allocate resources given to them by the central planning authorities. Thus, city authorities—within the limits of the resources given to them—have some ability to move those resources in response to expressed local wants and needs.

Another source of responsiveness in communist cities is the system of volunteer administrators. In all communist systems, ordinary citizens are encouraged to become part of voluntary public administration, with responsibilities to implement a wide range of public policies—health, fire prevention, welfare, propaganda, the inspection of public institutions, education, recreation, social services, and even public security and criminal justice. Thus, local residents' committees (one for every 300-400 households) in Chinese cities have performed a variety of functions at different times in such fields as

> *administration of rationing, street maintenance, dirt or snow removal, supplemental schooling and literacy training, sewing and cottage industries, welfare and funeral assistance.*[19]

They work closely with the precinct police station, which keeps close tabs on all aspects of neighborhood life through them.

In Soviet cities, volunteer auxiliary police patrols ("druzhiny"), over five million strong, much to the dismay of the regular professional police ("militsiya"), were brought not only into traffic control, parade duty, and neighborhood patrol, but also into the more serious aspects of law enforcement: the prevention of juvenile delinquency, vandalism, theft, and even murder. After Khruschev's removal, the supremacy of the professional police was reasserted and attempts made to curb the freewheeling activities of the amateur policemen.[20]

A measure of responsiveness is also provided by the system of secret police, with gigantic networks of informers in all institutions. Communist systems are highly concerned to know the moods of the various segments of the population, to prevent threats to public order, to identify potential troublemakers and dissenters, and to present an image of great efficiency and swift retribution against wrongdoers.[21] The Soviet secret police, the KGB—with its half million members (cf. the 17,000 of the FBI)—is reputedly one of the few efficient bureaucracies in the Soviet Union. But even secret police agencies such as the KGB are not always able to foresee and prevent explosions of mass anger. In communist cities, riots remain an ultimately irrepressible means of expressing public reactions to government policies.[22]

But, if there is some responsiveness in communist systems, the dominant fact is control from above. Every communist system is a system of *contained* responsiveness based on the unchallengeable machinery of coercion, surveillance, and repression. Although West European communists may argue that reliance on coercion and repression is not an inherent necessity under communism, there have been no examples so far of communist regimes which allowed the free expression, not to mention the free organization, of dissent.

COMMUNISM AND EFFECTIVE URBAN GOVERNMENT

To Marxists and radical economists, the crucial determinant of urban conditions is not the level of economic development, but rather the nature of the economic system. They argue that urban performance in a country is basically determined by whether or not the country is capitalist or "socialist."[23] Under capitalism, according to the radicals, many aspects of performance—such as occupation, place of residence, land use, property development, and industrial location—are left to the hazards of the market and the free choice of individuals and entrepreneurs. Under communism, such matters are decided by central government planners. Planners regulate the location of individuals, families, and entire social groups; locate commercial and industrial enterprises; and allocate capital and income among people and localities in accordance with a predetermined set of priorities. Where people live, what services they have access to, how much living space they occupy, how much privacy they enjoy, and what facilities they share with others—all these matters, under communism, are decided by government fiat rather than left to chance or choice, as in capitalist cities.

In theory, at least, under communism the whole urbanization process becomes a matter of man's control over his environment: planners determine the optimum size of cities, stop the growth of overcongested areas, and promote the growth of new centers as needed. Planners determine the optimum size and design of neighborhoods and dwellings and build new cities and rebuild old cities accordingly. Planners decide what the standard of living should be and allocate resources among individuals, families, and localities in accordance with that standard. Planners determine what the standards for public service should be to ensure that the public services are not starved in favor of unnecessary private consumption.

Since the state owns it all, land can be allocated in accordance with the needs of the community rather than as profits for real estate speculators. Planners can operate without hindrance from property interests. Likewise, since the state owns all major means of production, it can determine where it is most socially desirable to locate new industrial investments.

Other elements in the communist system would also seem favorable to high urban performance, in addition to central planning and state ownership of the means of production. According to Marxists, most social problems arise from the nature of the economic system. The basic source of crime, alcoholism, mental disease, juvenile delinquency, and family breakdown is said to be the capitalist mode of production. Under communism, serious social problems should, therefore, disappear. Communist stress on social equality and its eventual aim of a classless society should also favor performance for those with lower income, status, or education. One would expect to find no great contrasts in living standards between social groups or districts in communist cities. Likewise, communist stress on the communal—on shared goods and services and on free services—should mean universal access to all basic necessities in communist cities.

Then, too, under communism, there is a powerful state, armed with unlimited powers of surveillance, coercion, and repression—a state directed by a unified, disciplined, and zealous party elite. Presumably, in such a state, there is little power to dissent or deviate from the party line and state policy, especially since the state not only carries a big stick, but also has sole (legal) distribution rights for all the good things in society. To the extent that high performance involves changing and controlling people's behavior, one should expect under communism (with its lack of integrity and responsiveness) a high degree of effectiveness in securing desirable behavior (hard work, volunteer work, neighborhood cooperation, proper educational and health habits) and preventing undesirable behavior (crime, delinquency, alcoholism).

But in practice, the communist countries have not produced the ideal cities that, in theory, communism alone allows them to build. The record of performance is a mixed one, although given the communist penchant for secrecy and the manipulation of information for propaganda purposes, we cannot be sure. The record seems to be very good in some areas, such as education, health, and culture; medium in some other areas, such as crime, the mitigation of poverty, and transportation; and miserable in such areas as alcoholism, juvenile delinquency, housing, and consumer well-being.

There are several reasons for the gap between communist potential and communist achievement. The first is that, contrary to Marxist predictions, communist parties have been more successful in winning control of poor countries than rich countries. The advent of communism was supposed to take place at the peak of capitalist development, when the means of production had been most fully and completely developed; instead, communists have to come to power in less advanced nations. This means that communist regimes have had to devote their resources to investment in economic development (and defense) rather than in the creation of comfortable, affluent cities. Also relevant is the fact that many communist regimes have suffered severe disruption and devastation from war: still another negative legacy from the past. Current achievement levels in communist cities must be measured against a legacy of poverty, underdevelopment, and wartime devastation.

Emphasis on rapid economic growth has resulted in rapid growth rates at the expense of living standards and the environment. Communism in theory means that the government has complete mastery over the physical environment; but communism, in practice, means the dominance of production over consumption. Not only does national income flow into industrial investment rather than consumer goods, the government agencies responsible for production (the equivalent of our business corporations) are also given carte blanche to do with and to urban communities whatever they want as long as it increases production. The end result is that the optimum designs for dwellings, neighborhoods, and cities turned out by local city planners are completely ignored by local factory managers and their superiors in the central economic ministries. Business interests are powerful in capitalist cities, but in communist cities they combine economic power with government status and authority. In the interests of production, factories are given their own land, shopping facilities, schools, housing, water supplies, sports facilities, hospitals and clinics—all beyond the control of the local city planning authorities. Thus, communist cities are no better planned than cities in the West.[24]

Another problem derives from heavy reliance on bureaucracy rather than the market. Converting private enterprises into public enterprises has not made them more efficient or effective. To make the most of the scarce resources allotted to meet production quotas and satisfy the crushing demand for housing, quantity is heavily emphasized over quality. Thousands of standardized multistory apartment houses are churned out, using slapdash methods and producing the monotonous appearance of most neighborhoods in communist cities. Also standard, if not planned, is low quality construction and maintenance. Twelve percent of new Soviet apartments are regularly declared unfit for occupancy due to poor construction.[25] New housing generally requires considerable finishing and repair; joints are poor; dimensions are off; materials are defective; or important elements are left out.

Given the demand for housing, however, buildings and districts are occupied long before construction has been completed, equipment supplied, and utilities brought in—much as happens in systems without planning! The various government agencies and industrial firms that build and maintain housing are poorly coordinated so that housing is built before streets are paved, sewers dug, or water piped in—almost always before schools, playgrounds, or shops have been opened. Dwellings tend to be small and to be occupied by more than one family. However, rents are low in communist cities and take only a small proportion of family income.[26]

Reliance on bureaucracy rather than the market is counterproductive not only with regard to housing and consumer goods, but also with regard to consumer services. People producing services, such as clerks in stores, repairmen, and waiters and waitresses in restaurants have little incentive to please the customer because, in an economy of rationed scarcity, the customer is seldom right.

Moreover, communist regimes cannot easily do away with traditional elements of culture—political and otherwise—that impinge upon effectiveness: punctuality, discipline, carefulness, sticktoitivness. Despite fifty years of Bolshevik control, the Russians, for example, still have a casual attitude about time and orderliness. An English observer notes:

> *Things are still left to rust out of doors; in up-to-date air liners, the lavatories can be unspeakable; the general slatternliness persists alongside the most recent devices. One begins to suspect that untidiness, inefficiency, and the so often neglected appearance of towns and people cannot be altogether due to shortages of materials or of labor nor even to laziness; they must be due at least in part to a positive quality—to the undiscriminating energy and the undiscriminating concentration with which most Russians go about things. The dislike of being finicky and the desire to get on with what seems important causes gaps, fudges, untidiness, and mistakes which exasperate a Westerner and in the end lead to trouble which even Russians are obliged to acknowledge and to clear up.*[27]

Then, too, the stress on ideology in Communist systems prevents effective action on many severe problems or even acknowledgement that such problems exist. Marxist ideology posits that most social and individual problems derive from the nature of the economic system; once that system is changed and once the material conditions of life are changed, social problems should disappear. Attempts to explain a variety of forms of social maladjustment—hooliganism and alcoholism, for example—as "residues" from the bourgeois period become increasingly unconvincing, particularly in the USSR, more than a half-century after the 1917 Revolution. Ideology plays a role in Western systems, to be sure (for example, hostility to "welfare," rugged individualism, and grass roots, anti-Washington ideas in the United States), but this is a more pragmatic, problem-oriented approach to problems in which ideology eventually yields to pragmatism. There is greater ideological rigidity in communist systems.

As noted above, although there is probably far greater equality in Communist cities than in noncommunist cities and than in the same cities before communism, communist regimes have not been able to achieve as much equality as one might expect. No present-day communist regime claims to have established what is in their terms a "communist" society: a society based on the formula, "From each according to his abilities, to each according to his needs." Instead communist societies are to be built through the gradual transformation of "socialist" societies into communist forms. In the transitional period, the basic principle remains: "From each according to his abilities, to each according to his work." This means that communist regimes have retained the practice of differential rewards as the principle means of maintaining and improving productivity. Thus, in all the communist countries, there are considerable differences in the housing (and other consumer goods) afforded to the industrial, political, and cultural elites, on the one hand, and the mass of ordinary people, on the other.

In Shanghai, for example, the elites live in housing built since 1949, with over forty-three square feet per person; they pay lower rents than the 85% of the population forced to live in the pre-1949 housing with less than twenty-one square feet of dwelling space per person. Over 250,000 people live in traditional urban slum cottages with thatched roofs.[28] In North Korea, housing is divided into five types according to size and quality, with the best housing going to the party-government elite. Likewise, the Soviet elite enjoys a higher standard of living than rank-and-file Soviet citizens: better and more spacious housing, dachas in the countryside, special stores for shopping, special hospitals and clinics, child care, chauffered limousines, special rest homes, and clubs.[29]

Nonetheless, the gap in living standards between elite and masses is nowhere near so great and, certainly not so blatantly visible, so in the noncommunist countries, rich or poor. The Chinese elite may have two or three times the living space of the poorest Chinese, but even the amount of space given to the elite is probably only one-fourth the normal space per person in Western dwellings. As one commentator on Soviet life has written:

> *There is nothing in the Soviet Union like the range from people sleeping in doorways to others who have one mansion in Hyannis Port, another in Florida, a $40,000 penthouse, a ranch in the West and a home in the Riviera.*[30]

Likewise, if the poorest grade of North Korean housing includes one room and a half-size kitchen, the next-to-the-top grade (for factory managers, party functionaries, college professors, actors, and government bureau chiefs) consists of two heated rooms, one wood-floor room, a storage room, and a bathroom with toilet. The top elite receives a detached house with garden.[31] If the communists do not practice equality in the allocation of living conditions, they do not permit the kinds of inequality to be found in the noncommunist countries, especially the poor ones.

On the other hand, if power rather than income or perquisites is used to define class structure, then in communist cities, class inequalities are at least as severe as in the West. Few politicians or officials in the West have powers as absolute as those of politicians and officials in communist cities. Inequalities of power—involving control over jobs, housing, information, education, criminal sanctions, immunity from arrest, good medical care and medicines—match or exceed inequalities of income and wealth in capitalist cities.

A final reason for the gap between ideals and achievement under communism relates to the question of total control. In theory the party-government network controls everything in communist systems. But total control and total planning are ambitions rather than achievements. There are tradeoffs even in systems that strive for total, comprehensive planning. Stressing production, economic growth, and defense means that communist regimes have to give low priority not only to consumption, but also to environmental considerations. Communist cities often have worse air, water, and noise pollution than capitalist cities. Stressing economic growth also means that the central planners must allow considerable unplanned activity (unauthorized labor and resources) if targets are to be met. Official urbanization policy in the USSR has attempted since the 1930s to discourage the growth of the largest cities, but despite the system of internal passports and close police surveillance, planners have been unable to keep factory managers from hiring thousands of migrants precisely in the most congested centers or from hiring thousands of migrants who come (illegally) to those cities for employment.

Even when tied to food rationing, attempts to tell people where they can and cannot live have been ineffective—most of all in the largest cities, where illegal migrants most easily find employment, shelter, and obscurity. There are many ways around migratory controls, including marriage. Writes a western student who has studied in Moscow:

> *A great number of marriages are contracted in the [Soviet Union] because one of the partners is a legal resident of a city where the other wants to live. Moscow, Leningrad and several of the republic capitals and Black Sea resorts are 'closed' cities. That is to say one can move there only by securing a job that carries with it a residence permit or—considerably easier—by marrying a man or woman who has one. This is why a large number of undergraduates whose homes are in the provinces seek marriages of convenience during their final year of study. "I'll marry any old hag," said a student at my institute. "It doesn't matter, as long as she has a Moscow permit. I'll do anything to stay in the big city."*[32]

Under the 1935 General Plan for the City of Moscow, limitation of the city's growth was made a top priority of the regime; the population limit was set at five million. Moscow today has nearly eight million people.

The communist model of urban development stresses the ability of the centralized party-state to establish and maintain total control, but total control is, as we have seen, more a claim than an actuality. Even in communist systems, local officials retain the ability to go slow on unpopular central directives; to hide and hoard their own resources from the central planners; and to use their political connections to squeeze resources and autonomy from the central planners. Even in communist systems, private individuals retain the ability to flout and ignore the party line; to remain unreconstructed in patterns of antisocial or backward behavior; and to develop informal arrangements for coping with inadequate supplies and exhorbitant demands. Behind the facade of absolute discipline, there is considerable laxity; behind the facade of total dedication, there is considerable inefficiency and cynicism; and behind the facade of total harmony and coordination, there is considerable tension and conflict.

But in spite of laxity, inefficiency, and conflict, communist regimes manage to impose a large measure of control over urban society and to regulate rather tightly the allocation of resources to urban needs and demands. Performance is highly effective in a number of areas—especially when levels of socioeconomic development are taken into account. Given their level of economic development, people living in communist cities have excellent facilities; a relatively high sense of personal security (except in secret police matters); broad access to educational, cultural, recreational, day-care, and medical services of fairly high quality; and cheap, if overcrowded, public transportation. They pay very low rents, and they are able (and required) to find employment. There are few blatant or stark contrasts in living standards among city districts as can be seen in capitalist cities. There are also fewer insults to traditional urban decorum such as begging, prostitution, street sleeping, or porno shops.

On the other hand, the people in communist cities live in cramped and overcrowded housing; they have few conveniences for their homes; they pay high prices for clothing and many other consumer goods—when available; they spend hours in line shopping every day, after a full day's work; they find it difficult to get repairs done or to get a telephone; and most cannot take vacations abroad.

The communist impact on performance has been most dramatic in those areas where improvements can be made at relatively little financial cost. Thus, although the Castro regime in Cuba, reacted against the gap in living standards that had developed between Havana and the rest of the country and is strongly devoted to equalizing urban and rural conditions, nonetheless, it has made notable improvements in Cuban urban conditions. Rents are extremely low (never more than 10% of income); health care, education, electricity, and public telephones are free; there are no taxes; and entrance to all baseball parks is free. As in other communist countries, much of life is spent in line, waiting "for taxis, for buses, for ice cream, for cakes, for restaurants, for movies, or for picture postcards." Although some people have more privileges than others—better housing, the right to buy a new car, a 50% discount at Havana's one remaining night club—there is no ostentatious wealthy class. Havana is no longer a haven for the vicelords of the Mafia.[33]

Even more dramatic changes were carried out by the Chinese communists, at relatively little (financial, though not human) costs: law and order was established in Chinese cities for the first time in many decades; a rationing system was established to eliminate widespread starvation; prostitution, opium addiction, gambling and alcoholism—all of which had long plagued Chinese cities—were eliminated or drastically reduced; the power of organized crime was broken; and filthy, fly-ridden streets were cleaned. A major advance was made in the health, safety, and welfare of the urban masses, although housing became twice as overcrowded and severe unemployment persisted. These advances were achieved through the establishment of a pervasive system of public control over individual life.

6-3 PERFORMANCE DIFFERENCES
WITHIN THE COMMUNIST WORLD

One of the major performance differences among Communist cities is their differential willingness (and perhaps ability) to reveal performance statistics. Some communist regimes—notably, Yugoslavia, Poland, East Germany, and Hungary—publish a wide variety of rather candid statistical materials on their urban performance. Others—notably the Soviet Union, Cuba, Czechoslovakia, and Outer Mongolia—publish relatively few statistics useful for international comparison. The Asian communists—led by the People's Republic of China—publish no urban statistics. Thus, when statisticians in Eastern Europe publish data on comparative performance in communist cities, they omit Cuba, the Asian communist cities, and in many instances, Soviet cities.[34]

Even without statistical data, however, we know about some of the major performance differences within the communist world(s). Though the differences among communist cities in integrity and responsiveness are not very significant, the differences in effectiveness are quite striking. The same system of political economy produces quite different outcomes in different contexts. Most of the variance among communist cities derives from differential modernization: communist control came to Eastern European cities at a higher stage of development than it came to Cuba or Asia. Differences between European communist cities reflect differences in levels of economic development between relatively prosperous East Germany and Czechoslovakia and less prosperous countries to the east and south. Leipzig, Dresden, and Prague were advanced cities in 1900 and 1930—before communism—and remain today more advanced than cities in Poland, Hungary, Bulgaria, Romania, or Yugoslavia.

In the more advanced and prosperous communist countries, living standards are much higher; housing is less crowded; there are more automobiles, telephones, TVs and other modern appliances; the infant mortality rate is lower; and personal family income is higher. (See Tables 6-3 and 6-4)

The more modernized communist systems also tend to be much more urbanized. In most Asian communist countries, less than one-quarter of the population lives in cities and towns. (Of course, even the small percentage of the Chinese population living in towns and cities amounts to some 220 million people!) The European communist countries are much more highly urbanized as Table 6-3 shows.

But in addition to differences based on modernization—shares in world income—there are important performance differences based on ideology, politics, and policy, particularly between the European communist countries and the People's Republic of China.[35] The European communist movements were largely urban in origin and are today prourban in orientation. Inspired by the Marxist dream of a classless society, European communists seek to wipe out the sharpest inequalities inherited from the past—the inequalities between cities and countryside, urbanite and peasant, manual worker and mental worker, modern industry and commerce and agriculture. Equalization is sought by urbanizing the rural areas: mechanizing agriculture, providing peasants with urban services, and eventually changing peasants into modern workers. European communists have seen in industrialization the major means of building the abundance necessary for the eventual creation of the altruistic classless society. Industrialization, in turn, is to be promoted by differential rewards and statuses; the use of material incentives; a high division of labor; a heavy accent on professional training; and highly centralized planning through large-scale governmental bureaucracy. The city—in European communist thought—is associated with modernization, industry, the revolutionary working class, and the future.

Much of this thinking is alien to the Chinese, despite the common Marxist inspiration. The Chinese communists were defeated in their bid during the 1920s to capture the cities, and they turned instead to the rural areas to build their base of mass support. The city acquired an unfavorable set of associations for the Chinese communists. Cities were seen as the centers of foreign imperialism and counterrevolution in contrast to the patriotic and revolutionary countryside. Control over Chinese cities, after all, had been seized by several foreign powers during the nine-

Table 6-3   Comparative Modernization among the Communist Countries

	Per-Capita GNP	Percentage Urban	Telephones per 1000	Percentage of Literacy	Infant Deaths per 1000
Czechoslovakia	4011	56	162	100	20.4
Soviet Union	3285	61	57	98	27.8
East Germany	3058	74	137	100	16.0
Bulgaria	2020	56	74	95	25.4
Romania	1630	42	43	98	35.0
Hungary	1428	54	93	98	33.9
Poland	1350	54	67	98	23.5
Yugoslavia	1129	39	48	85	40.4
Albania	520	34	5	75	86.8
Cuba	520	61	32	97	28.9
Mongolia	380	46	20	100	—
North Korea	310	17	—	90	—
China	243	26	28	55	55.0
Cambodia	129	10	1	41	127.0
Laos	69	15	2	15	123.0
Vietnam	—	24	1	50	42.8

Source: *Reader's Digest Almanac and Yearbook 1977* (New York: Norton, 1977), pp. 482-486.

Table 6-4   Comparative Communist Urban Performance: The View from East Berlin

	Infant Mortality	MDs per 1000	Dentists per 1000	Pharmacists per 1000	Telephone per 1000	TVs per 1000	Living Space per New Dwelling (square meters)
East Berlin	20.6	31.3	5.7	2.8	326	315	60
Belgrade	31.0	N.A.	N.A.	4.0	N.A.	N.A.	N.A.
Budapest	41.8	46.1	5.1	4.8	210	237	53
Bucharest	43.0	29.3	N.A.	6.5	123	199	29
Gorki	17.0	54.8	4.4	N.A.	N.A.	N.A.	47
Kiev	16.4	80.0	1.1	N.A.	80	N.A.	45
Leningrad	18.8	71.5	4.1	N.A.	77	N.A.	46
Moscow	20.8	76.7	3.6	N.A.	135	N.A.	47
Prague	21.6	27.1	5.2	4.4	355	357	40
Sofia	23.1	N.A.	N.A.	N.A.	N.A.	N.A.	N.A.
Warsaw	25.9	49.5	14.2	13.4	145	237	45

Source: *Statistisches Jahrbuch der Hauptstadt der Deutschen Demokratischen Republik Berlin 1974* (East Berlin: Staatliche Zentralverwaltung für Statistik, Bezirkstelle Berlin), pp. 247-253.

teenth and twentieth century, and cities had become symbols of weakness and alien domination. The Chinese communists remained antiurban even after their conquest in 1949. To Mao, cities were centers of privilege, inequality, parasitic bureaucrats and intellectuals, and dangerous bourgeois values. The Soviet model of development, through city-based heavy industry and the creation of a new industrial and bureaucratic managerial class, came to be seen as a betrayal of Marxism. Instead, the Chinese turned to a developmental model that stressed rural development (agricultural and industrial), spiritual rather than material incentives, and amateur, spontaneous revolutionary enthusiasm or "Redness" over routinized, professionalized urban bureaucracy or "expertness." The Chinese reaction against urban-industrial-bureaucratic values reached a peak during the Great Cultural Proletarian Revolution of the mid-1960s, during which all major urban institutions—law courts, the police, schools, universities, hospitals, and factories—were disrupted by roving bands of amateur, spontaneous, and revolutionary "Red Guards." Only the Red Army remained intact to restore the rule of the Communist party. Since the mid-1960s, and particularly since the death of Mao, China has turned back somewhat from "Redness" to "expertness," admitting the need for stable institutions staffed with technically trained personnel for the development of the economy and the provision of effective services.

Mao's heritage, however, remains strong and the Soviet Union remains to the Chinese a model of what is to be avoided. Urban engineers, doctors, and bureaucrats are still sent into the countryside to work with and serve the peasant masses. Urban university students—much against their will—are still forced to spend their lives in peasant villages. Great efforts are still made to prevent urban elites from creating a privileged style of life and siphoning off a disproportionate share of national resources by exploiting the rural masses. The children of urban entrepreneurs, according to Laurence Ma, "are identified as products of Western and urban-based capitalism" and are "often denied fair treatment in education and in career advancement, in a way paying back to society the debts their parents had accumulated years earlier."[36] The residents of the city remain suspect as the symbols of "expertness," high living, and privilege compared to the denizens of the countryside—symbols of "Redness," hard work, and plain living.

But despite efforts to "rusticate" the urban elites and to check the growth of cities, antiurban feelings do not seem to be shared by the masses, and Chinese cities continue to grow. For, to many ordinary Chinese, thinking perhaps of better "living standards and quality of life, including practical things like medical care, education, and wages as well as perhaps equally attractive benefits like theatre, sports, department stores, and a sense of being where the action is," the city may still be the place to be.[37]

RAISING URBAN PERFORMANCE

7

The study of urban performance derives its appeal not only from its potential for explaining why cities are the way they are, but also from its promise that it may aid us in improving them. Whether we regard the state of cities or of particular countries as fraught with urban crisis; whether we rely for our definition of the existence of an urban problem on statistics about living conditions or on the gap between social expectations and present social realities; whether we believe society would pay the price for improving performance; or whether we believe that urban situations can be rectified by governmental action, understanding what is affected by government efforts to overhaul the performance of city systems is the inevitable burden of performance theory.

It is important to remember the limitation under which this burden is borne. Compelled by the need to describe an embarrassingly multifaceted reality, we have proposed a general paradigm for understanding urban performance. But, as we indicated in Chapter 1, an adequate theory of urban performance does not as yet exist. This makes the matter of proposing policies and programs for raising performance an uneasy task. The paradigm for the study of urban performance which we have presented does, we believe, indicate the principal forces which might be considered for inclusion in any reformist effort. But most of these forces have been studied in cross-sectional, static terms rather than in the longitudinal, dynamic terms which would be most useful for understanding how performance changes and can be changed over time. What we need is a comparative study of efforts to raise urban performance.

Furthermore, proposing policies involves an element of prediction; yet the magnitudes of the variables that are of most interest to policy—variables involving estimates of future population, employment, or revenues—are normally subject to dangerously large errors in estimation. Even more difficult estimates are involved in attempting to predict the concrete consequences of the particular programs adopted to achieve policy objectives; there may, in fact, be considerable uncertainty regarding the actual effectiveness of urban programs and, as we have recently seen in the United States, a considerable potential for letdown and dissatisfaction when programs fail to achieve the presumed goals of national policy. The difficulties of prediction in this case involve not inability to predict trends and developments, but inability to predict how particular programmatic actions will, in fact, work or not work. In rapidly changing and turbulent urban environments, it becomes increasingly difficult to use routine programs with tested efficacy and increasingly necessary to resort to experimentation. Unless the experimental nature of many urban programs is made apparent so as not to raise false hopes of improvement, efforts to improve urban performance may only generate increased dissatisfaction.

Then, too, prediction must be very sensitive to the *balance* of different factors, not just to their status or projected trend. Take, for example, the question: What is the effect of urbanization on democracy and the potential for democracy? The answer must be: it depends on the balance of contending forces that are set in motion by urbanization.

A further limitation arises not from the inadequacies of performance theory but from the possibly erratic character of the process of social change itself. As Albert Hirschmann has observed:[1]

> ... the ability of paradigmatic thinking to illuminate the paths of change is limited in yet another, perhaps more fundamental way.... ordinarily the cards are stacked so much against the accomplishment of large scale change that when it happens, be it a result of revolution or reform or some intermediate process, it is bound to be an unpredictable and nonrepeatable event, unpredictable because it took the very actors by surprise and nonrepeatable because once the event has happened everybody is put on notice and precautions will be taken by various parties so that it won't happen again....

Lenin's argument that "if the revolution has triumphed so rapidly it is exclusively because, as a result of a historical situation of extreme originality a number of completely distinct currents, a number of totally heterogeneous class interests, and a number of completely opposite social and political tendencies have become fused with remarkable coherence" describes a similar view. To the extent that urban change is in fact a product of uniqueness and not patterning, seeking to propose changes by paradigmatic thinking is subject to error.

What we believe can be most usefully conveyed here, then, is not a law of urban performance change, but an understanding of some of the cross-cultural experiences that involve attempts to change urban performance and an extrapolation of the forces on which they hoped to work.

> *The architect of social change can never have a reliable blueprint. Not only is each house he builds different from any other that was built before, but it also necessarily uses new construction materials and even experiments with untested principles of stress and structure. Therefore what can be most usefully conveyed by builders of one house is an understanding of the experiences that made it at all possible to build under these trying circumstances.*[2]

Central to the proposing of policies for changing urban performance is the basic perspective from which such change is approached. Three principal perspectives are typically applied to changing the performance of cities—radical, liberal, and conservative views of the urban polity. Each of these perspectives tends to identify different kinds and sources of urban performance gaps, and each then suggests different kinds of solutions.[3] The radical attack suggests that improvements in urban performance require alteration in the basic socioeconomic structure of the society in which cities operate. Liberal and conservative approaches focus instead on institutional imperfections.

Following Marx, radicals argue that the mode of production in capitalist societies produces dominant and subordinate classes. The nature of this class structure inevitably produces urban social problems. For example, Latin American Marxists believe that the problems associated with "los marginados," people marginal to urban life who form squatter settlements around major cities, can never be solved while large numbers of people remain economically outside the natural system of distributing income and property. In consequence, the problems associated with urban squatting cannot be solved without fundamental changes in national social and economic institutions.

The changes instituted by the urban reform laws of the Cuban government are an example of the basic program. Faced with the fact that only 45% of the urban population and 2.4% of the rural population had housing considered acceptable; that "belts of misery" surrounded all Cuban metropolitan areas; and that almost 1 million dwelling units would have to be built if each household was to be given a house with permanent usufruct, a threefold strategy was adopted. It involved the drastic restriction of the role of private rights in urban property; the imposition of central economic and land use planning controls in all cities; and the expropriation of urban and suburban land without compensation. Changed performance in urban housing is reflected in a reported rise from an annual production of 10,200 dwellings (1954-1958), only 1% built publicly, to the production of 17,089 units per year (1959-1963), half of which were built by government agencies. Since 1963, private enterprise in the housing construction industry has disappeared.[4]

The path to improvement in Cuban urban housing performance involves a general attempt to revolutionize legal, economic, and class relationships in Cuban national society. The program of social revolution also assumes a radical shift in the way of governing the national polity. An economically revolutionary society in the Cuban case is also one which has declared itself in favor of planned development through collective effort, equality, and participation in the production and consumption of urban goods and services; equality rather than hierarchy in social organization; and elimination of dependence on market forces and competition. The radical approach to changing urban performance, thus, involves not only a revolutionizing of national social and economic relationships, but the general reorientation of national public policy and the redistribution of national political power and authority.

In sharp contrast to the radical approach, both liberal and conservative prescriptions take the existing system of national, social, and economic relationships and attendant values as givens. Urban problems are seen as deriving from remediable imperfections in both the national and local system. Public policy is designed to remedy the imperfections and assumes that privileged groups will accede to the required changes, just as they have acceded to the series of changes involved in the establishment of the service state. Liberals in particular are optimistic about the possibilities for improving urban performance through governmental action, mostly to remedy the imperfections of the economic system. Liberals have fought for a wide range of government programs designed to equip people to compete in a competitive political, economic, and social order and to provide those unable to compete with minimal rights, services, and community influence.

Conservatives have less faith in national government programs; they tend to stress local and individual responsibility for coping with the pressures of competition. They would restrict the role of government to areas in which competition or individual enterprise may be socially destructive or injurious to individual rights. Thus, conservatives accept government action against air pollution where the pollution of the air by one party damages the interests of all others in a region, without possibility of compensation. Conservatives also tend to stress the positive features of the existing order, the degree to which things are running satisfactorily; they tend to discount the existence of a grave crisis in urban performance.

James Fesler has summarized the differences in these three schools of thought, which he calls sanguine (conservative), radical and moderate (liberal) as follows:

> *The sanguine assume that the necessary increment of changes will be effected automatically by the natural play of influences within and upon the ... political system. The radicals ... think fundamental changes necessary and are convinced that the present power holders in local governments, and even local citizens, will not act contrary to their perception of their short range interest— and so, they must be overcome. The moderates think that the needed changes will come neither automatically nor by a direct confrontation between radicals and those benefiting from present arrangements but that the landscape of local government can be significantly altered by deliberately fostering a succession of individual steps, none perceived by local power holders as seriously threatening their interests, but all together amounting to an outflanking of parochialism.*[5]

Views of change are associated with notions of what "the urban problem" is as well as with approaches to solving problems. Conservatives are quickest to attack rhetoric which puts numerous problems in the rag bag called "the city" or is overly generous in defining situations as "problems" or "serious problems." For example, the Advisory Commission on Intergovernmental Relations in the United States produced some fifty-three recommendations in the period from 1961 to 1965 for overcoming the fragmented structure of government in American metropolitan areas. Reviewing its work, an expert with a different philosophy comments:[6]

> *There is no denying that government in metropolitan areas is fragmented, of course, but that such fragmentation constitutes a "problem" for anyone but the people who write these kinds of reports is less self-evident. As the Commission recognizes, few residents of metropolitan areas pay much attention to reorganization proposals, and whatever inefficiencies there may or may not be, "local governments do ... keep the metropolis running." What then is the difficulty? In truth it is impossible to tell.*

Differing philosophies mean that what is a key to urban change for the liberal may be a relatively unimportant event for a conservative. Edward Banfield, commenting on the causes of dissatisfaction in American cities, argues that differences in race are unimportant as explanatory factors in comparison to income, education, place of origin, and attitudes.[7] Anthony Downs, commenting on the same "problem," identifies institutionalized racism (as opposed to overt racism) as key to many of America's urban relationships.[8] Thomas Anton, commenting on the causes of metropolitan imbalance, argues that efforts to change institutions in metropolitan areas amount to puny "organizational tinkering."[9] Bernard Frieden in reply argues that "present governmental arrangements have much to do with such problems as poverty and inequality of opportunity."[10] And even within a single philosophical camp there is disagreement on what is useful for eliminating urban problems. One radical commentator can praise the United States poverty program because of its emphasis on reallocating political power to the people as they engage in participatory institutions rather than in leaders of near autonomous and unrepresentative coalitions and parties, whereas others criticize it for the failure to relieve the economic problems of the poor.[11]

Clearly, we are not going to have a very good idea of what changes to make unless we can bring some coherence to these different views. In particular, we are not going to pursue a comprehensible course unless we know what kinds of urban performance we wish to emphasize.

Inequalities of performance may be seen as desirable or inevitable rather than signals of a need for change. They may be seen as desirable because they result from the varying patterns of consumer preference or because they have been deliberately established in order to favor a particular overall national pattern of growth. Thus, for example, needed investments may deliberately be discouraged in highly congested metropolitan regions, such as around Paris, in order to steer them to other regions of the country. Poor performance may be seen as the inevitable result of regional poverty and regional comparative disadvantages in development, and not as indicators of local inefficiency or malfeasance. Alternatively, political forces may deliberately attempt to destroy government performance within cities as a means of preparing for and executing a revolution in the national regime. There may be deliberate attempts to disrupt services, create terror, and destroy the authority of public officials. Low performance may be effected as a deliberate strategy. Thus, while discussing how to raise performance, some may work toward the destruction of performance in the short run in order to lay the basis for the total revamping of society or at least the destruction of an existing evil. Thus, policy prescriptions for the city are complicated to a significant degree by the relativity of judgments of its performance, problems raised originally in Chapter 1.

We have discussed the causes of performance variations as arising from two different sets of factors: those associated with economic and social modernization and those associated with political institutions and processes. We have also discussed both modernization and politics as factors operating at two different governmental levels: among nations and among cities within a single nation. The effort to raise urban performance is keyed to these causal factors. Governments can try to change urban performance by changing their policies with regard to national or local political institutions and power relationships or by attempting to alter the national or local socioeconomic environment. Thus efforts at change can involve the economy or the polity, the national level or particular cities within a nation, or some combination. To give the flavor of how actual urban performance change has been attempted, we shall examine and evaluate urban performance-raising policies, which implicitly rely on these different factors and governmental levels as presumed causes of urban performance variation. In summary form, these policies are:

7-2 RAISING URBAN PERFORMANCE
BY CHANGING CITIES

LOCAL INSTITUTIONAL REFORM

The most frequently urged policies to change urban performance involve changes in the local institutions which govern urban areas. For decades liberal reformers have toiled to devise institutions which provide better citizen inputs into city politics or maximize the technical and professional competence of city governments. To bring popular opinion more directly to bear, institutions like the referendum, the

Table 7-1   Changing Urban Performance: The Crucial Variables

| Level of Government | Causes of Performance Variation | |
	Economic	*Political*
National	Urbanization planning Migration policy New towns	Moral reform
City	Fiscal equalization Community development	Metropolitan government Community control

at-large election, and proposals for decentralization of functions to neighborhoods or socially defined subcommunities have been devised. To "rationalize" urban government, institutional changes are proposed for cities to raise technical competence and information capacity by the introduction of professional managers as urban executives, civil service systems for public bureaucracies, special districts for attracting and paying above-average salaries to functional specialists and the imposition of comprehensive, multifunctional planning. Reforms also look to annexation or consolidation of governmental units as the best hope for creating sufficient power and authority to do the requisite service job. In American cities, both these kinds of institutional changes have been pursued at once, creating tensions between the push for professionalization and the push for citizen responsiveness. For example, in 1971, technical studies by consultants in New York indicated that class size had little to do with student performance at the same time that several parent-controlled groups were demanding that class size be reduced. The mayor of the city was (as usual) caught between the conflicting priorities set before him by a reorganized school system which included both a highly professionalized central education board and decentralized community-oriented school board in the city.

The most widely discussed institutional reform in cities is the effort to replace splintered local authorities with a governmental jurisdiction which conforms to the social and economic limits of metropolitan areas. With the expansion in the number of city services and the spread of population beyond the traditional boundaries of the central city, the provision of integrated programs and policies for metropolitan areas has become more and more difficult. Political authority in the seven-county Milwaukee region is splintered among 153 local governments and 100 school districts; in Los Angeles county, among 373 units of government; and in the New York SMSA, among an estimated 1400. Urban Europe has had similar difficulties.[12] In Toronto, London, Stockholm, Rosario (Argentina) and elsewhere, new, two-tier metropolitan units have been created in which some functions, such as long-range planning and mass transit, are assigned to a metropolitan authority and others are shared or retained by smaller units.[13] The most dramatic example is the Greater London Council, created in 1965 to sweep away old boundaries and local authorities which had governed 8 million people, spread over 620 square miles. The Greater London Council shares functions with thirty-two elected borough councils. The British government, in 1974 extended this system to other large cities and reduced the existing 1210 local authorities in England to 365.[14] Similar efforts have been made in France, Italy, West Germany, the Netherlands, and Sweden.[15] The Swedes, on the basis of their experiences in creating a Stockholm metropolitan government out of 47 municipalities containing 1.3 million people, by 1974 reduced local units from 1037 to 278. Stockholm's metropolitan government, arising out of a joint regional-planning effort, takes care of water supply, sewage, transport, and health care, leaving other tasks to local units.

The advantage of having a unified metropolitan government lies in an ability to act in a wider area, with pooled financial resources for urban programs. For example, the Greater London Council has authority to relocate families in boroughs outside the crowded inner city without a borough's permission; central cities in the United States can disperse population only against the protest of suburban jurisdictions. The Stockholm metropolitan council is supported by contributions from the municipalities; in the United States, communities compete for tax resources, building factories where open space should be. In addition, whereas American voters have repeatedly turned down metropolitan arrangements at the polls, the citizens of cities outside the United States are seldom asked about reorganization. It is a matter of national parliamentary decision. In the Netherlands, a proposal for creating metropolitan-style governments specifically indicated that this will be done by central government fiat, if the communities do not agree on a scheme by a fixed date.[16]

Still metropolitan institutions have weaknesses. The Greater London Council, although equalizing performance within its own territory, is said to lack sufficient territorial reach to cover the burgeoning private developments and "new towns" which already lie beyond its borders. Despite extensive powers, the Toronto metropolitan government has avoided assuming functions which would involve coercing its subunits; in consequence it has been more successful with capital than with social programs. As in the voluntary Councils of Governments in which officials in most metropolitan areas in the United States are today organized, vetoes over specific policies are often informally retained by subcommunities. And, though metropolitan units eliminate the conflict among specialized functional bureaucracies for some services, not all functions actually are brought under one umbrella. Critics of the London scheme complain that education is still not well coordinated in the area. (The professional associations of teachers were among the most powerful critics of the original consolidation plan.)[17]

Other criticism arises from somewhat different interpretations of urban performance. Although larger authorities enjoy some advantages in terms of coordinative and resource effects, smaller units of government may be more approachable by citizens. The effect of local authority size on specific functions was examined for two services for minority groups—childrens' services and services for old people—in five urban areas in England, and it was found that a smaller authority was indeed associated with easier contact between authority and recipient, less resort to institutional solutions to care, the practice of more preventative work, and more placement of old people in institutions near their previous homes. Advocates of community control in the United States similarly argue that a highly decentralized administrative system is most appropriate for the provision of services to minority groups.[18]

LOCAL ECONOMIC REFORM

Closely linked to metropolitan integration, and indeed one of the evils it is frequently said to reduce, is fiscal disparity among jurisdictions within a metropolitan area. In the United States, fiscal inequalities in metropolitan areas reflect a decline in the relative economic standing of the central city. During the period 1959-1968, central city median family income dropped from 108.7% of the national average to less than the national average (94.6%). Simultaneously, there was a major redistribution of retailing and manufacturing activity to the suburbs, and central city expenditures on services rose. In those cases in which local units provide important services which have large effects on national development, such as education, the problem of unequal resources, unequal costs, or unequal needs can be important and severe.[19]

There have been many schemes for the reform of local finance. One solution lies in the transfer of the major functions of local governments to the central government, decreasing locality borne service costs. An alternative method for solving fiscal problems while maintaining the framework of a somewhat decentralized political system is for the central authority to tax areas of high income and transfer the surplus to areas of low income. This adjustment is generally made through a grant system so that the function of paying grants only to those with high need-low income is to some extent obscured. "Revenue sharing" is another technique for funneling money from the supposedly more affluent central government to less well-off lower units. This scheme, introduced in 1972 in the United States, has a long history in other countries. The Brazilian Constitution of 1946 contains provisions requiring the central government to share the revenues from several of its taxes with the municipalities: in 1965 subventions from these funds represented about 80% of the revenues of more than half of Brazil's 4300 municipalities.[20] Chilean municipalities are funded through similar provisions. Unfortunately, this apparently adequate flow of money often fails to materialize. In Chile the estimated total debt outstanding in 1967 from the central government to the municipalities was close to fifty million escudos (the equivalent of about nine million U. S. dollars).[21] Both the English and the Scots operate with more direct equalization systems in which the aim is to equalize fiscal potential in relation to needs. Opposition to financial equalization schemes in the United States remains, however, very strong.[22]

REALLOCATING LOCAL POWER

Fewer direct attempts have been made to change urban performance by reallocating local power in society than by restructuring local institutions, although some institutional reform has been specifically designed to achieve such a reallocation of power. The establishment of universal suffrage and elective governments was designed to promote widespread civic influence on urban performance, just as the establishment of career bureaucracies was designed to increase the impact on performance of technical and professional elements. The Progressive movement sought to abolish "the Shame of the Cities" by introducing "democracy, more democracy, and still more democracy" into urban government via the initiative, recall, and referendum; the direct primary; and nonpartisanship, designed to break the power monopolies of party bosses. In the same way, although for radically different purposes, the dicta-

torial movements of right and left have sought to improve performance by abolish-
ing free elections and installing in power a single political elite at all levels—national,
state, and local. Sometimes, of course, the consequences of institutional reform are
not necessarily those anticipated or desired by the reformers. The subjurisdictions
in metropolitan areas often manage to reassert their power in the metropolitan
councils designed to reduce localism in decision making. Nonpartisan institutions
have discouraged, rather than encouraged, widespread civic participation in city
affairs, especially on the part of low-income voters.

A recent attempt to change performance by upsetting the balance of power
was the "maximum feasible participation" provision of the Economic and Youth
Opportunities Act of 1964 (the "War on Poverty") in the United States. By requiring that the poor become participants in programs receiving federal funds and by
allocating funds directly to groups in subcommunities rather than through established governmental channels, some hoped reform would alter the decision-making
process in American cities. That this set of programs was deliberately intended to
be a reform in influence relationships seemed clear to Nathan Glazer, who in 1965
wrote:[23]

> *One of the most characteristic enterprises we have seen proposed in the Com-
> munity Action Programs to fight poverty consists of efforts to increase pres-
> sure on government bureaucracies. We are all acquainted with such programs;
> they organize the impoverished community to press its demands on the
> schools, the housing inspection services, the police and so on. . . . The best
> way to improve services is by attack from the outside rather than by reform
> from the inside. When local government protests that federal money is used
> to attack it and its services, the federal administration will have to explain:
> but that is the only way to get you to do your job.*

Another observer writes that "OEO personnel at the federal level 'operated on the
assumption that the involvement of the poor in policy making was necessary in
order to redistribute power in the cities; without power redistribution, they be-
lieved, there would be no great improvement in the lot of the Negro poor.'"[24]

Others concerned with reforming the allocation of power are concerned not
with power distribution, but with power fragmentation. Social critics in the United
States contend that cities are so divided that no authority or leadership exists which
can achieve consensus and get things done in the common interest. Milton Kotler
sees the problem as the failure of the city to be a whole polity:[25]

> *Social judgment is unable to govern [urban] contests of power because there
> is no municipal authority sufficient to rule and compose the dimensions of
> these conflicts. In the absence of sufficient authority there can be no prag-
> matic social judgment to achieve consensus and govern for the common in-
> terest.*

Many critics of this school yearn for a return to the old-style political machine
which, for all its failures, at least brought together enough centers of power to ac-

complish something. This emphasis on getting things done can also push urban systems toward the kind of bureaucratic domination that other urban analysts find alarming. Still others emphasize the need to arrive at a sufficient concentration of power in order to keep order, irrespective of whether services are provided. In unstable nations, a first consideration is achieving a concentration of power sufficient to maintain peace in the cities and to prevent significant numbers of urban residents from taking to the streets in protest.

In no cities, communist or noncommunist, rich or poor, Western or non-Western, have reformers achieved a satisfactory balance between the need for concentrated power in order to provide leadership and the need to diffuse influence among numbers of groups and participant citizens so as to ensure representativeness and a widespread sense of community involvement. In perhaps most cities of the world, community leaders hold on jealously to whatever little power they have managed to accumulate while outside groups and individuals become increasingly exasperated at their sense of impotence.

Like the poverty program in the United States, community development programs abroad are an example of an attempt at both local political and economic change. Such policies have been occasionally adopted by governments in developing countries and also have frequently been a requirement of many United States aid formulas for foreign assistance aimed at improving the quality of life for urban residents. Community development programs aim to improve urban services by providing financial and technical support for essentially self-help construction of urban housing and services. The goals are both to raise service levels and to provide experience in organization and community decision making. Whether or not self-help schemes efficiently improve urban services is a matter of debate. The Brazilian government has adopted largely non-self-help, centralized housing schemes because it argues that it can produce more housing units, at lower cost and of higher quality than through self-help. The Peruvian government has taken the opposite tack, arguing that although the housing produced via self-help means is of a different type (single-family rather than high-rise, fewer units are produced, and quality is more irregular), citizen satisfaction with these dwellings is higher than in the alternative type.[26]

There is also debate about the impact of community development experiences on political participation. In Latin America, many observers regard such programs as mechanisms not for organizing and politicizing the poor, but for coopting them into the existing system. General Manuel Odria, for example, who came to power in a military coup in Peru in 1948, promoted squatter settlements and the formation of dwellers associations as the organizational basis for the political party through which he hoped to perpetuate himself in power. Some argue that this has been the case in the United States as well. In many cities, poverty agencies became the base for new black organizations whose rhetoric was thunderous, but whose activities came to consist mainly of vying for position or patronage in the existing urban political system or for elective office where large numbers of black voters were concentrated. Participation was more closely related to demand making than in authoritarian regimes on the Odria model, but it also is, in an intricate fashion, a mechanism for securing support and channeling opposition into acceptable paths. But in the United States as in Peru, by turning some of the benefits of government to new groups, the apparatus of local government also is put to work for different parties in the national arena. In the United States, it was the national Democratic party that was supposed to benefit; in Peru, the opposition groups confronted the Christian Democratic APRA party.

Programs with mixed local economic and political goals have had rather checkered performance records. Most local government officials still operate with the assumption that promoting political participation must come at the cost of efficient, large-scale service gains. But again, the different views arise from different performance goals. An emphasis on participation, on an individual or group choice model for policy making, emphasizes subjective satisfaction with performance; an elite-choice model emphasizes objective measures of urban service production.

7-3 RAISING URBAN PERFORMANCE BY CHANGING NATIONS

SOCIOECONOMIC DEVELOPMENT

The sizeable differences among communist cities and noncommunist cities in urban performance suggest that political changes, like institutional reform or the reallocation of power, may have less relevance for raising urban performance than for raising the level of economic modernization. In the developing countries, therefore, there has been a tendency for urban policy to become subordinate to national economic development policy since the success of the latter has so much importance for urban performance.

Most national economic plans stress balanced regional development and the desirability of population dispersal into small cities. An ideological bias in favor of rural values, which can be found in many countries, expresses itself in efforts to recreate self-sustaining small communities (suburbs and small towns) by decongesting and limiting the growth of the large agglomerations, establishing new towns, and stimulating the growth of existing smaller population centers.

In national development plans, urban settlements are assigned the role of "growth poles," in which concentrated investment will create self-sustaining economic growth, which, in turn, will diffuse its benefits into the surrounding regions. Among the earliest and best known "growth pole" efforts was the creation of Brasília as the new capital of Brazil; the other well-known case is Guayana City, Venezuela, whose regional resources (hydroelectric power and iron ore) and heavy industry formed the base for a new city and, in theory, was to spread economic development throughout the surrounding undeveloped region in a manner supportive of national economic advancement.

Programs to create new regional development centers are tied mainly to the goals of economic growth, migration, and settlement policy. They deal less often with the internal structure and performance of the cities created as regional centers.

As a result, Brasília is already ringed with squatters. Guayana City, although performing efficiently as a center of steel production, functions much less well in terms of providing its citizens with social services, facilities, and opportunities for participation in decision making.[27]

National migratory controls are more directly related to urban performance in that they are designed to affect city growth rates and size, which are frequently associated with performance inequalities. However, migratory controls have not been as effective as might be imagined in easing the pressure on local housing, employment, and services. Even in the most tightly controlled societies, there is always considerable opportunity and incentive for evasion. In more liberal societies, such controls would most likely seem too costly a price to pay for improved urban conditions.

"New towns" policy is directly addressed to the problem of urban performance, which it aims to improve by decanting population from already congested centers into environments in which the parameters of urban performance are consciously designed from the outset to maximize urban amenity. There is no evidence, however, that even the most ambitious attempts to decrease major city size through the construction of new towns appreciably lessens the congestion in such cities. Furthermore, although many new towns do provide high levels of material comfort, few provide correspondingly high levels of psychological satisfaction for their inhabitants; nor do they normally meet the needs of those in society suffering most from service inadequacies.[28]

REFORMING POLITICAL ATTITUDES

Yet another approach to raising urban performance arises from the thesis that the central causal element is in the sector of national political values rather than in the economic structure. When the Kerner Commission suggested that the trouble with American cities was not streets and sewers, but "white racism," they were asking for a revolution in national attitudes about social, racial, and ethnic equality rather than a change in government structure or the economy. To reverse the chain of causality, the recent increase in strengthening law enforcement in United States cities is said to be a product of the great national preoccupation with crimes of violence and threats to personal safety. Perhaps the most frequently discussed prescription for urban society based on values and attitudes is Edward Banfield's list of measures for change.[29] Most of these—giving intensive birth control advice to the poor or paying problem families to send infants and children to day nurseries and preschools—are predicated on the assumption that a disproportionate amount of the things people call "urban crises" stem from the existence of a group with particular present-oriented values. In consequence, urban reforms must be devoted to progressively eliminating present-orientedness. But, such prescriptions run counter to another set of values: most of the Draconian resocialization and social control treatments that might make a difference to the present-oriented syndrome are so violative of civil liberties that it is to be hoped that the United States at present would not stand for them. Ironically, Banfield also argues that if it is lower-class culture which is responsible for the problems of the city, it is the "public-regarding middle and upper middle class ethos" which is responsible for making the situation worse. Through national policies conceived out of generosity—like minimum wages, late school leaving laws, limits on the arrest power of the police—the imposition of middle-class values has had the effect of exculpating the actions of the troublesome "lower class."

Banfield's suggestions for reforming lower-class morality are not the first instance of such a program in the United States. Clearly, the aim of progressive institutional reform around the turn of the century was also an attempt at moral reform designed to rid the cities of iniquitous political machines and to re-educate their misguided supporters. Whether Banfield's political value preferences will be as powerful in the future as were those of the reformers in the past is not yet clear. However, if Banfield's program is to be accepted, equally important programs must be designed and implemented to reform the moral values of middle-class suburbanites—to make the latter more aware of the realities of inner-city life that make "present-orientedness" a rational adaptation by the poor to insecurity and desperation.

7-3 CONSTRAINTS ON PERFORMANCE CHANGE

In reality, performance change is seldom approached, as here, by asking what variables control the system and what punishments or incentives will lead it, therefore, to move in a predictable way. By far the largest number of programs to change urban performance are not predicated on an approach to variables which control the way the city acts, but directed shotgun style to attack specific problems. Most programs are not "approaches" to urban performance but techniques for removing one or another commonly perceived problem. Program after program is adopted either in response to a visible crisis or in imitation of jurisdictions that are superficially alike.

The distribution of power also affects the style of performance proposals. Must programs be subjected to a process of bargaining among powerful organized groups in the population or among fragmented, highly differentiated groups, or are policies centrally determined and then effectuated by an attempt to command action? Can long-range programs, like the building of new towns in England or the construction of new national capitals in Turkey, Brazil or Pakistan, be sustained through changes in governments, or instead rise and fall as regimes vary? In the United States, where the balance is in favor of bargaining and an effort to associate widely publicized urban programs with party affiliation,[30]

> ". . . there exist well armed and strategically placed veto groups . . . which can prevent [these recommendations] from being seriously discussed much less adopted. The recommendations of the Moynihan report that government try

to strengthen the Negro family, is a case in point: official consideration of this idea had to stop abruptly when the civil rights organizations and their allies opposed its objectives. What these organizations did with this proposal organized labor could do with one to free up the labor market, organized teachers could do with one to reduce the school leaving age, organized social workers could do with one to define poverty in terms of hardship and so on.

Contrast the style implied in a description of decision making in Jalapa, Mexico, where government and official party functionaries with formal responsibilities for the *colonias proletarias* are subject to a continuous drumming of highly particularistic, unaggregated demands from residents.

"The confusion occasioned by this fragmented competition for attention and resources is complicated by the absence of developmental planning of the sort that might provide criteria for bringing together and judging conflicting claims on scarce resources. . . . There are no formally established guidelines by which needs are evaluated."[31]

Yet another type of performance decision making occurs in systems like that of Brazil. Despite the marked criticisms of such a tremendous effort and expense devoted to physical infrastructure development in the interior, Brazilian President Kubitschek was able to speed up the building of Brasília so that succeeding governments found it impossible to disregard the original commitment.

Still other constraints on the choice of programs inhere in value commitments. Can a program of deconcentration of large cities be imposed on areas where city life is revered and where the belief is that governments cannot be trusted to provide facilities over time in outlying areas? Can a city whose residents are convinced that most problems can be solved if we try, be led to accept a laissez faire government position?

Finally, some constraints are provided by the change process itself. The costs of reform itself are a factor. Given the obvious deficiencies in many cities, it is tempting to offer a series of legislative remedies which seek to start new programs or scrap old systems. In the United States, the temptation for frequent reform has not often been resisted. The costs of such changes include confusion, apprehension, lost time while new programs are prepared and staff recirculated, inadequate evaluation of what has gone on, and not least, money. The state of California once revised its welfare system in an effort to eliminate certain categories of recipients from the rolls. Each recipient was entitled to appeal his removal. In October 1971, over 7000 appeals were received and processed at a cost of about $1100 per appeal; this created an expense of $7,700,000 for that month alone. Performance may suffer from overdoses of performance change as well as from lack of innovation and institutionalization.

Perhaps most important, however, is the fact that no effort which seeks only to change one factor will succeed. Everything relates to everything else; all efforts to change performance have hidden consequences, some of which may undo what is being attempted.[32] Programs which go about the extraordinarily complex task of urban social intervention in a single-variable, simple-minded manner usually are turned around by the internal compensatory mechanisms of the same urban systems they are meant to reform.

What we have tried to do here is to describe some of the interrelations implicit in urban performance. We cannot yet describe the urban world in a way which varies all these factors and forces in all places at once, but our approach suggests that reformers should expect complexities and be alert for signals that they are in operation. If a view of the urban world through the lens of performance accomplishes this, we will not have changed the state of life in the cities, but we will have imposed a larger view of events, which is crucial to handling it. And that is no small thing.

CHAPTER NOTES

1. On the performance approach to comparative urban politics, see Robert C. Fried, "Comparative Urban Policy and Performance," in Fred I. Greenstein and Nelson W. Polsby, eds., *The Handbook of Political Science* (Reading, Massachusetts: Addison-Wesley, 1975), Ch. 6, vol. 6. For examples of the performance approach, consult the bibliography contained in that chapter. The performance approach is closely related to the public-policy approach to the comparative study of government and politics. See, e.g., Robert Lineberry and Ira Sharkansky, *Urban Politics and Public Policy* (New York: Harper & Row, 1978); Frank S. Levy, Arnold J. Meltsner, and Aaron Wildavsky, *Urban Outcomes: Schools, Libraries, and Streets* (Berkeley: University of California Press, 1974); Bryan T. Downes, "The Policy-Making Approach to the Study of Local Municipalities," in his *Cities and Suburbs* (Belmont, California: Wadsworth, 1971); James Q. Wilson, ed., *City Politics and Public Policy* (New York: Wiley, 1968); Brett Hawkins, *Politics and Urban Policies* (Indianapolis: Bobbs-Merrill, 1971); Marian L. and Howard A. Palley, *Urban America and Public Policies* (Lexington, Massachusetts: Heath, 1977).

2. Studies of cities outside the United States done with this perspective include William V. D'Antonio and William H. Form, *Influentials in Two Border Cities* (Notre Dame, Indiana: University of Notre Dame Press, 1965); Orrin Klapp and Vincent Padgett, "Power Structure and Decision-making in a Mexican Border City," *American Journal of Sociology*, Jan. 1960, pp. 400-406; Delbert Miller, *International Community Power Structures* (Bloomington: Indiana University Press, 1970); John Walton, "An Exploratory Study of Democracy and Development in a Mexican City," in F. M. Wirt, ed., *Future Directions in Community Power Research* (Berkeley: Institute of Governmental Studies, University of California, 1971); B. Michael Frolic, "Decision Making in Soviet Cities," *American Political Science Review*, March 1972, pp. 38-52; Donald B. Rosenthal, *The Limited Elite: Politics and Government in Two Indian Cities* (Chicago: University of Chicago Press, 1970); Richard R. Fagen and William S. Tuohy, *Politics and Privilege in a Mexican City*

(Stanford: Stanford University Press, 1972); Alejandro Portes and John Walton, *Urban Latin America: The Political Condition From Above and Below* (Austin: University of Texas Press, 1976).

3. See, for example, Annmarie H. Walsh, *The Urban Challenge to Government* (New York: Praeger, 1969) and *Urban Government for Paris* (New York: Praeger, 1968); Ivan L. Richardson, *Urban Government for Rio de Janeiro* (New York: Praeger, 1973); David T. Cattell, *Leningrad: A Case Study of Soviet Urban Government* (New York: Praeger, 1968); Hans Calmfors, Francine F. Rabinovitz, and Daniel Alesch, *Urban Government for Greater Stockholm* (New York: Praeger, 1968).

4. See, as examples, Arnold J. Heidenheimer, Hugh Heclo, and Carolyn Teich Adams, *Comparative Public Policy: The Politics of Social Choice in Europe and America* (New York: St. Martin's Press, 1975); Richard L. Siegel and Leonard B. Weinberg, *Comparing Public Policies: United States, Soviet Union, and Europe* (Homewood, Illinois: Dorsey, 1977); Robert J. Osborn, *Soviet Social Policies: Welfare, Equality, and Community* (Homewood, Illinois: Dorsey, 1970); Lloyd Rodwin, *The British New Towns Policy* (Cambridge, Massachusetts: Harvard University Press, 1956); Marcia N. Koth, Julio G. Silva, and Albert G. Dietz, *Housing in Latin America* (Cambridge, Mass.: MIT Press, 1965); and Charles Abrams, *Man's Struggle for Shelter in an Urbanizing World* (Cambridge, Massachusetts: MIT Press, 1964).

5. See, e.g., John Friedmann, "The Role of Cities in National Development," *American Behavioral Scientist,* May-June 1969, pp. 13-21; Norman Nie, G. Bingham Powell, and Kenneth Prewitt, "Social Structure and Political Participation," *American Political Science Review,* June 1969, pp. 361-383, Sept. 1969, pp. 808-832; Edward Soja, *The Geography of Modernization in Kenya* (Syracuse: Syracuse University Press, 1968); Glenn H. Beyer, ed., *The Urban Explosion in Latin America* (Ithaca: Cornell University Press, 1967); Samuel Huntington, *Political Order in Changing Societies* (New Haven: Yale University Press, 1968); Wayne Cornelius, "Urbanization as an Agent in Latin American Political Instability: The Case of Mexico," *American Political Science Review,* Sept. 1969, pp. 833-857; Robert Daland, ed., *Comparative Urban Research: The Administration and Politics of Cities* (articles by F. Rabinovitz and J. Guyot) (Beverly Hills: Sage, 1969); Gino Germani, ed., *Modernization, Urbanization, and the Urban Crisis* (Boston: Little, Brown & Co., 1973); and Lloyd Rodwin, *Nations and Cities* (Boston: Houghton Mifflin Co., 1970).

6. For some of the ambiguities of the term "city," see Kingsley Davis, *World Urbanization 1950-1970* (Berkeley: Institute of International Studies, University of California, 1969), vol. 1, pp. 10-24; and David Popenoe, "On the Meaning of 'Urban' in Urban Studies," in Paul Meadows and Ephraim Mizruchi, eds., *Urbanism, Urbanization, and Change: Comparative Perspectives* (Reading, Massachusetts: Addison-Wesley, 1969), pp. 64-75.

7. See, e.g., William A. Robson and D. E. Regan, eds., *Great Cities of the World: Their Government, Politics, and Planning* (London: Allen & Unwin, 1972); and H. Wentworth Eldredge, ed., *World Capitals: Towards Guided Urbanization* (New York: Anchor, 1975).

8. See, e.g., the volumes in the *Latin American Urban Annual* and the *South and Southeast Asia Urban Studies* series published by Sage in Beverly Hills. There are also relevant publications by the Economic Commissions of the United Nations for various world regions. For a delineation of twelve regional "families" of cities, see Lutz Holzner, "World Regions in Urban Geography," *Annals*. Association of American Geographers, Dec. 1967, pp. 704-712.

9. A large number of intranational comparative urban studies are referenced and analyzed in R. Fried, "Comparative Urban Policy," (cited above, n. 1).

10. Comparative studies across regions and countries are rare and sometimes controversial. See, e.g., one the best known, Gideon Sjöberg's *The Pre-industrial City* (Glencoe: Free Press, 1960) and two critics: Paul Wheatley, "What the Greatness of a City is Said to Be: Reflections on Sjöberg's 'Pre-Industrial City,'" *Pacific Viewpoint*, 1963, pp. 163-168; and Richard M. Morse, "A Framework for Latin American Urban History," in Jorge E. Hardoy, ed., *Urbanization in Latin America* (New York: Anchor, 1975), pp. 57-107.

11. An attempt to assemble some comparative performance data for major cities of the world can be found in Robert C. Fried's, *World Handbook of Cities* (New Haven: Yale University Press, 1980). Already available, but less performance-oriented, are the publications of the Tokyo Metropolitan Government *(Statistics of World Large Cities),* and those of the International Statistical Institute in The Hague. The ISI has been publishing comparative urban statistics for nearly a century. See e.g., its *International Statistical Yearbook of Large Towns* (The Hague: ISI, 1970). International comparisons can also be found in the statistical yearbooks of some cities like Belgrade, East Berlin, Göteborg, Warsaw, and Helsinki.

12. *Los Angeles Times,* May 12, 1975; La documentation Française, notes et etudes, "Moscou."

13. Ali Ashraf, *The City Government of Calcutta: A Study in Inertia* (London: Asia Publishing House, 1966), pp. 5-6.

CHAPTER TWO

1. Further elaboration of these criteria can be found in R. Fried, *Performance in American Bureaucracy* (Boston: Little, Brown & Co., 1976), Ch. 3.

2. See Arnold J. Heidenheimer, ed., *Political Corruption* (New York: Holt, Rinehart and Winston, 1970); and James C. Scott, *Comparative Political Corruption* (Englewood Cliffs: Prentice-Hall, 1972).

3. Hugh Tinker, *Race and the Third World City* (New York: Ford Foundation, 1973).

4. Willis D. Hawley, *Nonpartisan Elections and the Case for Party Politics* (Berkeley: University of California Press, 1972).

5. See Table 4-7.

6. See, e.g., Robert L. Lineberry and R. E. Welch, "Who Gets What: Measuring the Distribution of Urban Public Services," *Social Science Quarterly,* 1974, pp. 700-712; F. Levy et al., *Urban Outcomes* (cited above, n. 1); Robert Lineberry, *Equality and Urban Policy: The Distribution of Urban Services* (Beverly Hills: Sage, 1977); and various publications of the Urban Institute, Washington, D.C. From a different

perspective, see Frances F. Piven, "The Urban Crisis: Who Got What and Why," in Roger E. Alcaly and David Mermelstein, eds., *The Fiscal Crisis of American Cities* (New York: Vintage, 1976), pp. 132-144.

7. Gabriel A. Almond and Sydney Verba, *The Civic Culture* (Princeton: Princeton University Press, 1963).

8. Lineberry and I. Sharkansky, *Urban Politics,* Ch. 10; John C. Livingston and Robert G. Thompson, *Dissent of the Governed* (New York: Macmillan Co., 1972).

9. *Encyclopedia Britannica Yearbook,* 1974, p. 214; 1975, p. 219.

10. The situation in Western Europe, however, is getting worse not only with regard to urban terrorism, but to ordinary street crime as well. It is getting worse not only objectively (in terms of actual crime rates), but also subjectively (in terms of anxiety about those rates). Tolerance for street crime is much lower in Europe than in the United States and thus much lower rates of crime generate much greater anxiety. In some European countries, particularly Italy, there is little violent street crime, but there is a major problem with urban terrorists. Only Japan seems to have neither street crime nor much terrorism. Crime rates have actually been dropping! (See David Bayley, *Forces of Order: Police Behavior in Japan and the United States* (Berkeley: University of California Press, 1976), p. 7.

11. *The Fire Journal,* Nov. 1975, p. 25.

12. Hedrick Smith, *The Russians* (New York: Ballantine, 1976), p. 73.

13. The age structure of the community has an obvious impact on many performance measures, including the ratio of young people's deaths to total deaths. West European cities have very high proportions of people over 65, who therefore figure prominently in mortality statistics. However, better urban health conditions help create the longevity that eventuates in the preponderance of older people in mortality statistics.

14. Preference for single-family housing has been found in West Germany (58% of those surveyed), in France (70%), and in The Netherlands (78%). See Roland Ermreich, *Basisdaten: Zahlen zur Sozio-Ökonomischen Entwicklung der Bundesrepublik Deutschland* (Bonn: Neue Gesellschaft, 1974), p. 351; Dominique and Michele Fremi, *Quid?* (Paris: Laffont, 1974), p. 740; and Rijksplanologische Dienst, *Onderzoek naar Woonmilieus: Samenvating van de Resultaten* The Hague; Staatsdrukkerij, 1973), p. 30.

15. *Statistisches Jahrbuch der Hauptstadt der Deutschen Demokratischen Republik* 1974. See also the city yearbooks of Warsaw, Prague, Budapest, Prague, and Belgrade.

16. Calculated from AT&T Long Lines, *The World's Telephones* (New York: AT&T, 1972).

17. Rather large numbers of Americans answer "YES" to the question, "Have there been times during the last year when you did not have money enough to buy food your family needed?"

	Percentage YES
Sub-Saharan Africa	71
India	66
Mexico	42
Brazil	26

	Percentage YES
Italy	15
U.S.A.	14
Japan	14
U.K.	8
West Germany	7
Scandinavia	6
France	6
Canada	6
Australia	4

Source: Gallup International Research Institutes, *Human Needs and Satisfactions: A Global Survey* (June 1977), pp. 181-182.

18. H. Smith, *The Russians,* 471-472.

CHAPTER THREE

1. Some basic references in the theory (or theories) of modernization include: S. N. Eisenstadt, *Modernization: Protest and Change* (Englewood Cliffs: Prentice-Hall, 1966); Lucian W. Pye, *Aspects of Political Development* (Boston: Little, Brown & Co., 1966); Gabriel A. Almond and G. B. Powell, *Comparative Politics: A Developmental Approach* (Boston: Little, Brown & Co., 1966); S. Huntington, *Political Order;* Myron Weiner, ed., *Modernization: The Dynamics of Growth* (New York: Basic Books, 1966); Gabriel A. Almond and James C. Coleman, eds., *The Politics of the Developing Areas* (Princeton: Princeton University Press, 1960); Fred W. Riggs, *Administration in Developing Areas: The Theory of Prismatic Society* (Boston: Houghton Mifflin Co., 1964); Seymour M. Lipset, *The First New Nation* (New York: Basic Books, 1963); Talcott Parsons, *Structure and Process in Modern Societies* (New York: Free Press, 1959); Ira Sharkansky, *The United States: A Study of a Developing Country* (New York: Longmans, 1975).

2. This table builds on the models of "Agraria" and "Industria" explicated by Fred W. Riggs in William J. Siffin, ed., *Toward the Comparative Study of Public Administration* (Bloomington: Indiana University Press, 1957), pp. 23-110.

3. Almond and Verba, *The Civic Culture,* p. 185.

4. George H. Gallup, "Human Needs and Satisfactions: A Global Survey," *Public Opinion Quarterly,* Winter 1976-1977, pp. 459-467.

5. Gallup, "Human Needs," p. 463.

6. John A. Fairlie, *Municipal Administration* (New York: Macmillan Co., 1910).

CHAPTER FOUR

1. Richard Llewelyn-Davies, "The American City Through English Eyes," *Daedalus,* Fall 1972, pp. 185-193 at pp. 185-186.

2. Robert Heilbroner, "Benign Neglect in the United States," *Transaction,* Oct. 1970, pp. 15-22 at p. 16.

3. Daniel P. Moynihan, "Poverty in Cities," in James Q. Wilson, ed., *The Metropolitan Enigma* (New York: Doubleday, 1970), pp. 367-385 at p. 381.

4. Gallup, "Human Needs," p. 460.

5. Bureau of the Census, *Annual Housing Survey (1975), Part B (Indicators of Housing and Neighborhood Quality),* (Washington: United States Government Printing Office, 1977), pp. 1-42.

6. Dean S. Rugg, *Spatial Foundation of Urbanism* (Dubuque: Brown, 1975), pp. 238-239.

7. Frank J. Coppa, "Cities and Suburbs in Europe and the United States," in Philip C. Dolce, ed., *Suburbia: The American Dream and Dilemma* (New York: Anchor/Doubleday, 1976), pp. 167-191 at p. 174.

8. Ibid., p. 174. Marion Clawson and Peter Hall attribute lower European mobility rates to "a more settled career structure; smaller proportions of people with higher education and with professional qualifications; lower car ownership and hence a lower propensity to commute over long distances across country." (*Planning and Urban Growth: An Anglo-American Comparison,* Baltimore: Johns Hopkins Press, 1973, p. 123, note 2.) One should not exaggerate either the transiency in American cities or the stability in other advanced countries. Some neighborhoods remain quite stable in American cities, particularly the ethnic neighborhoods in such cities as Chicago, New York, and Philadelphia. And, in Europe, there has been for some time a growing tendency for people to leave the picturesque, but decrepit housing of the old centers for the newly built suburbs.

9. In most advanced countries, a person must notify the authorities of every change in address, even of a temporary stay overnight in a hotel. By law, every adult must carry an ID card. Thus there is much greater official control over individual movement and knowledge of individual whereabouts than in the United States.

10. Rugg, op. cit., p. 239.

11. G. A. Wissink, *American Cities in Perspective* (Assen, Netherlands: Royal Van Gorcum, 1962), p. 243.

12. Curiously Americans, despite their antiurban intellectual heritage, prefer living in or near cities more than do some Europeans. A Gallup International Survey found more preferences for city living among Americans than among the British, for example, who far preferred towns, villages, and rural areas to cities, (*Los Angeles Times,* Nov. 21, 1976). The American preference, of course, is not for living in the big city itself, but in the outlying suburbs, conveniently fragmented into a myriad of small towns.

13. David M. Potter, *People of Plenty: Economic Abundance and the American Character* (Chicago: University of Chicago Press, 1965).

14. The municipal activism of the 19th century predates the socialist movement and was carried out under the auspices of conservatives as well as liberal-radicals. Conservatives, for example, began the (socialistic!) practice in Stockholm of large-scale municipal acquisition of land ("land-banking") for future residential development. Conservatives under Bismarck created the basis for the modern welfare state in Germany.

15. On ethnic differences in the perception and evaluation of urban government services, see Nicholas P. Lovrich, "Differing Priorities in an Urban Electorate: Urban Service Preferences Among Anglo, Black, and Mexican American Voters," *Social Science Quarterly,* Dec. 1974.

16. Stephen Castles and Godula Kosack, *Immigrant Workers and Class Structure in Western Europe* (London: Oxford University Press, 1973).

17. N. H. Lithwick, *Urban Poverty* (Ottawa: Central Housing and Mortgage Corporation, 1971) p. 53.

18. Universal and equal male suffrage came to Bern, Switzerland, in 1846; to Chicago, 1870 (after the 15th amendment); Paris, 1870; Oslo, 1898; Helsinki, 1906; Copenhagen, 1908; Rome, 1912; Rotterdam, 1917; Brussels, 1917; Munich, 1918; Vienna, 1919; Stockholm, 1921; Yokohama, 1925.

19. Only in some West German cities (those occupied by the American military after World War II) and (since 1976) in Paris do the voters directly elect the mayor. The Governor of Metropolitan Tokyo is also directly elected—again as a legacy of the American occupation of Japan.

20. Seymour M. Lipset, "The Labor Movement and American Values," in John H. M. Laslett and Seymour M. Lipset, eds., *Failure of a Dream? Essays in the History of American Socialism* (Garden City, New York: Anchor Books, 1974), ch. 13.

21. P. J. Madgwick, *American City Politics* (London: Routledge & Kegan Paul, 1970), pp. 108-109.

22. Some of the reasons for lower registration in American cities include the following:

(1) In other countries, voter registration is automatic and tied to the system of registering the residence and location of every adult. Since every person is registered with the authorities at all times, it is a simple matter to convert the list of resident adult citizens into the list of eligible voters. In most American cities, registration is not automatic and requires periodic personal effort on the part of the voter.

(2) Residence requirements for voting, given the mobility of American households, cuts down on voting eligibility.

(3) Local elections in other countries are usually held on the same day throughout the country as part of nationwide election campaigns run by the national political parties. Local elections are often interpreted as a test of the relative power of national political parties. American city elections lack this kind of national political importance and thus American adults may see less reason to bother registering to vote.

(4) In some countries, voting is compulsory. In American cities, of course, it is not. There are no penalties for failure to register.

23. John Gardiner in *The Politics of Corruption* (New York: Russell Sage, 1970) argues that the lack of strong parties is just as conducive to corruption as was the old-style boss system.

"During the years when American cities were controlled by highly centralized political machines, it was possible for men seeking illegal privileges to control the entire city government simply by bribing the boss . . . [But] where, as is often the case in American cities today, the political system is not centralized enough to give total control to one or a few men, the next best hope for a criminal syndicate seeking protection for its illegal activities is a political system which is so decentralized that *no* political force is powerful enough to challenge individual officials who have been corrupted. . . . Such fragmented systems seem to attract more temptable leaders and to contain fewer forces, such as party organizations, interest groups and elite associations, which might persuade tempted officials to conform to legal norms." (pp. 7-8)

24. Harold Wilensky, *The Welfare State and Equality* (Berkeley: University of California Press, 1975), p. 13.

25. Willis Hawley, *Nonpartisan Elections;* J. David Greenstone and Paul E. Peterson, "Reformers, Machines, and the War on Poverty," in Wilson, ed., *City Politics,* pp. 267-292.

26. Archie Bunker is not totally implausible as a representative of some kinds of working-class attitudes.

27. Demetrios Caraley, *City Government and Urban Problems* (Englewood Cliffs: Prentice-Hall, 1977), Ch. 20.

28. Roy Lubove, *The Struggle for Social Security 1900-1935* (Cambridge, Mass.: Harvard University Press, 1968); Heidenheimer et al., Ch. 7.

29. Michael Harrington, *Socialism* New York: Bantam, 1973), Ch. 6.

30. Lipset, "The Labor Movement."

31. R. Fried, "Communism, Urban Budgets, and the Two Italies: A Case Study in Comparative Urban Government," *Journal of Politics,* 1971, pp. 1008-1051.

32. Heidenheimer, et al., *Comparative Public Policy,* Ch. 4 (Carolyn Adams).

33. J.-J. Servan-Schreiber, *The American Challenge* (New York: Avon, 1967), p. 222.

34. Charles R. Adrian and Charles Press, *Governing Urban America* (New York: McGraw-Hill, 1977), Ch. 6.

35. *Statistical Abstract of the United States 1977,* Tables 446-448.

36. John C. Bollens and Henry C. Schmandt, *The Metropolis* (New York: Harper & Row, 1975), p. 43.

37. Ibid., pp. 345-378.

38. Gardiner, *Politics of Corruption,* p. 9.

39. Welfare payments may vary on the order of five to one, but the cost of living varies on the order of less than two to one. (*Statistical Abstract of the United States 1977,* Table 715).

40. The crime rate, interestingly enough, did not drop during the period between the Civil War and the turn of the century when many American city police forces were brought under state-government control. See Bruce Smith, *Police Systems in the United States* (New York: Harper & Row, 1960), pp. 186-187.

41. Wilensky, *The Welfare State,* p. 1. See also Siegel and Weinberg, *Comparing Public Policies,* Ch. 6.

42. Marshall B. Clinard, *Cities with Little Crime: The Case of Switzerland* (Cambridge: Cambridge University Press, 1978), p. 116.

43. Richard Llewelyn-Davies, op. cit., p. 190.

44. One reason why European cities lack slums is that they were destroyed during World War II.

45. David Harvey, *Social Justice in the City* (Baltimore: Johns Hopkins Press, 1973); David M. Gordon, ed., *Problems in Political Economy: An Urban Perspective* (Lexington: Heath, 1977); James O'Connor, *The Fiscal Crisis of the State* (New York: St. Martin's Press, 1973); William K. Tabb and Larry Sawyers, eds., *Marxism and the Metropolis: New Perspectives in Urban Political Economy* (New York: Oxford University Press, 1978); Manuel Castells, *The Urban Question: A Marxist Approach* (Cambridge, Massachusetts: MIT Press, 1977).

46. M. Donald Hancock, *Sweden: The Politics of Postindustrial Change* (Hinsdale, Ill.: Dryden, 1972), pp. 99-100.

47. Marshall B. Clinard, *Cities with Little Crime: The Case of Switzerland* (Cambridge, Eng.: Cambridge University Press, 1978), pp. 103-107.

48. Castles and Kosack, *Immigrant Workers.*

49. *Annuaire Statistique de la Suisse 1977,* p. 556.

50. Jan DeAmicis, "It Just Happened: The Transformation of American Migrants in Australia from Sojourners to Settlers," *Australian and New Zealand Journal of Sociology,* June 1976, pp. 136-144 at p. 140.

51. Ibid.

52. R. J. Lawrence, "Social Welfare and Urban Growth," in R. S. Parker and P. N. Troy, eds., *The Politics of Urban Growth* (Canberra: Australian National University Press. 1972), pp. 100-128 at pp. 103-04.

53. William B. Munro, *Municipal Government and Administration* (New York: Macmillan, 1923), vol. 2, p. 225.

54. Ibid., pp. 238-40.

55. Ibid., p. 200.

56. Ibid., pp. 54-55.

57. Ibid., p. 77.

58. Frederic C. Howe, *The Modern City and Its Problems* (New York: Scribner's, 1915), pp. 271-272.

59. *Statistical Abstract of the United States* 1976, p. 17.

60. Howe, op. cit., pp. 58-59.

61. Ibid., pp. 52-54.

62. Ibid., pp. 287, 296-297.

63. *Statistical Abstract of the United States* 1976, p. xvii.

CHAPTER FIVE

1. Terence G. McGee, *The Urbanization Process in the Third World* (London: Bell, 1971).

2. Shanti Tangri, "Urbanization, Political Stability, and Economic Growth," reprinted in Jason L. Finkle and Richard W. Gable, eds., *Political Development and Social Change* (New York: Wiley, 1971), pp. 212-226.

3. Ibid., pp. 215-18.

4. United Nations, *1970 Report on the World Social Situation* (New York: United Nations, 1971), p. 153.

5. K. Davis, *World Urbanization 1950-1970*, vol. 1.

6. Gideon Sjöberg, op. cit.

7. R. Morse, "A Framework," p. 58.

8. A. Heidenheimer, *Political Corruption*, Chs. 4, 7, 10, and 11.

9. Eric Nordlinger, *The Military and Political Development* (Englewood Cliffs: Prentice-Hall, 1974), p. 126 and Ch. 4, generally.

10. Steffen W. Schmidt et al., *Friends, Followers, and Factions: A Reader in Political Clientelism* (Berkeley: University of California Press, 1977).

11. "Poly-communalism" is the term developed by Fred Riggs; see his *Administration*, pp. 158-164.

12. Aprodicio Laquian argues that patronage systems are highly functional for the success of Third World polities in "The Asian City and the Political Process," in D. J. Dyer, ed., *The City as a Centre of Change in Asia* (Hong Kong: Hong Kong University Press, 1972), pp. 41-55 at pp. 50-52.

13. Laquian, op. cit., p. 43.

14. Abrams, *Man's Struggle*, p. 5.

15. Tangri, op. cit.

16. Wayne A. Cornelius, *Politics and the Migrant Poor in Mexico City* (Stanford: Stanford University Press, 1975); Joan M. Nelson, "The Urban Poor: Disruption or Political Integration in Third World Cities," *World Politics*, April 1970, pp. 493-514.

17. Tangri, op. cit., p. 221.

18. Wayne A. Cornelius, "Urbanization and Political Demand-Making: Political Participation among the Poor in Latin American Cities," *American Political Science Review*, Sept. 1974, pp. 1125-1146.

19. Ibid., p. 1131.

20. Ibid., pp. 1139-1140.

21. International Bank for Reconstruction and Development, *World Bank Operations* (Baltimore: Johns Hopkins University Press, 1972), pp. 480-481.

22. Albert O. Hirschmann, *Development Projects Observed* (Washington: Brookings Institution, 1967), pp. 62-78.

23. Robert Sadove, remarks in Ranan Weitz, ed., *Urbanization and the Developing Countries* (New York: Praeger, 1973), p. 11.

24. David Epstein, *Brasília, Plan and Reality* (Berkeley: University of California Press, 1973), p. 69.

25. *Los Angeles Times*, May 18, 1966.

26. Ashraf, *The City Government of Calcutta*, pp. 9-14.

27. Joseph Lelyveld, "Can India Survive Calcutta?" *The New York Times Magazine*, Oct. 13, 1968.

28. Cornelius, "Urbanization," p. 1141.

29. Laquian, "The Asian City," p. 50.

30. Cited in Weitz, *Urbanization*, p. 22.

31. Population increase rates are taken from Fried, *World Handbook of Cities,* Ch. 12.

32. Gallup International Survey, *Los Angeles Times,* Nov. 21, 1976.

33. International Bank, *World Bank Operations,* pp. 476-77.

34. For cities over 100,000 population to double their population in a decade is extremely rare. Examples would be Philadelphia (1850-1860), Chicago (1880-1890), and Detroit (1910-1920). Two American cities with more than 100,000 people have actually tripled their population in a single decade: Chicago (1860-1870) and Los Angeles (1900-1910). No European city (except Cologne, 1880-1890) seems to have grown as fast as this, partly because Europeans were migrating to American rather than to European cities. (Source: L'Office Permanent de l'Institut International de Statistique, *Statistique Internationale des Grandes Villes,* The Hague, 1931, pp. 52-64.)

35. Calculated from International Bank, *World Bank Operations,* p. 484.

36. Kingsley Davis, "The Urbanization of the Human Population," in *Cities* (New York: Alfred Knopf, 1967), pp. 3-24 at pp. 19-20.

37. Tangri, op. cit., pp. 221-222.

38. *Statistical Abstract of the United States* 1977, p. 328.

39. Ronald E. Wraith, *Local Administration in West Africa* (London: Allen & Unwin, 1972), pp. 22-30.

40. Peter S. Cleaves, *Bureaucracy, Politics, and Administration in Chile* (Berkeley: University of California Press, 1974), Ch. 5.

41. Alan C. Purves and David U. Levine, *Educational Policy and International Achievement* (Berkeley: McCutchan Publishing Corporation, 1975), p. 70.

42. Ibid., p. 46.

43. Ibid., pp. 68-69.

44. Richard Musgrave, *Fiscal Systems* (New Haven: Yale University Press, 1969), Chs. 5-6.

45. *Los Angeles Times,* Nov. 9, 1977.

46. Cornelius, "Urbanization," pp. 1141-43.

47. D. J. Dyer, "Attitudes towards Spontaneous Settlements in Third World Cities," in D. J. Dyer, ed., *The City as the Center,* pp. 166-178.

CHAPTER SIX

1. These estimates are derived from K. Davis, *World Urbanization,* vol. 1.

2. Some works on urban government and politics in communist cities include: John W. Lewis, ed., *The City in Communist China* (Stanford: Stanford University Press, 1971); David T. Cattell, *Leningrad;* Jerry Hough, *The Soviet Prefects* (Cambridge, Mass.: Harvard University Press, 1969); William Taubman, *Governing Soviet Cities* (New York: Praeger, 1973); B. Michael Frolic, "Decision Making in Soviet Cities," *American Political Science Review,* March 1972, pp. 38-52; and Ezra Vogel, *Canton Under Communism* (Cambridge, Massachusetts: Harvard University Press, 1969).

3. Harold Berman, *Justice in the U.S.S.R.* (New York: Random House, 1963).

4. Adapted from the translation of the 1954 Constitution in Theodore H. E. Chen, ed., *The Chinese Communist Regime: Documents and Commentary* (New York: Praeger, 1967), p. 100.

5. Robert W. Clawson and David L. Norrgard, "National Responses to Urban Crime: The Soviet Union, the United Kingdom, and the United States," in Harlan Hahn, ed., *Police in Urban Society* (Beverly Hills: Sage, 1971), pp. 71-93 at p. 83.

6. Perhaps a crude indicator of comparative liberalism is the availability of legal counsel—potentially valuable in fighting city hall. In the United States there is one lawyer for every 626 people; in Canada, one per 1600; in Britain, one per 2200. In the USSR, there is a lawyer for every 17,000 people; in China, apparently, one per 286,000 people. Sources: Barry Richman, *Industrial Society in Communist China* (New York: Random House, 1969), p. 369; Frederick Barghoorn, *Politics in the USSR* (Boston: Little, Brown, 1966), p. 333; Seymour M. Lipset, "The Value Patterns of a Democracy," *American Sociological Review*, Aug. 1963, pp. 515-531 at pp. 525-526.

To be sure, Watergate indicates that the correlation between lawyers and liberalism is less than 1.0.

7. Gunnar Myrdal, *Asian Drama: An Enquiry into the Poverty of Nations* (New York: The Twentieth Century Fund, 1968), vol. 2, pp. 937-51.

8. Merle Fainsod, *How Russia is Ruled* (Cambridge, Massachusetts: Harvard University Press, 1953), Ch. 12.

9. Cattell, *Leningrad*, p. 48.

10. Smith, *The Russians*, pp. 111-112.

11. Clawson and Norrgard, "National Responses," p. 83.

12. Henry G. Schwarz, "The Treatment of Minorities," in Michel Oksenberg, ed., *China's Developmental Experience* (New York: Praeger, 1973), pp. 193-207 at p. 201.

13. Rinn-Sup Shinn, et al., *Area Handbook for North Korea* (Washington: United States Government Printing Office, 1969), p. 120.

14. Timothy Sosnovy, *The Housing Problem in the Soviet Union* (New York: Research Program on the Soviet Union, 1954); R. Osborn, *Soviet Social Policies*, pp. 221-222.

15. Henry W. Morton, "What Have the Soviet Leaders Done About the Housing Crisis?" in Henry W. Morton and Rudolf L. Tokes, eds., *Soviet Politics in the 1970s* (New York: Free Press, 1974), pp. 163-180.

16. James H. Oliver, "Citizen Demands and the Soviet Political System," *American Political Science Review*, June 1969, pp. 465-475 at p. 465.

17. "District and city soviets are the key link in the system of organs of state power and secure the practical implementation of Party and government policy at the local level." N. G. Starovoitov, "The District and City Soviets: Current Problems," *Soviet Law and Government*, Spring 1972, pp. 299-311 at p. 300.

18. Oliver, "Citizen Demands," p. 470.

19. Ezra Vogel, "Preserving Order," in J. W. Lewis, *The City in Communist China*, pp. 70-95 at p. 86.

20. Clawson and Norrgard, "National Responses," pp. 71-93. See also N. Bakhanskaia, "New Legislation on the Volunteer Auxiliary Police," *Soviet Law and Government,* Fall 1975, pp. 3-11.

21. F. Barghoorn, *Politics,* Ch. 9.

22. H. Smith, *The Russians,* Ch. 18.

23. See the authors listed in n. 45, Ch. 4.

24. R. Osborn, *Soviet Social Policies,* Chs. 6-7.

25. Manuel Castells, *La Question Urbaine* (Paris: Maspero, 1972), p. 94.

26. R. Osborn, *Soviet Social Policies,* pp. 550-551; Taubman, *Governing Soviet Cities,* Ch. 5.

27. Wright Miller, *Russians as People* (New York: Dutton, 1971), p. 93.

28. Charles Howe, "The Supply of Urban Housing in Mainland China: The Case of Shanghai," *The China Quarterly,* Jan. 1968, pp. 73-97; *Los Angeles Times,* March 17, 1979.

29. H. Smith, *The Russians,* Ch. 1.

30. Alexander Groth, *Comparative Politics: A Distributive Approach* New York: Macmillan Company, 1971), p. 208.

31. Shinn, *Area Handbook,* p. 120.

32. "An Observer," *Message From Moscow* (New York: Alfred Knopf, 1969), p. 125.

33. *Los Angeles Times,* May 19, 1975.

34. See the statistical yearbooks published by such cities as Warsaw, East Berlin, Budapest, and Belgrade.

35. The contrasts between Chinese and Soviet urban philosophies and policies are brought out in B. Michael Frolic's, "Communist Model(s) of Urban Development and Comparative Urban Research," paper presented to the Comparative Administration Group, City University of New York, April 26, 1971.

36. Laurence Ma, "Anti-Urbanism in China." *Proceedings of the American Association of Geographers,* 1976, pp. 114-118.

37. Ibid., p. 118.

CHAPTER SEVEN

1. Albert O. Hirschmann, "The Search for Paradigms as a Hindrance to Understanding," *World Politics,* April 1970, pp. 329-343, at pp. 341-342.

2. Ibid., p. 343.

3. David Gordon, *Problems in Political Economy,* pp. 1-15.

4. Ernesto Guevara, *Venceremos* (Havana: Libre Prensa, 1970); Rene Dumont, *Is Cuba Socialist?* (London: Deutsch, 1974).

5. James W. Fesler, "The Future of State and Local Government," in J. W. Fesler, ed., *The 50 States and Their Local Governments* (New York: Knopf, 1967), pp. 568-576, at p. 573.

6. Thomas J. Anton, review of Bernard J. Frieden, *Metropolitan America: Challenge to Federalism* (Washington: Advisory Commission on Intergovernmental Relations, 1966) in *American Political Science Review,* June 1968, pp. 623-624.

7. Edward C. Banfield, *The Unheavenly City Revisited* (Boston: Little, Brown, 1974).

8. Anthony Downs, *Urban Problems and Prospects* (Chicago: Rand McNally, 1976), Ch. 3.

9. Anton, op cit., p. 623.

10. Bernard Frieden's reply, *American Political Science Review,* Dec. 1968, pp. 1271-1272.

11. Frances Fox Piven and Richard A. Clowen, *Regulating the Poor: The Functions of Public Welfare* (New York: Random House, 1971) and *The Politics of Turmoil* (New York: Pantheon, 1974).

12. John C. Bollens and Henry J. Schmandt, *The Metropolis: Its People, Politics, and Economic Life* (New York: Harper & Row, 1975), pp. 43-45; Frank Smallwood, "Metropolitan Political Systems and the Administrative Process," in Simon Miles, ed., *Metropolitan Problems: A Search for Comprehensive Solutions* (Toronto: Methuen, 1970, Ch. 10.

13. Smallwood, "Metropolitan Political Systems," pp. 337-343; Orin F. Nolting, "Local Government Restructuring in Western European Countries," in International City Management Association, *The Municipal Yearbook 1976* (Washington: International City Managers Association, 1976), pp. 78-87.

14. Frank Smallwood, *Greater London: The Politics of Metropolitan Reform* (Indianapolis: Bobbs-Merrill, 1965); Gerald Rhodes, *The Government of London: The Struggle for Reform* (Toronto: University of Toronto Press, 1970); Jack Brand, *Local Government Reform in England 1888-1974* (London: Crown Helm, 1974); Jeffrey Stanyer, *Understanding Local Government* (London: Fontana, 1976); Lord Redcliffe-Maud and Bruce Wood, *English Local Government Reformed* (Oxford: Oxford University Press, 1977); Peter G. Richards, *The Local Government Act of 1972: Problems of Implementation* (London: Allen & Unwin, 1975).

15. Nolting, "Local Government Restructuring," On Stockholm, see Hans Calmfors, Francine F. Rabinovitz, and Daniel Alesch, *Urban Government for Greater Stockholm* (New York: Praeger, 1968).

16. Nolting, op. cit., pp. 78-82; Anne Marie Hauck Walsh, *The Challenge of Government,* pp. 80-82. Despite its great theoretical powers as a unitary state, the Dutch government has not, in practice, been able to impose strong metropolitan governments on the centuries-old accumulation of the spirit of local independence. See H. Van Ruller, *Agglomeratie-Problematik in Nederland* (Alphen: Sansom, 1972), pp. 230-232. On the weakness of national controls in the United States, see Douglas Yates, *The Governable City: The Politics of Urban Problems and Policy Making* (Cambridge: MIT Press, 1978), pp. 183-88.

17. Nolting, op. cit., pp. 82-84; Smallwood, *Greater London,* pp. 234-67.

18. Alan A. Altschuler, *Community Control: The Black Demand for Participation in Large American Cities* (Indianapolis: Bobbs-Merrill, 1970); Willis D. Hawley, "On Understanding Metropolitan Political Integration," in Willis D. Hawley, et. al.,

Theoretical Perspectives on Urban Politics (Englewood Cliffs: Prentice-Hall, 1976), Ch. 5.

19. Bollens and Schmandt, *The Metropolis*, pp. 66-70; Ursula Hicks, "Financing Metropolitan Government," in S. Miles, ed., *Metropolitan Problems*, Ch. 12; Julius Margolis, "Fiscal Issues in the Reform of Metropolitan Governance," in Robert Bish and Vincent Ostrom, eds., *Reform as Reorganization* (Baltimore: Johns Hopkins Press, 1974), pp. 41-70.

20. Ivan L. Richardson, *Urban Government for Rio de Janeiro* (New York: Praeger, 1973), pp. 27-47.

21. Peter S. Cleaves, *Developmental Processes in Chilean Local Government* (Berkeley: Institute of International Studies, University of California, 1969). See also Arturo Valenzuela, *Political Brokers in Chile: Local Government in a Centralized Polity* (Durham, N.C.: Duke University Press, 1977), pp. 44-52.

22. Laurence Boyle, *Equalisation and the Finance of Local Government* (Edinburgh: Oliver and Boyd, 1968); L. L. Ecker-Racz, *The Politics and Economics of State-Local Finance* (Englewood Cliffs, N.J.: Prentice-Hall, 1970), pp. 174-77; Anita S. Harder, *Federal Grants-in-Aid* (New York: Praeger, 1976), pp. 127-140; Ursula Hicks, "Financing Metropolitan Government."

23. Nathan Glazer, cited in Piven and Cloward, *Regulating*, p. 269.

24. Piven and Cloward, *Regulating*, p. 269.

25. Milton Kotler, "The Urban Polity," in Anselm M. Straus, ed., *The American City* (Chicago: Aldine, 1968), pp. 260-265 at pp. 262-263.

26. John F. C. Turner and Robert Fichter, *Freedom to Build: Dweller Control of the Housing Process* (New York: Macmillan, 1972). See also David Collier, *Squatters and Oligarchs: Authoritarian Rule and Policy Change in Peru* (Baltimore: Johns Hopkins Press, 1976).

27. Lisa Peattie, *The View from the Barrio* (Ann Arbor: The University of Michigan Press, 1968); Lloyd Rodwin, *Nations and Cities: A Comparison of Strategies for Urban Growth* (Boston: Houghton-Mifflin, 1970); David G. Epstein, *Brasília, Dream and Reality* (Berkeley: University of California Press, 1973).

28. William Alonso, "The Mirage of New Towns," *The Public Interest*, Spring 1970.

29. Edward C. Banfield, *The Unheavenly City Revisited*.

30. Ibid., p. 247.

31. Richard R. Fagen and William S. Tuohy, *Order Without Progress*, p. 63.

32. Daniel P. Moynihan, *Maximum Feasible Misunderstanding* (New York: Harper & Row, 1972), p. 238.

INDEX